SIGNS OF MASCULINITY

Rodopi Perspectives on Modern Literature

20

Edited by
David Bevan

SIGNS OF MASCULINITY
MEN IN LITERATURE
1700 TO THE PRESENT

Edited by

Antony Rowland
Emma Liggins and
Eriks Uskalis

Amsterdam - Atlanta, GA 1998

∞ The paper on which this book is printed meets the requirements of "ISO 9706:1994, Information and documentation - Paper for documents - Requirements for permanence".

ISBN: 90-420-0603-X (bound)
©Editions Rodopi B.V., Amsterdam - Atlanta, GA 1998
Printed in The Netherlands

CONTENTS

INTRODUCTION

I. Theorising Masculinity

Gender as an unstable category has been a central concern of literary studies from the late 1960s onwards, as the rise of feminist theory precipitated a widespread critical debate around the representation of women and femininity in literature. The formation of alternative feminist canons invites students to 'rediscover' classics of women's writing which have been overlooked and dismissed as trivial, or of limited literary value. However, it is now being recognised that in many instances gender studies has been fixated with femininity. Its binary opposite, masculinity, has to a certain extent been dismissed as an 'empty', redundant category of gender identity. Whilst the last ten years have seen important work by critics such as Alan Sinfield and Jonathan Dollimore on masculinities in Renaissance drama, research and interest in the signs of masculinity in texts from 1700 to the present is still a relatively new area of investigation.[1]

In the last fifteen years, theorists primarily from the disciplines of history, cultural studies, sociology and psychoanalysis have demonstrated that masculinity is broadly characterised by silences, crisis, uncertainty and invisibility. John Tosh has argued persuasively that, 'A profound dualism in Western thought has served to keep the spotlight away from men. In the historical record it is as though masculinity is everywhere but nowhere'.[2] This poses a problem for the study of literature in that, in more enlightened institutions, it takes account of cultural difference by considering a wide range of issues surrounding the representation of sex, gender, race and class. If masculinity is 'nowhere', hidden from the spotlight of critical investigation, then literary scholars seem guilty of exclusion, wilfully refusing to consider a prominent and fundamental aspect of gender identity. Feminist theory and books on the representation of Woman/women have threatened to monopolise gender criticism and gender studies: it seems essential to redress this balance by asking what the 'empty' category of masculinity can reveal about gender relations, sexuality and men's social roles, and how it can offer alternative ways of reading and evaluating literary texts.

Growing interest in masculinities in the late twentieth century relates to specific ways in which male identity and images of men are being negotiated and examined in the wake of the proliferation of feminism. In his discussion of men's silences, Jonathan Rutherford charts the 'emergence of a sexual politics of masculinity' in which predicaments in masculine identities are produced by a sense of cultural crisis and dislocation. He suggests that

> Feminism didn't so much remove men's powers and privileges as strip them of their legitimating stories [...] But if the old stories of masculinity seemed defunct, the disjunction between these apparently redundant vocabularies and men's lived experience, broke the continuity of men's historical sense of themselves. In their place were enigmas, gaps, absences and uncertainties.[3]

In the challenge to male power posed by feminism, men's stories and the cultural constructions of masculinity they encoded then seemed out of date, inappropriate, no longer an adequate reflection of men's 'lived experiences'. In trying to make sense of the absences and uncertainties involved in the representations of men, students of masculinity need to ask how to fill in the gaps, and to move towards new vocabularies and stories. This is very much a contemporary issue, as debates about fatherhood, male violence, impotence, house-husbands, gay identities, and a stream of other issues around men's lived experiences are constantly debated in the press and the media. In an article in *The Guardian*, ironically included in the pages for 'Women' (as if men have no interest in themselves as gendered subjects), Yvonne Roberts examines fatherhood in the 1990s, and the reasons why feminists and female academics rather than males have taken up the task of promoting the role of the father. She suggests that 'images of maleness' require 'radical alteration', that men are restricted in their roles by 'the traditional notion of what it is to be male - and the absence of cultural images that reveal the depth of men's emotional attachment to their children'.[4] Whilst masculinity and men's experiences are then a recognisable area of concern and interest in the 1990s, the need to radically alter our perception of men is paradoxically linked to the lack of available cultural images, or the existence of traditional, hence redundant images of maleness. As Lynne Segal succinctly puts it, 'Despite the explosion of writing on the topic, the category of "masculinity" remains deeply obscure'.[5] However, this obscurity, the 'inconsistent and contradictory meanings' which constitute male gender identity, also signals a crisis in contemporary culture, so that 'For some at least, "masculinity" has replaced "femininity" as the problem of our time – a threat to civilisation itself.'[6] Writers such as Ian McEwan and Tony Harrison have argued this in their readings of the atomic age as a product of fixed notions of masculinity; as John McLeod illustrates in his chapter on McEwan, the 'threat' manifests itself at an early age, as is evidenced by the adolescent fantasies about heterosexuality in *First Love, Last Rites*.

Difficulties in theorising masculinity relate to the restrictive and stereotypical ways in which men have been culturally constructed both in literature and society. Patriarchy proves an almost insurmountable stumbling-block for critics aiming to provide an affirmative reading of masculinity, as men have been historically categorised as oppressors, exercising their power over women at every opportunity and at every level of society. Segal's incisive commentary on the ambiguities of male identity is in many ways structured around an analysis of the operations of power, as she takes as her starting point 'men's attachment to the dominant masculine ideal of power and superiority'.[7] However, she is quick to point out that this is only an ideal, that the power attached to men and embedded in cultural images of masculinity is constantly being threatened or undermined by 'other men's assertion of contrasting gay, anti-sexist or Black male identities'.[8] Whilst it would be naïve to ignore the issues around patriarchy which underpin Anglo-American feminist theory, is it then productive to ask different questions about the constructions of masculinities, to focus on what Harry Brod and Michael Kaufman describe as 'the plurality and diversity of men's experiences, attitudes, beliefs, situations, practices, and institutions'?[9] Closer examinations of the literary representation of men may reveal not their unequivocal status and power over women and children, but the uncertainties and instabilities of their position within the text, and a mediation of the anxieties and ambiguities attendant on cultural constructions of masculinity. Totalised male dominance remains within the realm of fantasy, or it may be challenged and questioned by literature, set up as a misleading cultural myth.

One of the aims of this book is to draw out the wider implications of these anxieties and ambiguities in the context of theoretical debates around subjectivity and identity. The binary opposition between masculinity and femininity ensures that gender is defined and measured in terms of difference: typically, women have been defined by their 'otherness' to men, with men, ergo masculinity, functioning as the standard, the norm, the point of fixity. 'Normative masculinity' has come to exist as a measuring stick, and is often essentialised by feminist critics whose arguments rely on universalised notions of gender identity. However, critics from cultural history, literature and cultural studies have contested this version of events, often using ideas drawn from poststructuralism and postmodernism, to authorise their claims for a more pluralised, fluid conception of male identity. In his study of masculinity and subjectivity in modern culture, Peter Middleton focuses on the poststructuralist notion of the 'decentred subject', suggesting that identity is made up of a variety of subject positions: 'modern masculinites depend on the maintenance of discrete islands of subjectivity unconscious of one another'.[10] He goes on to provide a helpful account of the elusive definition of masculinity in the context of its ability as a concept to straddle different definitions and cultural constructions:

> Masculinity has been left behind the scenes, writing the scripts, directing the action and operating the cameras, taken for granted and almost never defined [...] As adjective, the term "masculine" moves between the identification of a person's sex as male and socially validated norms of acceptable behaviour for males. As noun, its referent will depend on what assumptions about subjectivity and society determine its context. For some sociologists masculinity is a role, for some poststructuralists it is a form of representation. Central to all usages seems to be an element of acculturation.[11]

Using the same metaphors of theatre and film which signified absence for John Tosh, Middleton describes the process by which masculinity becomes normative, at the same time that it is paradoxically hidden from view, unacknowledged, outside classification. It is associated with control, 'directing the action' and the act of looking, 'operating the cameras', perhaps as a strategy for diverting attention away from itself, 'left behind the scenes'. More significantly, its meaning changes chameleonlike as it is applied to different contexts; it can be linked to sexuality, social codes, performativity and representation. This collection testifies to the diversities of masculine identity explored in a range of literary and cultural texts, locating it within the shifting 'assumptions about subjectivity and society' which characterise literature in the modern period. As David S. Gutterman concludes in his discussion of gay male gender identity, what postmodern culture creates is 'a space where the scripts of normative masculinity can give way to a proliferation of masculinities'.[12]

II. Male Bodies and Sexuality

Binary oppositions used to define sexual difference have often equated femininity with the body. In traditional versions of Western culture, men have been classified in terms of attributes such as 'activity, culture, reason', whereas women are generally associated with 'passivity, nature, emotion', characteristics linked to concepts of the corporeal.[13] Hélène Cixous begins her famous essay 'Sorties: Out and Out: Attacks/Ways Out/Forays' with a similar list of such 'dual, hierarchical oppositions' where Woman's inferiority is signalled by her representation through almost the same terms: 'Passivity', 'Nature' and 'Mother', and

Man stands for 'Activity', 'Culture' and 'Father'. For French feminists, woman's body should be used 'to articulate the proliferation of meanings' because in the symbolic order 'woman is body more than man is'.[14] Anglo-American feminist accounts of sexuality have demonstrated the ways in which the medicalisation of women meant that they have been defined in terms of their menstrual cycles and their physical experiences of puberty, pregnancy and the menopause. The male body has remained largely hidden from view in line with the 'relative invisibility' which Tosh cites as a crucial feature of masculinity.[15] Feminist critics have, though, developed the model of the 'male gaze' in which men look at and admire (representations of) female bodies, thereby rendering their own invisible. Elizabeth Bronfen has argued that the beautiful and dead female body in art, literature and film has become an icon of Western culture. And yet men have not always been cast as spectators admiring the female object of desire, a version of culture which is of course reliant on the workings of heterosexuality. What is often overlooked is the representation of the male sexual body in art and sculpture, often the object of the homoerotic gaze and, more importantly, the variety of male bodies on display for both male and female eyes in literary and cultural texts. In this volume, contributors theorize the representation of the erotic bodies of the colonized slave and the remains left by cannibals, the 'muscular' criminal and the 'athletic' body of the executed murderer, and the ejaculating hero of the pornographic novel. Men's bodies can also be objectified, admired, put on show or subjected to violence. Perhaps it was the psychoanalytic delight in the male body, particularly the all-powerful phallus, which prompted a refusal to engage with the ways in which it has been represented. Lacan's theories of the phallus as transcendental signified, and Freud's notions of penis envy and castration complexes, may have been recognised as a valorisation of male dominance through theories of the body: women were defined by lack and therefore inferiority. That the objectification of the male body could be used to deconstruct male power seems a valid reason for its exploration in literature and art, precisely because the activity of looking at male bodies, whether by men or women, opens up a subversive arena of power relations where masculinity is no longer equated with subjectivity and control. Writing the male body is frequently the occasion for fracturing received notions of masculinity and introducing alternative narratives of desire and gender identity, involving effeminacy, impotence and homoerotic/homosexual attraction.

Even in the late 1990s it is still the case that the male body on display raises questions of censorship and indecency. Erect penises must be confined to the private home, rather than brought out into the open at the cinema and on television. Erections may be a commonplace of contemporary literature: an example from Hanif Kureishi's *The Buddha of Suburbia* (1990) is the line 'Pike's body was carrying his erection in my direction, like a lorry sustaining a crane'.[16] But they are banned from most cultural forms of representation, and associated with the unrepresentable. In his study of desire in modern narrative, Peter Brooks analyses the cultural differences between the representations of male and female sexual bodies and the obscenity still attached to the erect penis. He relates this back to models of normative masculinity:

> If the male body in patriarchy becomes the norm, the
> standard against which one measures otherness – and
> thus creates the enigma of woman – one might expect
> the male body to be more openly displayed and
> discussed [...] Precisely because it is the norm, the
> male body is veiled from inquiry, taken as the agent
> and not the object of knowing: the gaze is 'phallic', its

> object is not [...] Despite – or because of – the
> attention paid to viewing women naked, the paternal
> phallus may be the ultimate taboo object of our
> culture.[17]

What is fascinating in this account is the reversal of attitudes which seems to have occurred in our cultural preferences and pleasures. Whilst naked women now occupy centre stage signifying their objectification and vulnerability, the naked man, particularly in a state of 'obscene' arousal, is at once the norm and a 'taboo' object which should not be observed. Male bodies are the other, defined as both abject, horrifying and desirable. Filmgoers in 1998 waited anxiously for a fleeting and much publicised glimpse of the reputedly colossal member of Dirk Diggler in *Boogie Nights*. The desired appendage remains tantalisingly just off the edges of the screen until the end of the film, playing with the spectators' awareness of its 'taboo' nature. The ultimate phallic object and the masculinity it stands for then remains much more of an enigma than the images of breasts and vaginas which we have become accustomed to looking at for entertainment.

Reclaiming the male sexual body in gay literature is evidence of the shifts in representation: male bodies may be celebrated as objects of desire, brought back into the spotlight. In Judith Butler's alternative and challenging readings of gendered and sexual bodies, in both *Gender Trouble* and *Bodies that Matter*, the male heterosexual body seems to be the only body which *doesn't* matter. Gay and bisexual bodies, bodies which refuse to fit into binary models of penetrated/penetrator, are cause for celebration for their challenge to fixed categories and sexual identities, but in her view, male heterosexual bodies remain the invisible norm, and are not worthy of discussion. Theories of the ambiguities of masculinity, however, suggest that the male body is by no means fixed or normative, but instead stands as a significant and deeply ambiguous cultural sign. Whilst the male body can then function as an object of desire captured in the appreciative female/homoerotic gaze, male sexuality also needs to be reassessed and problematised and texts examined for their representations of male desire. Despite the aporia of heterosexual masculinity in *Bodies that Matter*, Butler's work has proved to be an important milestone for the study of men, with its discussion of decentred subjects, its refutation of a sex/gender binary, and its championing of performativity. Taking the latter, her theory can be applied to masculinity so that it becomes a fluid site for the performance of various identities, rather than a fixed norm. Rather than endorse a presumptive version of men, Butler argues that sex is actually a product of gender: both sexes, therefore, are able to perform masculinity, and 'man'. Identity is not prediscursive, but dialogic, a constantly changing assemblage of abstract concepts.

Middleton has voiced the need for a language in which men can articulate their emotions and sexual needs, suggesting that 'men's deafening silence about their own sexuality as opposed to the objects of their desire continues'.[18] Although it is certainly true that male sexuality does remain silenced in many literary texts, this lack has a tendency to announce itself, and draw attention to its own status. As Michel Foucault has demonstrated in his rereading of the Victorian 'repressive hypothesis', sexuality has been historically and culturally produced through silences: 'on the subject of sex, silence became the rule'.[19] He goes on to posit the theory that whilst nineteenth-century society sought to promote censorship and secrecy around sexual matters, this had the effect of producing 'a regulated and polymorphous incitement to discourse', a cultural pressure to talk about sex as much as possible.[20] Paradoxically in relation to sex, nineteenth-century society 'speaks verbosely of its own silence' and dedicates itself to 'speaking of [sex] *ad infinitum*, while exploiting it as *the* secret'.[21] To describe masculine sexuality as characterised by silences is then all too predictable for Foucauldian critics who would suggest that silences effectively produce more discourse on the subject, as the current interest in the 'empty', enigmatic category of male sexuality perhaps confirms. The accelerating interest in gay male sexual identity in the 1990s, also associated with censorship and secrecy and hence much talked and written about, has prompted an explosion of new fictional texts describing gay subcultures where sexuality and male bodies are openly discussed and delineated for the reader. Similarly, new renditions of sexuality, such as Eve Kosofsky Sedgwick's model of homosocial desire, have authorised new readings of canonical texts. In this volume, both Stephen Gregg and Emma Liggins provide readings of the representation of male sexuality and desire in which it is simultaneously figured through the body and silenced, displaced onto issues of race and cannibalism, or class and criminality.

Fears of homosexuality and effeminacy haunt representations of masculinity in many of the texts analysed here, as the myth of male dominance is propped up by a sharply defined heterosexuality used to maintain power over women. Theorists of sexuality from both sociology and cultural studies have highlighted the opposition between male heterosexuality and homosexuality for an understanding of male sexuality. In his study of the production of modern sexualities, Jeffrey Weeks argues that, 'Masculinity or the male identity is achieved by the constant process of warding off threats to it. It is precariously achieved by the rejection of femininity and homosexuality'.[22] Warding off the threat of homosexuality seems to be a constant of male sexual identity in many modern texts: both Defoe's Crusoe, fascinated by Friday's body, and the criminals of nineteenth-century Newgate novels shy away from a direct confrontation of the potentially sexual undertones of their attachment to other men. In the French film *Ma Vie en Rose* (1997), the threat to bourgeois society posed by uncertain masculinity is explored in the character of Ludo, a little boy who thinks girls have more fun, and thus dresses up in lipstick and skirts and voices his desire to marry his male friend. Whilst tomboys are treated with fondness and tolerance, the hostile and bigoted reactions to his exploration of his gender identity demonstrate the cultural value attached to a clearly defined masculinity. However, horror films allow a more transgressive playground for masculinity, since ostensibly male adolescents are given the opportunity to savour the parts, in the *Alien* sequence at least, of protective and disgusting mothers, strong heroines, weak men, and small penises bursting out of stomachs and running amok.

Relations between men in society and their potentially erotic nature are also a significant component of cultural constructions of male sexuality. Homosocial desire, in which the homoerotic is contained within the homosocial bonds between men, offers an alternative reading of the relationships between men. In her provocative rereadings of male-authored texts from Shakespeare and Wycherley through to Sterne, Tennyson and Dickens in *Between Men*, Sedgwick claims that 'patriarchy structurally *requires* homophobia', that, as opposed to relationships between women, the nature of bonds between men in modern society makes a sharp distinction between 'men-loving-men' and 'men-promoting-the-interests-of-men'.[23] This has not always been the case, since she demonstrates that patriarchy in ancient Greece did not preclude homosexuality; an essential linearity between male dominance and homophobia does not exist. She goes on to ask, 'If the relation of homosocial to homosexual bonds is so shifty, then what theoretical framework do we have for drawing any links between sexual and power relationships?'.[24] Her arguments and questions invite a closer examination of the bonds between men in literary texts, complicating issues surrounding the silencing of men's sexuality.

Not only do they alert us to the importance of analysing male-male relationships, they also form part of a larger theoretical project structured around breaking open what Gutterman refers to as 'the closed category of male, heterosexual identity'.[25] Debates around the implications of the binary opposites, heterosexuality and homosexuality, have centred around the 'incoherent' or 'discontinous' nature of gender produced by a fracturing of such binary models of sexual difference. Judith Butler, in particular, has demonstrated that in our society gender supposedly corresponds to what she calls 'the heterosexual matrix', a model built around normative conceptions of male and female heterosexual desire.[26] In this model female bodies are defined by their capacity to be penetrated, or permeated by male bodies so that gender and sexuality correspond without complications: 'A woman [...] only exists as a term that stabilizes and consolidates a binary and oppositional relation to a man; that relation [...] is heterosexuality'.[27] However, in her discussions of the sexual identities of lesbians, gays and bisexuals, she suggests that sexuality cannot be located so easily in gender, that a lesbian, for example, is 'neither a woman nor a man' but goes 'beyond the categories of sex'. In this line of reasoning, gender is theorised as 'the variable cultural construction of sex, the myriad and open possibilities of cultural meaning occasioned by a sexed body'.[28]

The question of the distinctions between sexuality and gender informs writing in this volume on masculine sexuality, exploring the cultural meanings attached to sexual bodies. In his analysis of the abjection of pornography, Matthew Pateman argues for a mitigated return to the biological rather than pursue a split between sex and gender. Responding to Butler's notions of the 'discontinuous' gendered bodies of homosexuality, Scott McCracken considers the sexual identity of the Uranian in the work of Edward Carpenter, a figure renowned for his progressive views on sexual categorisation, whose writing is typical of the climate of the 1890s in its focus on gender indeterminacy. Representations of individual sexual identities then serve to offer radical new versions of masculinity. As Gutterman maintains, 'the conflicts between individual nonnormative sexuality and cultural conceptions of normative maleness create interesting places of slippage where the standards of gender are undermined or contested'.[29]

III. New Men

In the post-war period there has been a flurry of activity seeking to identify and articulate the apparent crisis and sense of bewilderment experienced by some men, either collectively or individually, as to their contemporary identities and roles. Cultural shifts in class, family life, the rise of feminism, structural developments in the economy, changes in national identity and the nation-state, changes in aspiration, and patterns of consumerism, are all crucial and interrelated factors which have led to changes in models of masculinity, ranging from adjustment or to reinscribing patriarchy in other forms, or to complete retrenchment.

The 1950s saw contradictory impulses in the construction of
the mainstream man: he could be characterised as someone who
had 'returned from battlefield to bungalow with new
expectations of the comforts and the pleasures of the home', but
whilst he was more and more 'a man about the house', in the
home he was a silent and distant figure.[30] He lacked emotional
exchange with his wife, and to his children was often a figure
who would only be around to punish them when they stepped
out of line.

Although he criticises it as being too secular and lacking in
spirituality, dominant versions of the 1950s male - strong, hard-
working, controlling, and self-controlled - shadow the
controversial work of Robert Bly. This is precisely because he
sees a crisis, manifested by deeply troubled and unhappy men. It
arises from the reaction of 1960s men to the models offered by
the previous decade, a reaction which Bly sees as having
produced 'soft' males. For him the men of the 1950s were at
least centres of authority, good teachers and role models, able to
guide their children into adult life. Bly's work, best known for his
Iron John, has been validly characterised as 'a crude, muddled,
and almost mock-parodic response for "masculine" development
in feminine men', but he does raise the point that masculinity is
mostly condemned as coercive and negative, and that many men
feel ashamed of expressing any form of it, an action which has
led to a kind of self-paralysis.[31] He argues that 'many of these
men are unhappy. There's not much energy in them. They are
life-preserving but not exactly life-giving'.[32] Culture's missing
centres of authority are identified with fathers by Bly, and a large
part of his bonding camps involve men trying to come to terms
with or overcome alienation from the father, whether personal,
mythical or archetypal. The metaphors Bly uses of hairiness,
wildness, of the need to rediscover the wildman at the bottom of

the pool, are extremely primitive and dangerous in their open-
endedness. David Tracey is right to point out that they are also
close to the primitive mysticism of some fascist rhetoric, saying
that if 1950s man was secular, 1930s man in Europe was not,
and fascism 'was very much a quasi-religious, ritualistic
celebration of the archetypal masculine spirit in all its rawness
and pristine glory'.[33] If Bly has identified a problem, and it is at
least arguable that what for him is a problem is rather a healthy
response to feminism and changes in dominant masculinities, then
the dangers of his responses are clear.

Bly feels that we are living in an age in which traditional and,
for him, comforting and enabling centres of authority are no
longer available, or are deeply suspected, an age which can be
glossed with the term postmodernity. Suggestions that we are
now living in a postmodern world has given rise for optimism,
that we are now freed from the tyranny of living through binary
opposites, which position people unequally in power
relationships. Sabina Lovibond suggests that the claim made by
the constructors of postmodernism that the Enlightenment
project of rationality and egalitarianism has run out of steam
should be one of disappointment for people caught in unequal
power relations, but she also feels that the claim should be
treated with suspicion: 'How can anyone ask me to say goodbye
to "emancipatory metanarratives" when my own emancipation is
such a patchy hit-and-miss affair ?'[34] To gloss this, it has been
argued that the 'programme' of the Enlightenment and modernity
was disastrous and male-centred, that its attempts at 'social
engineering' ended in abuses, and, at an extreme level, in the
Gulags. Lovibond argues that the attempt to discredit the
narratives of rationality and egalitarianism also discredits
narratives used by feminism in the form of analysis and self-

empowerment. In other words men, feeling threatened, have dismissed modernity and embraced postmodernity, a state which leaves their power intact.

An alternative challenge to the concept of the power-driven male became apparent in the 1980s with the coming of the 'New Man', mainly produced by advertising campaigns and magazines. The male as consumer of a much wider range of products has emerged, and been constructed and targeted, over the past decade or so, and this has been linked to ways in which advertisers focus as much on life-style as on product and individual consumer. The New Man - a male who wipes down the surfaces, listens attentively, goes shopping, and goes down without expecting or demanding 'tit-for-tat' oral sex - cannot be simply written off as the result of innovations in advertising copy. Advertising reflects *and* produces social trends after all, but his coming into being is generally seen as inextricably linked to changing patterns of consumerism, and to the male being more and more recognised and targeted as a consumer. The phenomenon of the New Man is connected to the ways in which males have become much more willing to be looked at, and to look at themselves, which signals shifts in some males' relationships with their bodies. Despite the fact that *Playboy* magazine, encouraging men to experience pleasure in spending money, appeared in the 1950s, the male in this era was hardly recognised as a consumer, as some of the main forms of masculinity were built around the idea of conformity, emotional fixity and self-denial. This began to change in the 1970s as some men began to react positively to feminism, and began to explore differing forms of subjectivities, and as advertising began to respond to, and construct, males as sensitive, emotional and as full of needs and desires.

Many have been scornful of the very idea of the New Man,
seeing him purely as the construct of advertising campaigns, or
arguing that they have never met one, or that he promised much
but delivered pitifully little. Responding to media representations
and ideals, some contemporary fiction has attempted to redefine
the hero by dismissing normative images of powerful, aggressive
men. In John McLeod's chapter, he argues that, in McEwan's
fiction, while sensitive New Men are beginning to recognise and
value their feminine side, this has the potential danger of
collapsing back into a patriarchal vision where 'a complicit
masculinity' threatening the female with elision prevails.
Whatever characteristics the New Man is said to possess in
McEwan's work, they are similar to those of the 'soft' male so
despised by people like Robert Bly. Nevertheless, the concept
can be seen as positive if, at the very least, it is seen as 'a fraught
and uneven attempt to express masculine emotional and sexual
life'.[35] The phenomenon of the New Man has more recently been
superseded by the rise of 'new laddism', organised around and
encouraged by several magazines directed at men, such as
Loaded. In a recent *Guardian* article, 'We're all lads now',
questioning the influence of *Loaded* on more 'classy mags' such
as *Esquire* and *GQ*, the editor of the latter is quoted as saying,
'We undermine men all the time,' while Bryan Appleyard claims
that, 'In these new mags, maleness has become a pitiable
speciality - onanistic, isolated and enfeebled'.[36] Debates about
such lads' magazines continue to revolve around their
articulation of sexist attitudes to women, even if they do
simultaneously seek to revise images of the New Man. In many
ways, the New Lad of the 1990s is a particularly insidious
phenomenon, and can be seen as an attempt to reinscribe

traditional forms of masculinity, only this time wrapped up in postmodern irony.

IV. Masculinity and Class

Another aspect of masculinity which deserves attention is its social contexts and the ways in which men's social roles and codes of behaviour are shaped and interrogated. Sedgwick's *Between Men* highlights the issue of social relations as essential to an understanding of male homosocial desire in literature, claiming that 'the emerging pattern of male friendship, mentorship, entitlement, rivalry, and hetero- and homosexuality was in an intimate and shifting relation to class'.[37] Her reading of Sterne's *A Sentimental Journey*, for example, concentrates on the master-servant relationship between Yorick and LaFleur, and the ideological threat of the latter's effortless conquests of the servant women Yorick himself desires. Social configurations of masculinity raise a series of questions about hierarchical structures, about the use and abuse of power in public and private spheres, about the family, education, crime and work. An important element of the essays in this volume is their engagement with male roles made available within social structures and with the struggle to socialise boys into men. The delegitimisation of men's stories and vocabularies to a certain extent depends on the reader's awareness of men's social identities and the cultural images of masculinity disseminated in and to different classes. Antony Rowland's chapter explores cultural constructions of masculinity within a working-class district of Leeds in the 1960s, and how they emasculate a scholarship boy who senses, and deplores, his dissemination into the bourgeoisie.

An examination of men's social roles also precipitates a deeper appreciation of men's relationships with women. This area of enquiry has been recently considered by social historians who have begun to look at shifting gender roles in the home, as well as men's experiences in all-male institutions such as the public school and the army. John Tosh and Michael Roper, and the feminist historians Leonore Davidoff and Catherine Hall, have been instrumental in directing critical attention to men's roles and experiences of domesticity. Lynne Segal concentrates on men's responses to fatherhood between the wars in relation to changes in women's lives; like Sedgwick, she believes that it is difficult and unproductive to only conceptualise men in relation to other men. Contributors draw on material from cultural history to locate their analysis of men in changing social and economic circumstances, using newspaper reports, conduct-books, political tracts and socialist manifestos to ground their ideas. Daniel Duffy considers the dangers of uncontrolled masculinity within the middle-class home in relation to Anne Brontë's fiction and poetry, linking her male characters' fiendishness to the failure of woman's influence, her inability to minister to her husband. He argues that masculinity depends upon specified versions of female weakness inherent in the middle-class feminine ideal and that violations of the opposition between the husband's authority and the wife's weakness produced hellish versions of the middle-class household.

Most historical accounts of Victorian masculinity have concentrated on the middle-class ideal of manliness, a code of conduct built on 'qualities of physical courage, chivalric ideals, virtuous fortitude with additional connotations of military and patriotic virtue'.[38] Mangan and Walvin tentatively suggest that working-class labourers and servants were too busy to think about ideals of masculinity and femininity, surely a reductive way of disallowing interest in the lower classes. Their view of masculinity has been criticized by John Tosh who has argued that manliness is 'an *elite* cultural form' which ignores issues of sexual identity, the body, and most importantly, men's *relations* with women.[39] Indeed, Michael Roper and John Tosh stress the importance of masculinity as a 'relational construct, incomprehensible apart from the totality of gender relations', and call for an 'understanding of mutations of male dominance over time and their relation to other structures of social power, such as class, race, nation and creed'.[40] The widening debates around different social definitions of masculinity encourage us to reconsider stereotypical versions of working-class men, such as the wife-beater, the drinker, the criminal, the hooligan and the delinquent. If such men have no interest in gender as Mangan and Walvin claim, how do they define themselves: by their work, their strength, their position, their violence? As Tosh asks in a slightly different context, 'In which sphere was a man really himself?'[41] In her chapter on Dickens, Emma Liggins considers the ways in which working-class boys turned to crime out of a lack of sexual and economic choices, as theft and murder seemed to be viable alternatives to the marriages denied to penniless young men dissatisfied by work. Eriks Uskalis, in his analysis of Graham Swift's *Waterland* (1983), discusses some of the ways in which economic strength and autonomy was an integral aspect of the masculinity of the ruling class in the nineteenth century, and how this was linked to citizenship.

Economic choices for men in the post-war era have also weakened support structures for traditional models of masculinity. Threats to the 'wages of white maleness' have permeated across all social classes, and small fault-lines appearing in them in the years immediately following the war have become significant cracks in the last decades. 'The wages of white maleness' is a phrase used to describe what used to be the unquestioned given that white men, no matter from which class or how poor, could take for granted that they would have a job, more or less for life, and that, no matter how excluded by, and distant from, 'real' power, and no matter how necessarily limited their aspirations, they could at least count on being the boss and having power within the home. In the context of America, it is a mistake to state that all the male militias are primarily fuelled by racism and misogyny; instead they are driven by threats to these 'wages of whiteness', and their ire is primarily aimed at a government felt to be increasingly uncaring and distant. In Britain, these threats have been felt through differing processes; the decline in industries offering 'man's' work, the increasing dominance of distant multinationals, the move away from work for life towards part-time work and short-term contracts, and the fact that governments have progressively moved away from the idea of full employment as absolutely essential to the health and wealth of the nation-state and its citizens. The erosion of this stable factor - more or less guaranteed work for men - has had massive social effects, as work was, and still is, in many ways a source of male self-esteem and integrity.

Working-class masculinities in the last thirty years have been increasingly policed, particularly in the exemplary deployment of both ideological and repressive forces to control the 'unruly' male body as articulated through the punk movement, the miners' strike of 1984-85 (amongst other strikes), and the caging of predominantly male football supporters. There are problems with claiming these examples of masculinity as being policed, perhaps particularly as these sectors exhibit precisely the entrenched elements of 'traditional' masculinity, but perhaps they do so precisely because they spring from areas of controlled brutalisation.

Punk had its seeds in a variety of uniquely converging environments, amongst them the ranks of the excluded, and council states populated by males increasingly suspicious and disillusioned with their prospects, and increasingly inclined to refuse the line that education and work were noble things to aspire to, and that they were in any way available. This disaffection was given voice in The Clash's 'Career Opportunities'. Grundy's establishment provocation for the Sex Pistols to say something controversial on live TV was an attempt to court moral condemnation, and the same establishment manipulated the figures to prevent 'God Save the Queen' topping the charts during the Jubilee celebrations. To its credit punk never aspired to establishment status and, in true Situationist style, was already over before the date established in its canonisation, 1977. In its attempt to foster further politicisation through links with reggae, it also played on the white establishment's anxiety of being undermined by immigrant cultures. This genuine attempt, which had longer-term effects in ska revivals, Two-Tone, and Rock Against Racism, was in some ways remarkable, given that it was fostered by sections of the male working class which has, not without justification but often too simplistically, been seen as a breeding-ground for racism. Increasingly marginalised and powerless, white male youths were attracted to the traditions of dissent within West Indian music, which was much more used to articulating resistance. Punk, at the same time as it was a manifestation of disaffected male youth which was threatening enough to be policed, also dismantled gender divisions in its rejection of stereotypes, and its fostering of asexuality and an anti-fashion standpoint. The phenomenon Punk, 'forever condemned to act out alienation, to mime its imagined condition, to manufacture a whole series of subjective correlatives for the official archetypes of "the crisis of modern life"', holds a particularly ambivalent and fascinating position in the history of cultural constructions of masculinity.[42]

Turning to the miners' strike, given that the Conservative government had increased the production of dual-fired power stations, and had ensured plentiful stocks of coal prior to any strike, it is 'hard to avoid the conclusion that the miners fell into a well laid trap', a year-long strike the Conservatives spent twenty million a week on to ensure it would win.[43] The case must not be overstated, nor must the significant role of women in the strike be ignored, but at the same time this battle was one waged against the trade union movement as a whole, and therefore in many ways against a form of traditional and (anti-establishment) dissenting masculinity.[44] The Conservative government chose to target the miners because their union had a symbolic role at the heart of sections of the working class, who were perhaps particularly tied to the ideal of the 'wages of white maleness', and if it could be crushed, fierce anti-union legislation could be more easily passed, and differing working practices throughout the industries and beyond could be developed.[45] Any argument that attacks the trade union movement, and the communities built around the large industries traditionally associated with it, is also an assault on a particular, and potentially dissenting masculinity. It needs to address the fact that the culture of the labour and trade union movement has been strongly masculine, and in such a deep-rooted manner that changes have been slow. But whilst the trade union movement has represented large numbers of men in full-time employment, its treatment of part-time workers and jobs traditionally associated with women has been at least inadequate.

V. Male Violence

Male violence has also been a commonplace of historical accounts of masculine social identity; many recent books on masculinity include some discussion of the gendered nature of violence and its social origins and ramifications. Jonathan Rutherford selects the representation of violence in films as another 'predicament in masculinity', exploring the myth and popularisation of Rambo and the male viewer's identification with such an 'icon of popular culture'.[46] Lynne Segal voices the feminist unease with men's continuing violence and aggression towards women and the implications of this iconisation, asking the leading question, 'Is Violence Masculine?' In her perceptive commentary on this aspect of male behaviour, she considers 'the social and cultural linkages between "masculinity" and violence' which are often bolstered by the state violence carried out by men.[47] Whilst suggesting that 'the majority of men [are] enthralled by images of masculinity which equate it with power and violence', she locates this more specifically in the social environment by arguing that 'It is the sharp and frustrating conflict between the lives of lower working-class men and the image of masculinity as power, which informs the adoption and, for some, the enactment, of a more aggressive masculinity'.[48] Other writers such as Roger Horrocks have considered serial murderers such as Jack the Ripper as exaggerated but symbolic examples of men's dangerous conceptions of the masculine role where male dominance is taken to frightening extremes. The essays in this volume by Matthew Pateman and Emma Liggins offer divergent readings of the celebration/execration of male violence in western culture, as male murderers become unacknowledged objects of desire, and pornography reveals the violent implications of sexuality. Pateman responds to Andrea

Dworkin's radical and infamous claim that 'all sex is rape', and that pornography reinforces and displays men's sexual enjoyment of violence towards women.

Writers such as Segal and Middleton have also drawn attention to fighting in wars as revelatory of men's social/gender identity; divorced from their emotions, men are often crudely represented as fulfilling their masculine urges through atrocity, becoming men by killing in the service of their country. Whilst violent masculinity is then officially condemned and vilified in our society, its cultural representation often reveals an alternative vision where killers such as Rambo and Bill Sikes enjoy a certain glory. The fact that violence helps to shore up male identity is an aspect of modern culture which is difficult to assimilate. In Brontë's fiction, as Duffy argues, violence is something that is passed on from father to son, part of the socialization of boys into men which always horrifies women. In the film version of Patrick McCabe's *The Butcher Boy*, the main character's mimicking of his father's violence at an early age means that the audience is treated to horrific visions of his self-definitions through murder, though here his behaviour is seen as excessive and evidence of psychological disturbance, inappropriate for a young boy. Tarantino's hugely popular films also depend upon an enjoyment and celebration of male violence. Men who hide in toilets, and are shot before they shoot, are emasculated in *Pulp Fiction*; in *Jackie Brown*, jokes are made at the expense of a female character, Melanie, who is killed, in a moment of dubious postmodern irony, because she nags too much.

Working-class masculinity has been typified, particularly by the tabloid press in the 1980s, with the elusive figure of the violent football hooligan. Bill Buford's exposition of hooliganism in *Among the Thugs* begins with a delineation of this nightmare for the

discerning bourgeois: Manchester United fans setting out for Italy
are lager louts and 'tourist trash', exposing indecent expanses of
flesh.[49] Football offers, for Buford, an arena for class war, as in this
depiction of a train journey amongst drunken fans:

> Hoping to avoid trouble, I sat in a first-class carriage at
> the very front of the train, opposite a man who had paid
> for his first-class ticket. He was a slim, elegant young
> man with a thin moustache, wearing a woollen suit and
> expensive, shiny shoes: a civilised sort of fellow reading a
> civilised sort of book - a hardback novel with a dust
> jacket. A supporter had been staring at him for a long
> time. The supporter was drunk. Every now and then, he lit
> a match and threw it at the civilised man's shiny shoes,
> hoping to set his trousers on fire. The civilised man
> ignored him, but the supporter, puffy and bloodshot,
> persisted. It was a telling image: one of the
> disenfranchised, flouting the codes of civilised conduct,
> casually setting a member of a more privileged class
> alight.[50]

'Telling' maybe in terms of Buford's narrative: surely drunkenness is
stereotyped here as a sign of working-class insobriety. The offending
fan could be a naughty bourgeois: as Buford illustrates throughout
the book, many of the most violent fans hold down traditionally
middle-class occupations. Hence, in a peculiar echo of Dworkin, he
offers a classless vision of masculinity as the trigger for violence.[51] In
contradiction, he concludes that the crowd violence of the 1980s
was due not to a political act by a stable working class, but due to its
decline, and the beginning of industrial recession. (A similar point is
discussed by Rowland: Harrison's depiction of hooliganism in 'V'
correlates the decline of Leeds United and working-class solidarity
in the early 1980s.) Economic deprivation takes its toll on formerly

stable roles for working-class men, so they become, according to Buford, 'so deadened that [they] use violence to wake [themselves] up'.[52]

The tragedy at Hillsborough on 15th April 1989, in which ninety-five people attending a football game were crushed to death, happened precisely because a culture had developed which was already predetermined to see any group of males as threatening to the social order, but without any sense of understanding the social context. Hooliganism did occur, of course, but it is necessary to see it as mainly articulated at either end of the working-class scale, the underclass and the aspiring class. The experience of being caught in 'downward mobility' fostered 'the kind of tribal aggression that soccer fans, deprived by education and social experience of any other focus for their personal identities or frustrations, exhibit towards each other'.[53] At the other end of the working-class strata this masculine 'posturing' arises from the 'upwardly-mobile, individualistic fraction [...] which has done relatively well out of the restructuring of British industry and business in the last twenty years'.[54] The term 'working class' is in some ways a misnomer, given the large ranks of the unemployed youth who are seen as unruly 'in large part because of their untutored, unchallenged "masculinity"'.[55] The suggestion here is that it is the lack of an identity, or the loosening of identity, which has resulted in a retrenchment of various forms of masculine behaviour. Blanket condemnation of football hooligans is unhelpful unless it is analysed through looking at the context of the breakdown of traditional masculine structures, and unless the fears and anxieties of these people are addressed. The rhetoric of condemnation and moral outrage may play well to the galleries, and be effective in gaining votes, but is irresponsible if it helps to feed into constructions of men, either excluded or cut adrift, as always already dangerous. In a related area, rhetoric concerning 'zero tolerance' tactics can be seen as legislation directed mainly at men, who are being constructed as dangerous subjects in need of fierce policing.

VI. Men in Literature

Whilst it certainly seems clear that cultural constructions of masculinity merit serious attention, there is still a noticeable reticence to address such issues in literature. Students tend to shy away from deep discussions of masculinity, perhaps because they have internalised a 'men as misogynists' credo, or because they are predominantly female themselves and feel that they have little to offer on the subject. As male students of literature at universities seem to be dwindling at an alarming rate, we should perhaps ask ourselves why this particular area of enquiry, in a culture obsessed with gender and its performance, seems so threatening. Relating masculinity to notions of the literary canon, arguments against the study of masculinities appear particularly forceful. Feminists might respond that English degrees have always been structured around the study of works by white, middle-class male European writers, that students have been bombarded, almost exclusively, with men's stories and poems, with cultural manifestations of masculinity, until fairly recent creations of alternative feminist canons and the (re)discovery of women's writing. Suzanne Moore has also argued that men have even hijacked gender studies to talk about women in an insincere version of gender tourism.[56] However, the purpose of this collection is to encourage male and female readers to reassess men's stories and representations of masculinity. Gender studies is still in its infancy, so that simplistic humanist accounts of such

texts, applauding their discussions of non-gendered human nature
and moral values, have taken no account of their implications for
gendered and sexual identities. If the study of literature is to be
committed to the exploration of culturally constructed
'difference', then it is vital that we include analysis of masculinity
and its ramifications with regards to class, sexuality, race, history
and nationhood.

David Gutterman suggests that postmodernism enables us to
produce rewrites 'in the cultural scripts of masculinity', that late
twentieth-century culture is intent on 'creat[ing] a space for a
variety of different masculinities to be performed'.[57] In his
representational metaphors, the performance and textualisation of
masculinities offer radical revisions of normative gender identity,
gesturing towards new versions of representation. His ideas can
be productively applied to a range of canonical and non-canonical
texts, enabling a reevaluation of our interpretations of men in
literature from *Beowulf* onwards (surely a fascinating bundle of
gender contradictions: the great warrior ultimately unmanned by a
dragon!) Whilst cultural-studies scholars such as Antony
Easthope and Roger Horrocks have used masculinity to theorise
twentieth-century popular culture and its icons, the attention paid
to literature's representation of masculinity, apart from isolated
areas such as Renaissance drama, has been scant. The editors
hope that this book will provide students with an introduction to
some of the signs of masculinity particularly relevant to literary
studies, and that it will promote awareness of their implication for
class, race, sexuality and gender.

Courses on masculinity available on degree schemes in English
are slowly beginning to establish themselves, particularly with the
very contemporary interest in gay identity and rights, and the
widening field of sexual politics. We hope that this book will

inspire a renewed interest in male writers who have been vilified for their representations of women. Authors such as Dickens and Lawrence (and more recent ones, such as Harrison) now seem to be greeted with cries of horror by students angered by their reductive and patronising versions of femininity. Rather than dismiss such work as patriarchal, the anxiety of the male author in relation to his work, as addressed by William Stephenson and Liz Hedgecock, testifies to the complexity and 'anxiety' of influence experienced as men seek to rewrite cultural scripts. Such rewriting includes revisions of stereotypical versions of 'mateship' in the Australian fiction discussed by Eriks Uskalis, fantasy yobs that Rowland tackles in Harrison's 'V', and the gushing penises in Pateman's porn. These last three examples are pertinent to recent changes in conceptions of masculinity; the first five chapters in the book are concerned with historical redefinitions of male identity in the eighteenth and nineteenth centuries. As a whole the book reflects the diversity of critical approaches to men in literature from 1700 to the present. Cannibals, criminals, fiendish fathers, hacks, Uranians, porn stars, errant clergymen, yobs, New Men and 'mates': these are models of masculinity which inform the readings of the individual texts in this book.

[1] Alan Sinfield, *Cultural Politics - Queer Reading* (London and New York: Routledge, 1994), *Faultlines: Cultural Materialism and the Politics of Dissident Reading* (Oxford: Clarendon Press, 1992) and *Political Shakespeare: Essays in Cultural Materialism*, ed. by Jonathan Dollimore and Alan Sinfield (Manchester: Manchester University Press, 1985). See also *Romantic Masculinities*, ed. by Tony Pinkney, Keith Hanley and Fred Botting (Keele: Keele University Press, 1997).
[2] John Tosh, 'What should Historians do with Masculinity? Reflections on Nineteenth-century Britain', *History Workshop Journal*, 38 (1994), 179-202 (p.180).
[3] Jonathan Rutherford, *Men's Silences: Predicaments in Masculinity* (London: Routledge, 1992), pp.3, 5.

[4]Yvonne Roberts, 'Father's little helper', *The Guardian*, 9 April 1998, p.5.

[5]Lynne Segal, *Slow Motion: Changing Masculinities, Changing Men* (London: Virago, 1990), p.x.

[6]Segal, p.60.

[7]Segal, p.xi.

[8]Segal, p.xi. She helpfully points out that ideals of masculinity derive from the social meanings which accrue to these ideals and that men's attachment to their own power is necessarily ambiguous. Her work as a whole is careful to take account of the many 'differing relations of power – class, age, skill, ethnicity, sexual orientation' which impact upon men's experiences. See pp.x-xi.

[9]Introduction to *Theorizing Masculinities*, ed. by Harry Brod and Michael Kaufman (London/California: Sage, 1994), p.4.

[10]Peter Middleton, *The Inward Gaze: Masculinity and Subjectivity in Modern Culture* (London: Routledge, 1992), p.152.

[11]Middleton, p.153.

[12]David S. Gutterman, 'Postmodernism and the Interrogation of Masculinity', in Brod and Kaufman, p.229.

[13]Gutterman, p.221.

[14]Hélène Cixous, 'Sorties: Out and Out: Attacks/Ways Out/Forays', in *The Feminist Reader: Essays in Gender and the Politics of Literary Criticism* ed. by Catherine Belsey and Jane Moore (London: Macmillan, 1989), pp.101, 113.

[15]Tosh, p.180.

[16]Hanif Kureishi, *The Buddha of Suburbia* (London: Faber and Faber, 1990), p.202.

[17]Peter Brooks, *Body Work: Objects of Desire in Modern Narrative* (Cambridge, Mass.: Harvard University Press, 1993), p.15.

[18]Middleton, p.126.

[19]Michel Foucault, *The History of Sexuality: An Introduction*, trans. by Robert Hurley (1976; Harmondsworth: Penguin, 1981), p.3.

[20]Foucault, pp.8, 35. His arguments about censorship and discourse are particularly illuminating in the context of how sexuality becomes transgressive.

[21]Foucault, p.35.

[22]Jeffrey Weeks, *Sexuality and its discontents: Meanings, myths and modern sexualities* (London: Routledge & Kegan Paul, 1985), p.190.

[23]Eve Kosofsky Sedgwick, *Between Men: English Literature and Male Homosocial Desire* (New York: Columbia University Press, 1985), pp.4, 3.

[24]Sedgwick, p.5.

[25]Gutterman, p.229.

[26]See Gutterman, pp.225-31 for a clear explanation of Butler's arguments about the heterosexual matrix. He also provides an incisive discussion of Sedgwick's theories of the closet and the culture of cross-dressing.

[27]Judith Butler, *Gender Trouble: Feminism and the Subversion of Identity* (London: Routledge, 1990), p.112-13. She is actually paraphrasing the work of Monique Wittig here, but the explanation can also stand for her own model of heterosexuality.

[28]Butler, pp.113, 111-12. See also Gutterman's discussions of the 'freedom to reimagine sexuality apart from gender'.

[29]Gutterman, p.227.

[30]Lynne Segal, 'Look Back in Anger: Men in the Fifties', in *Male Order: Unwrapping Masculinity*, ed. by Jonathan Rutherford and Rowena Chapman (London: Lawrence & Wishart, 1988), p.166.

[31]David J. Tracey, *Remaking Men* (London and New York: Routledge, 1997), p.90.

[32]Robert Bly, *Iron John: A Book About Men* (Reading, Mass.: Addison-Wesley, 1990), p.4.

[33]Tracey, p.87.

[34]Sabina Lovibond, 'Feminism and Postmodernism', *New Left Review*, 178 (November/December 1989), 5-28 (p.12).

[35]Jonathan Rutherford, 'Who's That Man?', in Chapman and Rutherford, p.32.

[36]Libby Brooks, 'We're all lads now', *The Guardian*, 13 July 1998, p.8. (Bryan Appleyard is a writer for the *Sunday Times*.)

[37]Sedgwick, p.1.

[38]*Manliness and Morality: Middle-Class Masculinity in Britain and America, 1800-1940*, ed. by J. A. Mangan and James Walvin (Manchester: Manchester University Press, 1987), p.1.

[39]Tosh, p.181, 182-83.

[40]Introduction to *Manful Assertions: Masculinities in Britain since 1800*, ed. by Michael Roper and John Tosh (London and New York: Routledge, 1991), pp.2, 7.
[41]Tosh, p.188.
[42] Dick Hebdige, *Subculture: the Meaning of Style* (London and New York: Routledge, 1979), p.65.
[43]Malcolm Pearce and Geoffrey Stewart, *British Political History 1867-1995: Democracy and Decline* (London and New York: Routledge, 1996), p.541.
[44]Obviously it can be very persuasively argued that the trade union movement is part of the establishment, but never completely, and establishment attacks on the working class need little recounting here.
[45]This loss, and this period, has been painfully and wittily caught in the film *Brassed Off* (1996).
[46]Rutherford, pp.185-87.
[47]Segal, p.267-68.
[48]Segal, p.265. She also considers issues around football hooliganism, rape and sexual violence, detailing the destructive ways in which violence becomes linked to 'men's endeavours to affirm "masculinity"' (p.269). Her argument also takes account of the growth of a permanent under-class in many Western societies, and finishes by locating male aggression in the conditions of 'the increased barbarism of public life' and 'contemporary capitalism' (p.271).
[49]Bill Buford, *Among the Thugs* (London: Secker and Warburg, 1991), pp.33-34.
[50]Buford, p.21.
[51]Buford, p.116.
[52]Buford, p.265.
[53]Ian Taylor, 'Hillsborough, 15 April 1989: Some Personal Contemplations' *New Left Review*, 177 (September/October 1989), 89-110 (p.104).
[54]Taylor, p.105.
[55]Taylor, p.106.
[56]Suzanne Moore, 'Getting a Bit of the Other - the Pimps of Postmodernism', in Rutherford and Chapman, p.167.
[57]Gutterman, pp.231, 234.

1.

'STRANGE LONGING' AND 'HORROR' IN *ROBINSON CRUSOE*

As early as 1957, in *Mythologies*, Roland Barthes analysed the bodily attributes of masculinity in the chapter upon 'The Romans in Films'. It seemed to Barthes that although bodily signs of masculinity passed for the natural, they were lying.[1] It is this simultaneously over-determined *and* empty nature of the signs of masculinity that enables what Jonathan Rutherford calls 'the myth of masculinity'.[2] It is also this double nature which, at a recent conference upon masculinity, perhaps gave rise to questions over whether the category of masculinity was in fact a useful starting point at all in cultural analysis: were there categories more substantial able to articulate the workings of culture without the seeming reductiveness of the category 'masculinity'?[3] Perhaps what is needed is a recognition that this category is absolutely 'nominal' in Locke's words: and also that as a unit of analysis it is practically useless without the perception that it is the concatenation with other categories that provides the useful 'work' of analysis.[4] Whilst I recognise that the study of gender cannot be conflated or subsumed under studies of sexuality, race, class, nationhood, or any other axis of analysis, it still performs a necessary task. As Eve Kosofsky Sedgwick comments in *Epistemology of the Closet*, the conflation of sexuality with gender risks

> obscuring yet again the extreme intimacy with which all these available analytic axes do after all mutually constitute one another: to assume the distinctiveness of the *intimacy* between sexuality and gender might well risk assuming too much about the definitional

> *separability* of either of them from determinations of,
> say, class or race.[5]

This essay, then, will tease out the intertwined threads of male sexuality and race, and of gender and nationhood, in Daniel Defoe's rich, almost mythic, text from 1719, *The Life and Strange Surprizing Adventures of Robinson Crusoe*.

It may, therefore, seem strange that I want to concentrate on eating. But I want to argue that *Robinson Crusoe* revolves around issues of imagined boundaries: for Crusoe, control over his body is the control over his imaginary bodily boundaries that are invested with the symbolic significance of nominal categories such as gender, sexuality, race, and nationhood. Yet the anxious metaphors and displacements throughout the novel are traces of a double movement of longing for, and horror of, the other, theorised by Julia Kristeva in *Powers of Horror* as abjection. Further, they are a kind of textual haunting.

Critics of Defoe's *Robinson Crusoe* have long pondered over the perceived 'problem' of Crusoe's sexual relations, or lack of them. This 'silence', as it were, has been given many varying interpretations.[6] Most have presumed an automatically, or naturally, heterosexual economy of desire for Crusoe to inhabit. I am not about to claim that Crusoe was homosexual. Rather, I want to suggest that *Robinson Crusoe* is haunted by a textual silence: it shapes, and is shaped by, a definition of masculinity that is structured by societal violence towards 'unnatural' sexual practices.

Defoe himself presented a rather ambivalent attitude towards unnatural sexual practices being represented in print at all. In an edition of his *A Review of the State of the British Nation* in 1707 (the year of the Society for Reformation of Manners' purge of sodomites in London), in opposition to the 'large

Description' afforded the crime of arson in that essay, he laments the publicity given to the trials of sodomites such as Captain Rigby and the opportunistic reprinting of the 1631 trial of the Earl of Castlehaven:

> I think 'tis in its Nature pernicious many Ways, to have this Crime so much as named among us; the very Discourse of it is vicious in its Nature, abominable to modest Ears, and really ought not to be entertain'd, far less should be so openly discuss'd, so publickly try'd in the Courts of Justice, and the Accounts of it exposed as a Subject to the vulgar Discourse of the People.[7]

As Ian McCormick has commented in relation to this piece, 'behind these comments is the sense of a concealed category which called for, excited and sanctioned the need to unmask'.[8] Sedgwick has also noted this almost paradoxical nature of same-sex desire, describing it as '*the* open secret'.[9]

Robinson Crusoe, then, can be set against this powerful silence, and also against a background of changing ideologies of male sexuality. As Randolph Trumbach notes, between around 1660 to around 1750,

> Europe was switching from adult male libertines who had sex with boys and with women to a world divided between a majority of men and women who desired only the opposite gender, and a minority of men and women who desired only the same gender.[10]

Yet it is important to be aware that such changes do not occur in isolation. The axis of gender saw parallel changes in the conception of 'effeminacy'. Broadly speaking, in the late-seventeenth century, a perception that too much heterosexual contact with women, and knowledge of feminine society, was a sign of effeminacy - a sign which encompassed debauchers and fops - had changed, by the mid-eighteenth century, to a conception that equated effeminacy with men who exclusively desired other men.[11]

Set against this background, Crusoe's signs cluster around eating and, more especially, horror, for cannibalism is *the* subject of horror in *Robinson Crusoe*. The spectacle, and spectacular signs, of cannibalism - bones, blood and flesh - haunt Crusoe. Yet it is an altogether more insubstantial object that first predominates Crusoe's anxieties:

> I was exceedingly surpriz'd with the Print of a Man's naked Foot on the Shore, which was very plain to be seen in the Sand: I stood like one Thunder-struck, or as if I had seen an Apparition.[12]

The amazing singularity of the footprint hyperbolically underlines its strangeness, its spectacular improbability: 'how it came thither, I knew not, nor could in the least imagine'. For Crusoe, 'wild Ideas were found every Moment in my Fancy', the source of which utter strangeness he finds 'must be the Devil; and Reason joyn'd in with me upon this Supposition: For how should any other Thing in human Shape come into the Place?' (p.154). However, he finally concludes 'that it must be some more dangerous Creature, (*viz.*) That it must be some of the Savages of the main Land' (p.155). Yet a level of metonymic association has built up in the movement from 'Devil' to 'Savages', and the exact nature of this association is not for long withheld, for Crusoe's fear is that they will find and 'devour me' (p.155).

It is here that *Robinson Crusoe* rehearses the automatic linking of the natives of the Antilles with 'cannibalism', so that 'Carib' becomes metonymic for 'cannibal' and vice versa. Indeed, the appellation 'Savage' denotes a particular definition of 'cannibalism' associated primarily with colonial discourse: cannibalism, according to Hulme, is 'the image of ferocious consumption of human flesh frequently used to mark the boundary between one community and its others'. The footprint, the sign of irrationality itself, materialises as the sign of the cannibal: the spectre of the footprint is the signifier of the 'other', all that is not 'self'.[13]

Ultimately, the episode triggers Crusoe's reflections upon God's providence and omnipotence, and he finds comfort in the words of the Bible to *'Wait on the Lord, and be of good Cheer, and he shall strengthen thy Heart; wait, I say, on the Lord'* (p.157). Even in the face of two injunctions to *'wait'*, Crusoe cannot resist going back to check that the footprint has not all along been a print of his own foot: torn between fear and a desire to know and therefore to know himself *as* a 'self', Crusoe is horrified at discovering all over again that the footprint is the unassailable sign of the other; there is no 'Similitude', only difference (pp.158-59). As in the first encounter, Crusoe feels his sense of self dissolving. At his first sight of the spectacle he is 'like a Man perfectly confus'd and *out of my self'* (my emphasis, p.154). The second encounter highlights the degree of loss of bodily control, having 'the Vapours [...] to the highest Degree' (p.159).[14]

Torn between desire and horror, Crusoe marks the boundary between self and the other. More properly, it is a movement that precedes and initiates self and other: the narrative reiterates the pre-oedipal process that heralds the beginnings of subjecthood and individuality that Julia Kristeva terms 'abjection':

> There looms, within abjection, one of those violent,
> dark revolts of being, directed against a threat that
> seems to emanate from an exorbitant outside or
> inside, ejected beyond the scope of the possible, the
> tolerable, the thinkable. It lies there, quite close, but it
> cannot be assimilated. [...] Unflaggingly, like an
> inescapable boomerang, *a vortex of summons and*
> *repulsion places the one haunted by it literally*
> *beside himself.*[15]

Through the flow of bodily fluids - urine, faeces, tears, mucus -
the 'I' comes to recognise the 'not I'. These fluids become
things of horror, loathing, 'abject'. The abject comes to
represent an 'other' and effectively establishes the body's
boundaries. However, it is through this same motion that this
incipient self senses that its boundaries are permeable, that what
is expelled - the abject - is a constant threat. Importantly, it is
not only fluids which signal the abject but the spectacle of the
dead body:

> as in true theatre, without makeup or masks, refuse
> and corpses *show me* what I permanently thrust aside
> in order to live. [...] the corpse, the most sickening of
> wastes, is a border that has encroached upon
> everything. It is no longer I who expel, "I" is
> expelled.[16]

Sickening, yet irresistible, the signifiers of cannibalism - the
footprint, but more spectacularly the human remains - mark
Crusoe as vital, whole, while threatening to destroy that vitality
and wholeness.

Crusoe's reaction to the sight of human remains is always one of horror:

> I was perfectly confounded and amaz'd; nor is it possible for me to express the Horror of my Mind, at seeing the Shore spread with Skulls, Hands, Feet, and other Bones of humane Bodies. (pp.164-65)

The need to describe these horrors is not offset by the apparent dread of the spectacle: far from it, the descriptions increase in their ghoulish fascination with the detail of dismemberment.[17] Nowhere is the narration of self and 'abject' more clear than at Crusoe's first encounter with human remains:

> I was so astonish'd with the Sight of these Things, that I entertain'd no Notions of any Danger to my self from it for a long while; All my Apprehensions were bury'd in the Thoughts of such a Pitch of inhuman, hellish Brutality, and the Horror of the Degeneracy of Humane Nature; which though I had heard of often, yet I never had so near a View of before; in short, I turn'd away my Face from the horrid Spectacle; my Stomach grew sick, and I was just at the Point of Fainting, when Nature discharg'd the Disorder from my Stomach; and having vomited with an uncommon Violence, I was a little reliev'd. (p.165)

At first we might wonder why Crusoe seems unconcerned about any threat to himself, for the sight of human remains does not provoke a reflection that his very own body's dismemberment may be prefigured in this 'horrid Spectacle'. Instead, like the footprint, this depiction produces a link between the violently fragmented bodies - the supposed products of cannibalism - and

the native Caribs themselves. The tokens of the abject come to
signify the 'inhuman, hellish Brutality, and the Horror of the
Degeneracy of Humane Nature'. Crusoe violently ejects, or
abjects from the boundary of his self, the threat of the cannibal
by locating the source of the abject - the human remains - not
within himself - but as a signifier of the 'Savage Wretches'. So
the potential threat that Crusoe *and* the human remains *and* the
cannibals are psychically closer than imaginable, is ejected:
proving to himself that the 'Degeneracy of Humane Nature' is
not a Hobbesian state of nature common to all humankind, but
by virtue of his bodily cleanliness is located within the abject.
This *corps propre* is achieved by vomiting: 'Nature discharg'd
the Disorder from my Stomach'.[18] The 'Disorder' is peculiarly
charged here, as if the material in his stomach is metonymic for
the spectre of cannibalism itself.

This Galenic, humoural psychology is pressed into service by
Defoe to construct a private consciousness. Commenting upon
dreams in *Robinson Crusoe*, Armstrong and Tennenhouse point
to the way in which a certain kind of individuality was invented
by fiction which 'saw fit to designate an interior domain of
"self" as separate and apart from everything else that was, by
definition, not such a self'.[19] This interior domain is dependent
upon the control of bodily boundaries: in this case, vomiting and
non-cannibalism stand in close association. Oral functions which
European and Carib males might have in common are sharply
differentiated.[20] Racial identity in this text is a function of
alimentary control: the delineation of a regulated internal 'space'
is constructed as a distinctly European trait, where those abject
bodies and appetites are in fact the founding condition of that
identity. Mobilising Judith Butler's theorisation of gendered
identity in *Bodies That Matter*, such an identity can be termed
performative, where performativity is understood as 'that

reiterative power of discourse to produce the phenomena that it regulates and constrains'.[21] The many episodes where Crusoe regulates his self argue that subjectivity comes into being through repetition, exclusion and the policing of an 'imaginary morphology': the repetition of anthropological myth, the exclusion of the abject Caribs, the policing of appetite, are bound up with the category of gender.[22]

Bodily control was perceived as especially problematical for women in the eighteenth century: women's bodies were conceived as being perpetually on the verge of losing self-control, the weakness of their fibres and nerves apparently rendering their bodies far more liable to hysteria. 'That is why', the physician Sydenham noted, 'this disease attacks women more than men, because they have a more delicate, less firm constitution [...] and because they are accustomed to the luxuries and commodities of life and not to suffering'.[23] In *The Ladies Dispensatory: or, Every Woman her own Physician* (1740), alimentary metaphors were strangely mixed with the functions of the womb:

> That lax and pliant Habit, capable of being dilated and contracted on every Occasion, must necessarily want that Degree of Heat and Firmness which is the Characteristick of Man, and which enables him to digest and evacuate his Nutriment in due Time and Proportion.[24]

Self-control also intertwined moral and bodily codes, where laxity in body control led inevitably to the precipice of immodesty at least, and very probably immorality. This perceived lack of bodily control parallels a perceived lack of

sexual control in the misogynist trope of the insatiable woman
employed by Robert Gould:

> That Whirl-pool Sluce which never knows a Shore,
> Ne're can be fill'd so full as to run ore,
> For still it gapes, and still cries - room for more![25]

Importantly, it also bespoke a fear by the male of a kind of
engulfment, a fear of being consumed, of being *eaten*.

Much was made of the control of appetite in the ideology of
the Society for Reformation of Manners, an organisation that
targeted most especially male manners in its heyday from the
1690s to the 1720s. 'National Fast Days' were proclaimed,
especially during times of national anxiety such as the wars of
Austrian, then Spanish Succession, then during the French
plague of 1720, which received ideological backing from the
Societies. Fasting, the ultimate in bodily self-denial, is in Josiah
Woodward's 1695 sermon on a fast-day, 'a natural expression
of self-abhorrency'.[26] It has its symbol perhaps in Crusoe's
almost ritualistic fasting on each anniversary of his shipwreck on
the island, an emblem of *corps propre*:

> I kept this Day as a Solemn Fast, setting it apart to
> Religious Exercise, prostrating my self on the Ground
> with the most serious Humiliation, confessing my
> Sins to God, acknowledging his Righteous Judgments
> upon me, and praying to him to have Mercy on me,
> through Jesus Christ. (p.103)

The importance of cleanliness, healthiness and autonomy as an
image for the rising bourgeoisie is noted by Foucault in *The
History of Sexuality*, but this also interacts with aspects of

British Protestant nationhood.[27] For within the reformist
ideology the manners of the nation's men reflected the state of
the English nation. Lapses in masculine virtue led to an inlet of
effeminacy, and a weakening of England's defences against
Popery.[28] Fasting relied, not only upon Christian models of self-
mortification, but on Galenic models of the body. An excessive
diet increased the 'heat' in the male body, leading to an excess
of sexual desire. If such desires were assuaged through sex with
women, there was always the danger of an enervated and sickly
male. Too much sexual contact with women rendered men
'effeminate'.

Some interesting crossings between the axes of gender and
sexuality and the theme of appetite can be gleaned from Defoe's
*Conjugal Lewdness: or Matrimonial Whoredom. A Treatise
Concerning the Use and Abuse of the Marriage Bed* (1727). In
this, the narrator fulminates against marriage for sex instead of
for procreation:

> where was the Religion of all this? [...] where the
> Soul is governed by the Body, where the spiritual Part
> is over-ruled by the fleshly, where the sensual directs
> the rational [...] The Order of Things is inverted;
> Nature is set with her Bottom upward; Heaven is out
> of the Mind, and Hell seems to have taken
> Possession.[29]

The narrator spares thirteen pages exclusively to the excesses of
diet: 'it is an undeniable Maxim, that a luxurious Appetite in
eating and drinking raises an ungoverned Appetite in other
Pleasures', and he recommends a 'Doctrine of Discipline and
Mortification' (pp.310, 315). Yet, like Defoe's anxieties over
sodomy trial reports, a concealed category is very near the

surface, emblematised, I think, in the phrase 'Nature [...] set
with her Bottom upward'. The 'Crime of Sodom', although
standing in for all the depredations of the marital bed, inevitably
raises the spectre of sodomy, and that too becomes associated
with excessive appetite:

> The Crime of *Sodom*, however unnatural the Vices
> are which they practised, is laid all upon a Cause,
> which was of the same Kind with ours, Pride and
> Idleness, and Fulness of Bread. By which I
> understand, that their lascivious Wickedness
> proceeded from their luxurious Diet. (pp:317-18)

Indeed the anxieties of appetite seem to take on something of
the abject for Defoe:

> We not only dig our Graves with our Teeth, by
> mingling our Diseases with our Food, nourishing
> Distemper and Life together, but we even eat our
> Way into Eternity, and damn our Souls with our
> Teeth; gnawing our Way through the Doors of the
> Devil's Castle with our Teeth. (pp.323-4)

For Defoe, loss of alimentary control does not only indicate a
fall from ideal manliness, that is, a corruption along the axis of
gender, but a fall from heterosexual manliness: a corruption
along the axis of sexuality.

Anxieties over orality had further connotations. G. S.
Rousseau has pointed out the interaction of the discourses of
cannibalism and sodomy, and notes how the sodomite 'became
the *new cannibal* of the age - by attributing to him a whole
series of practices originating in and around the mouth,
especially kissing, masturbation, and eating' (his emphasis).[30]

Some idea of this can be glimpsed in a text from 1691, *Mundus Foppensis: or, The Fop Display'd*:

> The World is chang'd I know not how,
> For Men kiss Men, not Women now;
> And your neglected Lips in vain,
> Of smugling *Jack*, and *Tom* complain:
> A most unmanly nasty Trick;
> One Man to lick the other's Cheek;
> And only what renews the shame
> Of *J.* the first, and *Buckingham*:
> He, true it is, his Wives Embraces fled
> To slabber his lov'd *Ganimede*;
> But to employ, those lips were made
> For Women in *Gomorrha*'s Trade;
> Bespeaks the Reason ill design'd,
> Of railing thus 'gainst Woman-kind:
> For who that loves as Nature teaches,
> That had not rather kiss the Breeches
> Of Twenty Women, than to lick
> The Bristles of one Male dear *Dick*?[31]

As a text that straddles changes in effeminacy and sodomy it is a pot-pourri of ideologies of gender and sexuality. But the emphasis on orality clearly owes something to other excesses in appetite.

For Defoe, there are other similarities between sodomy and cannibalism: namely the concept of Nature abandoned by heaven, which we have seen in the excesses of appetite in *Conjugal Lewdness*. However, here is his opinion on sodomites, from 1707:

> As for the Persons, I leave them to Justice. I believe,
> every good Man loaths and pities them at the same
> time; and as they are Monuments of what human
> Nature abandoned of Divine Grace may be left to do -
> So in their Crime they ought to be abhorr'd of their
> Neighbours, spued out of Society, and sent expressly
> out of the World, as secretly and privately, as may
> consist with Justice and the Laws.[32]

Here he is describing the Caribs in *Robinson Crusoe*:

> who [...] have no other Guide than that of their
> own abominable and vitiated Passions; and
> consequently were left, and perhaps had been so
> for some Ages, to act such horrid Things, and
> receive such dreadful Customs, as nothing but
> Nature entirely abandon'd of Heaven, and acted by
> some hellish Degeneracy, could have run them
> into. (p.170)

Haunting this text, 'the conditions of the possibility of the
work', in Pierre Macherey's words, is that silent category of
sodomy, for other cultural links exist between cannibalism and
sodomy in the accounts of West Indian exploration.[33]

Richard Trexler noyes that in an early reference to Carib
culture, in 1494, Columbus's doctor, Diego Alvarez Chanza,
claimed that when the Caribs captured islanders they 'first
castrated them, then used them sexually until they grew to
adulthood, at which point they were killed and eaten'.[34] In 1495,
Michele di Cuneo commented that the natives were 'largely
sodomites'.[35] In 1525, Tomás Ortiz also noted that the Caribs
'were sodomites more than any other race'.[36] While not using
these accounts as anthropological facts, I would like to suggest

that such narratives, like the narratives of cannibalism, are of the order of available cultural myths.

Is, however, Crusoe's experience of cannibalism *only* one of horror? If for Defoe unnatural and excessive appetites lead to unnatural and excessive sexual practices, then Crusoe's fear of cannibalism, his fear of being eaten by another man, bespeaks a fear of sodomy. Yet Crusoe is simultaneously drawn to, and repulsed by, the image of Carib sodomy; he needs this image to identify himself against, in the same motion that he removes himself from this image: that is the movement of abjection. That Crusoe needs to desire that which must not exist within himself - the excessive sexuality denominated by Defoe as sodomy - puts the text under some strain. I believe such a need existed because *Robinson Crusoe* produces, and is produced by, a culture which was beginning to conceive of an ideal bourgeois manliness as exclusively heterosexual. Since Crusoe's bodily perfection must appear as a co-operation between nature and reason, that which is unnatural appears when we glimpse ambivalent textual moments. The peculiarly charged atmosphere surrounding Crusoe's sight of a shipwreck off the island is one of those moments.

After viewing the shipwreck during the night off the island's shore, Crusoe concludes that all the seamen have died, and the loss of potential company is almost insupportable:

> I cannot explain by any possible Energy of Words, what a strange longing or hankering of Desires I felt in my Soul upon this Sight; breaking out sometimes thus; O that there had been but one or two; nay, or but one Soul sav'd out of this Ship, to have escap'd to me, that I might but have had one Companion, one

> Fellow-Creature to have spoken to me, and to have convers'd with! (pp.187-88)

Crusoe's longing for company after being alone for many years seems only a 'natural' expression for homosocial bonding. However, the furious 'Energy of Words' and emotions are startling:

> Such were these earnest Wishings, That but one Man had been sav'd! *O that it had been but One!* I believe I repeated the Words, *O that it had been but One!* A thousand Times; and the Desires were so mov'd by it, that when I spoke the Words, my Hands would clinch together, and my Fingers press the Palms of my Hands, that if I had had any soft Thing in my Hand, it wou'd have crusht it involuntarily; and my Teeth in my Head wou'd strike together, and set against one another so strong, that for some time I cou'd not part them again. (p.188)

Nowhere else in the novel does Crusoe balance so precipitously on the edge of his desires, for here is a body ruled by its own movements. The intense repetition of the phrase *'O that it had been but One!'* at once testifies to the strength of his desires, *and* to the ineffectiveness of those desires being controlled by the will that names them. Indeed, speaking those words energises his body beyond control: his hand is no longer his to control, but merely 'it', emphasising the extent to which his body is 'involuntarily' expressing his homosocial longings.

What is the link between Crusoe's 'strange longing' and involuntary bodily movements? 'Let the Naturalists explain these Things', Crusoe says, 'I knew not from what it should proceed' (p.188). Given that for Defoe the body that no longer responds to control is a potential source of aberrant sexual desire, then this particular aberration in the text is the effect of abjecting from Crusoe's body any excessive sexual desire. Suspended between the voluntary and the involuntary, Crusoe's body is suspended between heterosexuality and homosexuality. It is the trace of what cannot be signified openly, the unconscious cultural expression of a need to differentiate ideal heterosexual manliness from the man who exclusively desired other men. Pushed to create a perfectly wholesome, autonomous body, and therefore unable to signify erotic desire for men *or* women, yet also pushed by the needs for Crusoe to display an ideal heterosexual manliness, *Robinson Crusoe* displays a body hysterically miming a desire without aim.

Crusoe is also suspended between paralysis and action, torn 'between Fear and Desire' whether to risk the dangerous excursion to the shipwreck (p.190). For in the shipwreck is the abject: dead and possibly dismembered bodies, but also the reverberating silence of erotic contact with other males. As in abjection, Crusoe is drawn to that which he fears, for therein also lies self-definition: 'I must venture out in my Boat [...] it could not be resisted [...] I should be *wanting to my self* if I did not go' (my emphasis, p.189). What he finds on board the shipwreck is two men who have drowned, 'with their Arms fast about one another' (p.191). As an emblem of all that Crusoe has lamented over, the wish for male company, it is perfect: the sorrowful expression of two men in their last moments of life clinging to each other. Yet it curiously receives no comment from Crusoe apart from his dispassionate conjecture that when the storm struck the ship they 'were strangled with the constant rushing in of the Water' (p.191). Instead Crusoe's longing seems temporarily silenced as his attention is diverted onto the utilitarian material inside the shipwreck.

What happens, then, to his desire for company? After the shipwreck Crusoe is visited by 'an Impetuosity of Desire' to sail to the mainland which is the product of impulses characterised as irrational:

> Pray note, all this was the fruit of a disturb'd Mind, an impatient Temper, made as it were desperate by the long Continuance of my Troubles, and the Disappointments I had met in the Wreck, I had been on board of; and where I had been so near the obtaining what I so earnestly long'd for, *viz.* Somebody to speak to [...] All my Calm of Mind in my Resignation to Providence, and waiting the Issue of the Dispositions of Heaven, seem'd to be suspended. (p.198)

Again, the force of these irrational desires to sail towards the abject, the site of cannibalism and sodomy, manifests itself in his body: 'it set my very Blood into a Ferment' (p.198). The result is a dream in which there is a premonition of the rescue of Friday. However, there are notable differences between the dream and the reality of Friday's rescue. In the dream 'Friday' escapes without Crusoe's help:

> I thought in my Sleep, that he came running into my little thick Grove, before my Fortification, to hide himself; and that I seeing him alone, and not perceiving that the other sought him that Way, show'd my self to him, and smiling upon him, encourag'd him. (pp.198-99)

Notably, Crusoe's desire for company does not manifest itself in a willed action to rescue him; rather, Friday magically comes to

Crusoe. Similarly, he hopes this 'Servant' will act as a pilot for his venture to the mainland, and 'will tell me what to do', a process that seems a disavowal of Crusoe's desire, yet echoes his loss of bodily control and his somnambulant state (p.199).

The most notable point of agreement between dream and reality is, however, Friday's willing subjection to Crusoe. When Crusoe does actually rescue him a year and a half later, Friday 'kneel'd down [...] kiss'd the Ground, and laid his Head upon the Ground, and taking me by the Foot, set my Foot upon his Head; this it seems was in token of swearing to be my Slave for ever' (pp.203-4). Yet as Hulme points out, Friday's 'self-interpellation as a subject with no will' removes the need for violence and force on Crusoe's part, in effect re-writing the history of colonisation and slavery where such violence and force were absolutely necessary.[37] It also papers over Defoe's anxieties of the social order between master and servant. In a passage from *Augusta Triumphans* (1731), he complains of the '*Sunday* Debauches' at the market around the 'Hundreds of *Drury*'. Defoe's fear of the potential instability of this relationship is graphically portrayed as instabilities in sexual and gender roles:

> While we want Servants to do our Work, those Hundreds, as they call 'em, are crowded with Numbers of idle impudent Sluts, who love Sporting more than Spinning, and inveigle our Youth to their Ruin: Nay, many old Lechers (Beasts as they are) steal from their Families, and seek these Harlot's lurking Holes, to practice their unaccountable Schemes of new invented Lewdnesses: Some half hang themselves, others are whipt, some lie under a Table and gnaw the Bones that are thrown 'em, while

others stand slaving among a Parcel of Drabs at a Washing-Tub.[38]

These instabilities, whilst testifying to Defoe's anxieties, also signal the precariousness of the social order. That the relationship between master and servant *can* be overturned by desire, as Sandra Sherman notes, indicates the contingent and performative nature of social power. It also suggests that in displacing the agency for master/slave relations in *Robinson Crusoe* away from Crusoe onto Friday himself, making Friday the 'addict', instabilities in sexual and gender roles are displaced too. Crusoe's active desire for companionship is disavowed by Friday's self-subjection, displacing the potential for homoerotic desire surfacing in the text onto an apparently peaceful master/slave relationship.[39]

Yet the trace of the belief that Carib sodomy is contagious pervades Crusoe's relationship with Friday. Crusoe's description of Friday has the effect of re-shaping Friday himself, of de-othering him, producing a body less threatening, less cannibal, less sodomiser:

> He was a comely handsome Fellow, perfectly well made; with straight strong Limbs, not too large; tall and well shap'd, and as I reckon, about twenty six Years of Age. He had a very good Countenance, not a fierce and surly Aspect; but seem'd to have something very manly in his Face, and yet he had all the Sweetness and Softness of an *European* in his Countenance too, especially when he smil'd. His Hair was long and black, not curl'd like Wool; his Forehead very high, and large, and a great Vivacity and sparkling Sharpness in his Eyes. The Colour of his Skin was not quite black, but very tawny; and yet

> not of an ugly yellow nauseous tawny, as the
> *Brasilians*, and *Virginians*, and other Natives of
> *America* are; but of a bright kind of dun olive Colour,
> that had in it something very agreeable; tho' not very
> easy to describe. His Face was round, and plump; his
> Nose small, not flat like the Negroes, a very good
> Mouth, thin Lips, and his fine Teeth well set, and
> white as Ivory. (pp.205-06)

This superlative description is both misleading and ambiguous, at best. That Friday is set apart from the rest of the native Caribs is expressed constantly throughout the portrait, and at one level this could be in the tradition of the idealised 'noble savage' (similar, for example, to the eponymous hero in Aphra Behn's *Oroonoko* and the figure of Yarico in *The Spectator* no. 11). However, such depictions were overbalanced by the dominance of less benign portrayals from the seventeenth century.

It is my contention that this description of Friday abounds with an ambivalent desire. On the one hand the language is, as Hulme notes 'tinged with erotic delight', even if it is inseparable from the master surveying a healthy slave.[40] Yet I believe the eroticism cannot be denied. Friday is 'a comely handsome fellow', and while 'very manly' has 'all the Sweetness and Softness of an *European*'; he has also 'a great Vivacity and sparkling Sharpness in his Eyes', and the colour of his skin 'had in it something very agreeable'. This eroticism is the trace of the irrational and dangerous passion within Crusoe that must be produced in order for it to be displaced from his body, for the production of a heterosexual male whose borders will not be contaminated by cannibal sodomy. The production of an erotic cathexis between Crusoe and Friday and the trace of cannibal sodomy are displaced by shaping Friday as European and not that threatening savage: by displacing the actual Carib body from the narrative. There is no mention of the 'normal Carib practices of ear and lip plugs, flattened foreheads and noses, as well as scarification', notes Boucher.[41] Because such a description would reinstate the threat of cannibal sodomy and the threat of a potential homoerotic cathexis, such bodies are reserved for the mainland natives who must always exist as a distanced threat for Crusoe's self-definition.

However, the fear and horror of contamination by cannibal sodomy never leaves. Crusoe, after he sees the human remains of a cannibal feast, fears with 'Abhorrence' that Friday 'had still a hankering Stomach after some of the Flesh, and was still a Cannibal in his Nature' (p.208). In an important way Friday is perceived to be in a state of addiction, implying a lack of control over appetite, both alimentary and sexually, in opposition to Crusoe's control over his bodily appetites. Even in the face of contrary evidence, Crusoe still evinces a paranoia of cannibalism. When Friday tells him of the Spanish castaways on the mainland who live alongside the natives there, Crusoe asks how it is that they are not eaten. Friday explains that they have made a truce, and besides they only eat men who fight them and are taken prisoner in battle. Yet when Friday sees the mainland from the island one day, all of Crusoe's fears return:

> I made no doubt, but that if *Friday* could get back to
> his own Nation again, he would not only forget all his
> Religion, but all his Obligation to me; [...] and come
> back perhaps with a hundred or two of them, and
> make a Feast upon me. (p.224)

The over-turning of the master/servant 'Obligation', as in *Augusta Triumphans*, signals a potential threat to sexual roles. Crusoe's horror of cannibalism, his fear of being eaten, his fear of being used sexually by another male, his fear of a contagion that pierces his bodily self-containment, are all bound up here.

The images of Crusoe's fasts, his Protestant bodily reverence, the vomiting of cannibalism, the sodomites 'spued out of society' and his body, suggest the myth of an impossibly hermetic self: impossible because those very movements, these gut reactions, are absolutely necessary. Early eighteenth-century masculinity thrived, in order to construct its identity, on the unnameable; manliness longed for those abject silences because therein lay definition.

[1]Roland Barthes, *Mythologies*, trans. by Annette Lavers (London: Vintage, 1993), pp.26-28.

[2]Jonathan Rutherford, 'Who's That Man?', in *Male Order: Unwrapping Masculinity*, ed. by Jonathan Rutherford and Rowena Chapman (London: Lawrence & Wishart, 1988), pp.21-67 (p.23).

[3]'European Masculinities', Department of History Research Colloquium, University of Manchester, 22 February 1997.

[4]I am drawing upon John Locke's distinction between '*real*' and '*nominal* *Essence*', where 'nominal' suggests a linguistic label, see *An Essay Concerning Human Understanding* ed. by Peter H. Nidditch (Oxford: Clarendon Press, 1975), III.vi.2-3, pp.439-40. For a discussion of Locke's theory, see Diana Fuss, *Essentially Speaking: Feminism, Nature and Difference* (New York & London: Routledge, 1989), pp.4-5.

[5]Eve Kosofsky Sedgwick, *Epistemology of the Closet* (Harmondsworth: Penguin, 1990), p.31.

[6]Ian Watt, in his portrait of Crusoe as an embodiment of economic individualism, finds that economic priorities necessitate the expulsion of personal and sexual relationships. Citing Weber, he notes 'sex [...] being one of the strongest non-rational factors in human life, is one of the strongest potential menaces to the individual's rational pursuit of economic ends', *The Rise of the Novel: Studies in Defoe, Richardson, and Fielding* (Harmondsworth: Penguin, 1957), p.70. J. Paul Hunter believes that Crusoe

is named after the divine, Timothy Cruso, and that any reference to sexual relations only brings to mind that religious man's past sexual exploits, to the detriment of the allegorical naming, *The Reluctant Pilgrim: Defoe's Emblematic Method and Quest for Form in Robinson Crusoe* (Baltimore: The Johns Hopkins Press, 1966), pp.205-7. Robyn Weigman proposes that male sexuality is voiced by Crusoe's domination and fashioning of a feminized landscape, 'Economies of the Body: Gendered Sites in *Robinson Crusoe* and *Roxana*', *Criticism*, 31:1 (1989), 33-51, (pp.43-45). Christopher Flint notes a 'strange double focus' in Defoe's narratives which depend upon, and yet continually reject, the conjugal family, 'Orphaning the Family: The Role of Kinship in *Robinson Crusoe*', *ELH*, 55 (1988), 381-419 (p.382). Peter Hulme, whilst noting that 'the masculinist ethos of European colonialism is probably explanation enough of *Robinson Crusoe*'s lack of women', glances at the eroticized portrait of Friday, *Colonial Encounters: Europe and the Native Caribbean, 1492-1797* (London & New York: Methuen, 1986), pp.211-12. Hans Turley, finally, locates Crusoe's desires as torn between *homo economicus* and normative ideals of domestic identity, 'The Homosocial Subject: Piracy, Sexuality, and Identity in the Novels of Daniel Defoe' (unpublished doctoral dissertation, Washington University, 1994; abstract in *Dissertation Abstracts* DAI-A 54/04 (Oct. 1995), p.1373), pp.230-290.

[7]Daniel Defoe, *A Review of the State of the British Nation*, ed. by Arthur W. Secord, 9 vols (London, 1703-14; New York: Columbia University Press, 1938), 27 November 1707, pp.495-96 (p.496), vol. IV.

[8]Ian McCormick, ed., *Secret Sexualities: A Sourcebook of 17th and 18th Century Writing* (London & New York: Routledge, 1997), p.50.

[9]Sedgwick, p.22.

[10]Randolph Trumbach, 'The Birth of the Queen: Sodomy and the Emergence of Gender Equality in Modern Culture, 1660-1750', *Hidden from History: Reclaiming the Gay and Lesbian Past*, ed. by M. Duberman, M. Vicinus, G. Chauncey (Harmondsworth: Penguin, 1989), pp.129-40 (p.130).

[11]See Michael McKeon, 'Historicizing Patriarchy: The Emergence of Gender Difference in England, 1660-1760', *ECS*, 28:3 (1995), 295-322 (p.308).

[12]Daniel Defoe, *The Life and Strange Surprizing Adventures of Robinson Crusoe*, ed. by J. Donald Crowley (London, 1719; Oxford & New York:

Oxford University Press, 1972), p.153. Further references are given after quotations in the text.

[13]Hulme, p.86. Hulme notes that the footprint is 'like a pure trace of the idea of otherness' (p.201).

[14]The 'vapours' were considered to be a form of exhalation from the lower part of the body and were both cause and symptom of mental disorders such as hypochondria and hysteria, although hysteria was generally assigned to women. See Robert James M.D., *A Medicinal Dictionary*, 3 vols. (London: 1743-45).

[15]Julia Kristeva, *Powers of Horror: An Essay on Abjection,* trans. by Leon S. Roudiez (New York: Columbia University Press, 1982), p.1. (My emphasis.)

[16]Kristeva, pp.3-4.

[17]See also pp.183, 207.

[18]Kristeva, p.53. The translator renders *corps propre* as 'one's own clean and proper body'; see 'Translator's Note', viii.

[19]Nancy Armstrong & Leonard Tennenhouse, 'The Interior Difference: A Brief Genealogy of Dreams, 1650-1717', *ECS*, 23:4 (1990), 458-78 (p.458).

[20]That differences in eating practices are culturally determined is suggested by the fact that Africans thought that it was Europeans themselves who were cannibals. See *The Life of Olaudah Equiano, or Gustavus Vassa the African*, ed. by Paul Edwards (Harlow: Longman, 1988), pp.22, 26-27, 31-32. Also, see Nick Rowe (rowen@ENC.EDU), 'Re: cannibals, European, citation', in C18-L (C18-L@LISTS.PSU.EDU), 12 May 1997.

[21]Judith Butler, *Bodies That Matter: On The Discursive Limits of 'Sex'* (New York & London: Routledge, 1993), p.2.

[22]Butler, p.13.

[23]Thomas Sydenham, *Médecine pratique* (French trans., Paris, 1784, p.394), cited in Foucault, *Madness and Civilization: A History of Insanity in the Age of Reason*, trans. by Richard Howard (1961; London: Routledge, 1989), p.149.

[24]*The Ladies Dispensatory: or, Every Woman her own Physician* (London, 1740), in *Women in the Eighteenth Century: Constructions of Femininity*, ed. by Vivien Jones (New York & London: Routledge, 1990), p.83.

[25]Robert Gould, *Love Given O're: or, a Satyr against the Pride, Lust, and Inconstancy, etc. of Woman* (London, 1682), in Jones, p.62.

[26]Josiah Woodward, *Sermon Preached before The Right Honourable the Lord-Mayor and Aldermen of the City of London, At St. Mary le Bow. On Wednesday the 19th of June, 1695. A Day appointed for a Solemn Fast* (London, 1695), p.7, see also pp.27-28. Woodward was a tireless campaigner for the Societies for Reformation of Manners.

[27]Michel Foucault, *The History of Sexuality: Vol. 1, An Introduction*, trans. by Robert Hurley (1961; Harmondsworth: Penguin, 1981), pp.122-7.

[28]See, for example, John Shower, *A Sermon Preach'd to the Societies for Reformation of Manners in the Cities of London and Westminster, Nov. 15 1697* (London, 1698), p.49.

[29]Daniel Defoe, *Conjugal Lewdness; or, Matrimonial Whoredom. A Treatise concerning the Use and Abuse of the Marriage Bed*, (London, 1727; Gainsville, Florida: Scholars' Facsimiles and Reprints, 1967), p.271.

[30]G. S. Rousseau, 'Cannibal discourse, the Grand Tour, and literary history', *Studies on Voltaire and The Eighteenth Century*, 303 (1992), 35-69 (p.58).

[31]Anon., *Mundus Foppensis: or, the Fop Display'd* (1691), The Augustan Reprint Society, no. 248 (Los Angeles: University of California, 1988), pp.12-13.

[32]Defoe, *Review*, 27 November 1707, p.496, vol. iv.

[33]Pierre Macherey, *A Theory of Literary Production*, trans. by Geoffrey Wall (1966; London: Routledge & Kegan Paul Ltd., 1978), p.92.

[34]Richard C. Trexler, *Sex and Conquest: Gendered Violence, Political Order and the European Conquest of the Americas* (Cambridge: Polity Press, 1995), p.65.

[35]Cited in Trexler, p.65.

[36]Cited in Jonathan Goldberg, *Sodometries: Renaissance Texts, Modern Sexualities* (Stanford: Stanford University Press, 1992), p.193. See especially pp.179-222 for Renaissance texts of sodomy and the 'new world' from Mexico to Peru.

[37]Hulme, p.206. Within these terms of self-subjugation Friday, in a legal and symbolic sense, is in a state of addiction. 'Addiction' in the *OED* (2nd ed.) is defined as 1. 'a formal giving over or delivery by sentence of court. Hence, a surrender, or dedication, of any one to a master'. And 2. 'the state of being (self-) addicted or given *to* a habit or pursuit'. As we shall see, Crusoe also fears Friday is literally addicted to cannibalism.

[38]Daniel Defoe, *Augusta Triumphans: The Generous Projecter* (London, 1731), pp.41, 42. See also Sandra Sherman, 'Servants and Semiotics: Reversible Signs, Capital Instability, and Defoe's Logic of the Market', *ELH*, 62:3 (1995), 551-573 (pp.566-67).

[39]See also Turley, pp.267-68.

[40]Hulme, p.212.

[41]Philip P.Boucher, *Cannibal Encounters: Europeans and Island Caribs, 1492-1763* (Baltimore & London: The Johns Hopkins University Press, 1992), p.126.

2

'SUCH FINE YOUNG CHAPS AS THEM!' REPRESENTATIONS OF THE MALE CRIMINAL IN THE NEWGATE NOVEL

Popular fascination with the male criminal was a cultural commonplace of the early Victorian period. Crime news was a growing feature of the newspapers, which officially condemned the criminals, but seemed to take a perverse delight in their wicked deeds all the same. The exploration of the links between masculinity, class, crime and violence in the nineteenth-century press exposes an uneasiness about society's reactions to discourses of criminality which continues today. Lynne Segal suggests that 'We need to ask why a type of working-class aggressive masculinity seems such a perennial feature of our social environment'.[1] I shall be suggesting that stereotypes of the male criminal, the twin focus of admiration and horror, contributed towards received notions of masculinity, and that the public execution became the site on which the traumas of male, working-class identity were played out. The hanged bodies of the criminal classes became the sign of their uncertain sexualities, as discourses on criminality dwelt on the muscular appearance of the criminal. Anxieties about women's reactions to reports of male violence and their attendance at executions will be considered in relation to the ambiguities of male sexual identity in both newspaper reports and popular fiction.

Recent discussions of Victorian masculinity have tended to concentrate almost exclusively on middle- and upper-class male experience, as John Tosh has acknowledged.[2] However, Victorian popular fiction often confronted aspects of class and gender identity which remained at the margins of more traditional texts. The detailed examination of working-class experience in the Newgate novels of the 1830s raises a series of questions about the socialisation of working-class men, and the lack of economic and sexual choices available for them. Michael Roper and John Tosh suggest that 'masculinity is never fully possessed but must perpetually be achieved, asserted or renegotiated'.[3] In the Newgate novel, these assertions and renegotiations are channelled through criminal impulses and violence out of frustration at economic and sexual deprivation. Whilst the popular novel then duplicated the easy admiration of criminal-heroes, and the celebration of the working-class lifestyle endorsed by contemporary plebeian texts such as street-ballads and broadsheets, it also cast an ironic eye over such representations of masculinity, and its shifting relation to class. Execution scenes, in both novels and factual accounts, had a propensity to emphasise the hero's emasculation, and to suggest that the power and sexual attraction of the working-class man was a facade. Crime is then linked to the performance of masculine power. As Segal argues, 'It is the sharp and frustrating conflict between the lives of lower-class men and the image of masculinity as power, which informs the adoption, and, for some, the enactment, of a more aggressive masculinity'.[4]

Executions and Male Bodies on Display

Fevered debate on the social usefulness and moral effect of public executions spanned the period of the Newgate novel's popularity, as the increasing levity and indifference of the crowd to the death of the criminal undermined the middle class's capacity for legal and social control of its inferiors. Most of the readers of such texts would have witnessed executions, or at least have read numerous newspaper accounts of them. As V. A. C. Gatrell confirms, 'Until the collapse of the capital code in the 1830s no

ritual was so securely embedded in metropolitan or provincial urban
life. Nor was any so frequent.'[5] Part of the hostility towards the
Newgate novel stemmed from the pretence that executions were not
attended by respectable people, that they had no interest in criminals
beyond a desire to discipline them. I suggest that the reading of the
novels parallels the activity of going to see criminals hanged, that
the texts stage a similar assessment of the hero in terms of bravado
and weaknesses, and that the sense of horror, excitement,
celebration and anxiety is common to both experiences.

Renowned for the diversity of responses they inspired, public
executions appealed to people from all walks of life, as the body of
the hanged felon inspired a range of emotional and erotic responses.
The following extract from *The Times* of 1837, describing the
execution of John Smith, 25, and George Timms, 22, for the
'barbarous murder' of Hannah Manfield, is typical in its illustration
of crowd reaction:

> Timms was the first led up - a stout athletic man, in
> apparently perfect health, and habited in the usual garb of
> his class of life; he walked with slow and staggering
> steps, hanging down his head, and crying bitterly [...]
> Suddenly the fatal bolt was drawn; and as the bodies
> swung round, and exhibited themselves in a short
> convulsive struggle with death, a piercing cry of horror
> rose from the dense mass of people of both sexes, who, to
> the number of several thousands, thus witnessed the
> awful sacrifice indispensably due to injured society, to
> outraged humanity, and to public justice, in the capital
> punishment of these two most atrocious murderers.[6]

Whilst the men are officially condemned for the barbarity of their
crimes, their age and appearance militate against such a reading of

their deaths. As historians have confirmed, many criminals executed in this period were 'in the prime of manhood'; commenting on the male criminal's body became a commonplace of such accounts, as did the use of adjectives such as 'muscular' and 'athletic' in this context.[7] Suggesting that Timms was in 'apparently perfect health' both testifies to the physical hold criminals enjoyed over the crowds, and elicits sympathy for his predicament, as a lament for lost possibilities is staged by his body's failure to display the signs of disease and want, the usual bodily signs of a man 'of his class of life'. The admiration of the murderer's body, however, is at odds with the vision of Timms crying and hanging down his head as he approaches his death; the scaffold then becomes the site of the failure of masculine defiance where signs of feminine weakness and impotence (his inability to walk) are displayed. The uncertainty of the body as sign is further conveyed by the crowd's reaction to the swinging bodies. The 'piercing cry of horror' emitted by men and women alike is the culmination of a series of contradictory messages about men, murder, class, the law and sexuality, which are anchored in the body of the criminal.

Executions then made available the viewing of the male body for erotic purposes. Gazing on male bodies 'exhibiting themselves in a short convulsive struggle' does not seem like a proper pastime for women, especially in the light of the men's youthfulness. Bodies were left to hang above the crowd for an hour before they were cut down, supposedly as a warning against the evils of crime, but they had more impact as sexual objects. Gatrell notes Dickens' appreciation of the corseted form of Maria Manning after she had been hanged, and Thomas Hardy's disturbed memories of the bodies of other hanged women.[8] Executions became the breeding-ground for dangerous passions, and hence a potent political and sexual arena. An aura of political uncertainty generated by the mixed classes of the crowd surrounded the scaffold, which intensified the erotics of the event. The activity of 'going to see a man hanged' was seized upon by Thackeray as a signifier of cultural decline, partly because of the numbers of women present.[9] At the execution of Bishop and Williams for the murder of bodies to be sold for dissection, the number of women from a variety of classes spectating was an identifiable cause for concern, as:

> amongst the immense assemblage might be noticed several females, most of them of that *caste* whose attendance on such an occasion might be naturally expected, but some of them, we regret to state, of a class that decency, if not humanity, should have kept away from a scene so revolting to these delicate sensibilities that generally characterise females.[10]

In attending executions women were liable to be mistaken for prostitutes enjoying scenes of 'revolting' indecency. By reading Newgate novels, they laid themselves open to similar charges. While male bodies on display remained a rarity for most women, the convulsive jerks and quiverings of the (well) hung men, not to mention the erections and ejaculations occasioned by the feel of the noose and the advent of death, bordered on obscenity.[11]

The dangers of attending executions spiralled out from these multiple interpretations of the body of the criminal and the codes of manliness it endorsed. In the aftermath of the hanging of William Thurtell for murder in 1824, a *Times* leading article highlighted the contradictory stance of admiring murderers, unable to account for this unorthodox impulse in modern life:

> Not many days ago, it did appear to us that nothing could present itself to our observation more fitted to affect a

well constituted mind with disgust and horror, than the
late assassination for which *Thurtell* has been executed.
We regarded it as a murder most heartless, most
treacherous - in its motives the most sordid and base - in
its details the most inhuman and revolting [...] the justice
of the punishment was as clear as the atrocity of the
criminal; yet, to our amazement, we now discover the
greatest *sympathy* expressed in a thousand quarters for
him by whom the crime was perpetrated. "Manly,
dignified, consistent, courageous" *Thurtell*! Such are the
misplaced epithets bestowed profusely upon a being
whose only title to distinction above the common herd of
desperadoes was just a more animal indifference to pain
inflicted on himself or others [...] that such an exhibition
should have been admired - that the callous performer
should have been, as he has since been applauded - not
only among the ill taught and unreasoning vulgar, but by
some of those whose duty it is to correct their errors and
to imbue their minds with right notions of morality, is a
subject of bitter and mournful meditation.[12]

Baulking at the provision of an explanation for the appeal of
murderers, the piece emphasises the cross-class nature of their
attraction, as middle-class opinion mimicked the vulgar adulation
of its social inferiors. Thurtell's ordeal generated discourses on
manliness because it was primarily associated with the practice of
watching men die, the universal pursuit for which Thackeray
coined the phrase, 'Going to see a *Man* Hanged'. Adjectives
collectively ascribed to Thurtell's heroism were 'misplaced
epithets', socially threatening, because they altered the terms under
which criminality could be assessed and revealed an alternative
agenda to the law's view of the scaffold as a place where justice
was done. As in the account of the hanging of Timms and Smith,

attempting to draw a moral from the scene of violence by invoking the 'justice' of the event was doomed to failure as the attractions of the criminal outweighed the lesson his punishment was supposed to deliver. His body cancelled out remembrances of his past violence, becoming victimised by the cruelty of the penal codes, which was itself subject to violence. Working-class atrocity paled into insignificance in comparison to the relentless and unremitting operation of criminal policy, sacrificing the nation's youth to 'right notions of morality'

The Sexual Attractions of the Newgate Criminal-hero

Despite their obvious relation to the changing penal codes of the 1830s, Newgate novels were usually set in the eighteenth century, when the youth of male offenders was particularly noticeable, and the long list of capital offences tallied with the frequency of public executions. Edward Bulwer-Lytton, William Harrison Ainsworth and others pandered to the demands of the public with tales of highwaymen and murderers, where 'our hero' is a glamorised version of a historical criminal, from the same school of lovable rogues as the infamous Dick Turpin. In effect, the Newgate novelists highlighted a significant aspect of the dynamics of masculine narrative, in which the hero's progress depends upon a rejection of the temptations of crime and the allure of the working-class adventuring lifestyle.[13] They were in debt to Fielding's manipulation of his notorious swashbuckler hero, Tom Jones, who is only rescued from the gallows by the revelation of his middle-class origins and the love of a good woman. Like his counterpart Oliver Twist, his illegitimacy and uncertain parentage generate comments that he is 'born to be hanged', rather as if this were the fit conclusion to the male working-class plot. The gallows then cast an ominous shadow over the working-class male, as the criminal-heroes battle to escape their author's intimations of such an untimely end.

In Edward Bulwer-Lytton's novel *Paul Clifford* (1830) and William Harrison Ainsworth's *Jack Sheppard* (1839), the limitations of heroism are explored in the context of such oscillations between failure and confidence, as the men of the titles struggle to escape the destiny offered by their class position. Clifford, in particular, shares many characteristics with Tom Jones, being presumed illegitimate, thwarted in love because of his lower-class origins, and renowned across the land for his seductive manner. He is also frequently referred to as 'our hero', as eighteenth-century representations of the criminal are self-consciously invoked. Paul models himself on such representations; it is noted that 'Nothing could wean him from an ominous affection for the history of Richard Turpin' (p.30).[14] He also styles himself as a Smollett hero, feeling the need to 'leave the house, and seek his fortunes alone, after the manner of the ingenious Gil Blas, or the enterprising Roderick Random' (p.41). Bolstered by their picaresque associations, both plots solicit admiration and sympathy for their heroes by a celebration of the energy, intelligence and youth of men intent on fighting against a society which singles them out for blame and contempt. Positioned firmly within a lower class scapegoated as potentially dangerous, the boys are marked out for crime from the moment of their births; the gallows infiltrates their upbringing, used as both warning and temptation. In the early chapters of *Paul Clifford*, Mrs Lobkins worries about the consequences 'if little Paul should be scragged!', admonishes him for consorting with more practised criminals like Long Ned 'already on the way to the scragging post', and concludes, 'I tell you, child, you'll live to be hanged in spite of all my love and 'tention to you!' (pp.24, 81). In Ainsworth's novel, Sheppard's untimely end is signalled both by the handbills and woodcuts of his father's execution adorning his walls and the dire threats of Jonathan Wild that the son will follow in the footsteps of the father. His family origins emphasise the likelihood of his initiation into crime; he was born in the women felon's ward in Newgate on the very day that his father fell victim to the law, ensuring that his birth was attended by his mother's thoughts of 'halters, and gibbets, and coffins, and suchlike horrible visions' (p.5).[15] Their proximity to the gallows is held over the two heroes of the texts as a never-ending threat; Jonathan's power over Mrs Sheppard and her family is anchored in his ability to carry such threats through: 'If that sickly brat should live to be a man [...] I'll hang him upon the same tree as his father' (p.37). The notion that both boys will 'live to be hanged' as they attempt to live to be men locates the criminal impulse within male sexual development, as achieving the status of manhood is jeopardised by the presence of the gallows in urban society.

The performative aspect of criminality abhorred by *Times* reporters was essential to both Clifford and Sheppard, who owe their dominance over the reader to their flamboyance and indifference to fear. Kneebone describes Jack as 'the talk and terror of the whole town [...] the most daring and expert house-breaker that ever used a crowbar' whose 'exploits and escapes are in everybody's mouth' (p.168). In an eulogy to his associate's qualities, Blueskin paints Jack as the epitome of all that is glamorous and fascinating about criminals, claiming 'there isn't his fellow, and never will be again. I've seen many a clever cracksman, but never one like him. If you hang Jack Sheppard, you'll cut off the flower o'the purfession [sic]' (p.192). Ainsworth looks back nostalgically to an age when the youth of the condemned smoothed over their potential for violence. As Gatrell confirms, 90% of men hanged in London in the 1780s were aged under 21.[16] Clifford's crimes are diminished by his charming manner; he is 'one of those accomplished and elegant highwaymen of whom we read wonders, and by whom it would have been delightful to have been robbed' (p.217). Assessing his criminal character, Long Ned proclaims, 'he be a fine chap and I'll go to his hanging!', suggesting that masculine 'fineness' might be a criterion for a gallows death (p.322).

Erotic appreciation of the fictional criminal was anchored in the cultural fascination with the bodies of those condemned to be hanged. Both Sheppard and Clifford are blessed with outstanding physiques which facilitate their escapes from prison and ensure them a constant stream of attention. We are told of Clifford that he looked:

> a man in whom a much larger share of sinews and muscle than is usually the lot even of the strong had been hardened, by perpetual exercise, into a consistency and iron firmness which linked power and activity into a union scarcely less remarkable than that immortalised in the glorious beauty of the sculptured gladiator. (p.304)

During his confinement in Newgate, Jack is visited by Hogarth whose artist's eye swiftly appraises the litheness of his form, exclaiming, 'Look at that light, lithe figure - all muscle and activity, with not an ounce of superfluous flesh upon it' as if he were 'designed by nature to plan and accomplish the wonderful escapes he has affected' (p.282). Ainsworth's novel started a craze for its leading male, what *Fraser's Magazine* called 'a Jack Sheppard mania', as the novel was transferred to the stage as a means of capitalising on his attractions.[17] Anticipating the final display of their bodies to crowds of thousands, the texts linger on the physical attractions offered by the men, promoting an image of men as muscular, well-built and energetic.

This corresponds to the presentation of criminal bodies in contemporary newspaper accounts of executions. Perhaps as a shorthand for indicating the youth of the malefactors, *The Times* drew on a similar range of adjectives to describe the figures of hanged men. The twenty-eight year-old William Howell choking to death for murder in 1845 struck the reporter as being a 'fine, athletic, well-proportioned fellow'.[18] In 1839, the body of the condemned Michael Slattery elicited comment because he was 'so weak [...] that he could not hold his body in an erect position', and he appeared 'as if deprived of all nerve'.[19] Whilst such sentiments pointed towards the demise of the sexual function of the man's body - that at the moment of execution, he was nervous and could not remain erect - the report concludes with the information that 'He was a man of about 5 feet 11 inches high, and proportionably robust and muscular'.[20] Immaterial as it is to the way in which the men died, such information was often proffered in such reports, and was even privileged over descriptions of the death - the time it took to die, or evidence of struggling - in some shorter pieces, like that covering Howell's death. Such predictable comments added to the rituality of the deaths and their reporting, but used this rituality to announce the alternative agenda of sexuality. As the Newgate plot demonstrated, men indulged in crime at the expense of sexual activity, using their bodies to escape from prisons or facilitate highway robberies from admirers, rather than to reproduce or offer sexual pleasure. The gallows is only the visible sign of a certain unproductive and self-obsessed strain to Victorian masculinity, which sacrificed bachelors to the noose when they were no longer socially useful. Inept in their dealings with women, unable to conceive of sexuality unattended by violence or force, the men were upbraided by the gallows for their failures to add to the population, as the reports lamented the waste of their bodily strength and health.

In Lytton's later novel *Eugene Aram* (1832), sexual anxieties are also mobilised by premonitions of hanging, offering up an alternative image of the male criminal as one unmanned by the demands of his social position. Riding home, Aram sees before him in a lightning flash 'the gibbet, immediately fronting his path, with its ghastly tenant waving to and fro' (p.194).[21] Masculine sexual identity is threatened by the potential for crime, as men like Aram struggle with the consciousness that:

> at any hour, in the possession of honours, by the hearth of love, I might be dragged forth and proclaimed a murderer; that I held my life, my reputation, at the breath of accident; that in the moment I least dreamed of, the earth might yield its dead and the gibbet demand its victim. (p.339)

Crime in this scenario is a means of cancelling out socially sanctioned sexuality in the form of marriage - 'the hearth of love' - where the murder victim may be unearthed at any moment and demand the murderer's dead body to balance things out in social terms. Accounts of criminal activity in the press perpetuated such images of the criminal as a working-class male ever aware of his proximity to the gallows. A typical case recorded in *The Times* in 1832, 'the frightful murder [...] perpetrated on the body of Elizabeth Randal by her husband, Thomas Randal', includes Randal's exclamation of success and resignation: 'I have done it: I have done what I intended to do, and am now ready for the gallows'.[22] Here the direct route to execution for the working man is stressed, almost as if Randal's violence were a necessary confirmation of his social status and gender. Similarly, Lytton's novel suggests that Aram is victimised into playing the criminal, unable to offer any resistance to fate, so that marriage and reputation are but an 'accident' to be corrected by execution and its concomitant reordering of social categories. It is in this context that the gallows and the gibbet come to symbolise the scarcity of sexual and economic choices for lower-class men.

Sexuality is used to anchor the delights and pressures of crime and murder, as the text plays on the erotics of violence. Houseman's sexual attractions frighten Elinor and Madeline, as their fears of his potential for violence are confused with their awareness of his body; Elinor confides with a kind of terrified delight to her sister after their encounter with him, 'I saw the barrel of the pistol quite distinctly' (p.12). Criminality is used to mediate images of virility, employing the same sensationalist tactics of the press by weaving together stories of murders and the sexual relationships that preclude them. Interchanges between Aram and his partner-in-crime Houseman largely consist of threats of violence and death, and paradoxically display far more passion than any of the love scenes between Aram and Madeline, the conventional heroine. The tie between male criminals is 'stronger than that of friendship' partly because each of them admits to living 'with the rope around his neck', uniting them through their fear of execution and their awareness of the potential glamour of their situation. In one revealing scene, Aram taunts Houseman with the ease with which he could kill him: 'Two nights since, when my blood was up, and the fury upon me, what should have prevented me tightening the grasp that you so resent and laying you breathless at my feet?' (p.187). Their homosocial tie then slips over into the homoerotic as the shared knowledge of their deeds of blood encourages them to toy with the idea of the other's dead body. The relationship between Aram and Houseman exceeds the limits of male bonding or criminal association, supporting the view that men turn to crime and the company of men out of a fear of sexual commitment. The male reader of the Newgate novel, like the male spectator of an execution, hides his homoerotic urges behind his admiration of criminality, built on the exclusion of women and marriage in a world which denies the existence of responsibility. As women gravitated towards marriage to give them a sense of social purpose, the Newgate plot suggested that men increasingly turned to crime as an alternative means of gratification. Marriage is perceived to be a middle-class pleasure, unavailable to those with lower-class social credentials or uncertain parentage. Producing and inspiring its own set of erotic responses, criminality is imaged as an essential stage of male, working-class sexual and social development.

Violence and Emasculation

Execution scenes in the Newgate novel trod a fine line between admiration for the glamorous heroes of the hour and execration for men who had transgressed social codes in such a way that sympathy was withdrawn. Arguably, the focus on the male murderer, particularly in Charles Dickens' *Oliver Twist* (1837), helped to deglamorise this cultural icon, who, shorn of his charms and deprived of his muscular body, highlighted the more sinister and violent aspects of working-class sexuality. Ainsworth's account of Jack's final moments is poised on the brink between nostalgia for an era in which crime was associated with virility, and a growing awareness of the inconsistencies of criminality and the true basis of notoriety. His fame now appears uncontested, the word on everyone's lips: 'By this time, Jack's reputation had risen to such a height with the populace - his exploits having become the universal theme of discourse - that the streets were almost impassable for the crowds collected to obtain a view of him' (p.330). One of the benefits of setting Newgate novels in the eighteenth century was the observance of the convention of the ride to Tyburn. In 1783, this practice was abandoned, partly because it encouraged the carnivalesque aspects of the execution, giving the criminal the opportunity to enjoy his fifteen minutes of fame. Gatrell is somewhat dismissive of the claims that the Tyburn cart was a platform for glorification of the working man, and points out that bravado was often a result of drunkenness and that 'dying game' was a falsity which only thinly concealed the quaking terror of the condemned.[23] Dying game *was* a defence mechanism, admittedly, which it was difficult to believe in, but it was more specifically a discursive construct perpetuated by certain Newgate novels and broadsheets as a means of restoring that recognition of working-class experience and making it meaningful. Jack's final procession uses his control over his body and the crowd's appreciation of that control as an illustration of this recognition:

> Though encumbered by his irons, his step was firm, and his demeanour dignified. His countenance was pale as death, but not a muscle quivered, nor did he betray the slightest appearance of fear. On the contrary, it was impossible to look at him without perceiving that his resolution was unshaken [...] [a shout is heard as he leaves Newgate] He looked around, and as he heard that deafening shout - as he felt the influence of those thousand eyes fixed upon him - as he listened to the cheers, all his misgivings - if he had any - vanished, and he felt more as if he were marching to a triumph, than proceeding to a shameful death [...] Words of encouragement and sympathy were addressed to Jack, who, as he looked around, beheld many a friendly glance fixed upon him. (pp.336, 338, 339)

Rather than using the scaffold as an arena of repentance and suffering, Ainsworth celebrates the idea of community, as the onlookers forget class distinctions in their eagerness to applaud the bravery of a man who chose to break the rules of social decorum. It is ambiguous as to whether Sheppard is actually experiencing the terror Gatrell posits as an inevitability of the Tyburn ride, but succeeds in disguising it, or whether his heroism is bolstered by his capacity to face his fate with dignity. The crescendo of adjectives of self-control - 'firm', 'dignified', 'unshaken', - coupled with the negation of the image of the quivering body, the fearful countenance and the expression of misgivings, constitutes a rejection of the stereotype of the criminal unmanned by his plight. They suggest rather that the cheering of the crowd elevates him above the ordinary felon and acknowledges the strength of character required to cover up his fears. There is a sense that the shouting, words of encouragement and friendly glances have the power to dictate the mood of the occasion, ensuring that his death is a triumph rather than a shameful experience.[24]

Execution scenes tended to displace issues of punishment onto those of sexual excitement, as the display of the criminal bodies encouraged comments on male sexuality, and deviant behaviour in the crowd. Ruminating on the inhabitants of a Smithfield jail, Nancy in *Oliver Twist* comments on the attractiveness of those condemned to be hung: 'such fine young chaps as them!' echoing descriptions of Clifford (p.95).[25] The vision of her lover meeting his death in this way inspires romantic devotion: 'If it was you that was coming out to be hung [...] I'd walk round and round the place till I dropped, if the snow was on the ground, and I hadn't a shawl to cover me' (pp.95-96). Bolstered by such literary adulation for the criminal, murderers occupied a definite place within sexual fantasy. Bourgeois attempts to protest too much about the 'offensive and foul behaviour' of the crowds attending hangings similarly exhibited a kind of sexual arousal masquerading as horror in which the deviancy of the working classes also seemed erotically charged. Dickens' angry anti-execution letter to *The Times* in 1849 dwelt lasciviously on the obscenities generated by the hanging of the Mannings, particularly on the 'tumultuous demonstrations of indecent delight when swooning women were dragged out of the crowd by the police with their dresses disordered'.[26] What was then intended as the confirming of social categories became a carnival of disruption, simultaneously 'odious spectacle' and exhibition of indecency, where dangerous sexualities held sovereign sway.

And yet such elements of carnival were persistently undermined by the gravity of the occasion, as the 'faintings, fightings [and] whistlings' failed to drown out the obvious agony and fear of the condemned men.[27] Crime as an emasculating activity figures strongly in *Oliver Twist*, as the hangings of Fagin and Sikes are anything but glamorous, shifting the emphasis away from the sexual towards the social repercussions of the event. The gallows became a symbol of political oppression which unmanned the working classes by jeopardising their capacity for crime and violence. Fagin's ruminations on his impending fate confirm such suggestions as in his lonely cell he sits and thinks:

> of all the men he had known who had died on the scaffold; some of them through his means. With what a rattling noise the drop went down; and how suddenly they changed, from strong and vigorous men to dangling heaps of clothes! [...] It was like sitting in a vault strewn with dead bodies - the cap, the noose, the pinioned arms, the faces that he knew, even beneath the hideous veil - Light, light! (p.343)

In this scenario, execution is an emasculation procedure as the 'strong and vigorous men' are deprived of body, becoming nothing more than their clothes. Virility gives way to impotence of both the social and sexual variety, as the clothes 'dangle' pointlessly; Fagin and Sikes are just the last in a long line of unremarkable male criminals who have been punished in this way. The dead bodies with which the condemned cell seems to be strewn have no uniqueness, since execution requires that men are deprived of identity once dressed in the customary cap as their bodies are faceless and indistinguishable. The gibbet's victims have no honours to boast of, as they are subsumed beneath the generalisations of working-class masculinity.

The scenes leading up to Sikes' accidental hanging and the viewing of his body bear a strong resemblance to the behaviour of the Newgate crowds awaiting the execution of the infamous James Greenacre, sentenced in 1837 for the mutilation of his fiancée Hannah Brown. Awareness of men's horrific violence towards women was registered in the execration both men aroused - the killing of Nancy is a harrowing and detailed account of male domestic violence. United by their vilification of the murderer, the crowd chasing Sikes mimics the behaviour of the crowd watching Greenacre die, registering their vehement disapproval of his unrestrained violence. It is the force of their shouts which initiates the hanging, rather than the other way around, as Dickens repeatedly refers to the 'multitude of angry voices', 'the cry of the infuriated throng' and the 'terrific yells' (p.326). Articulated within the same language as the hatred expressed by the crowd outside Newgate, the screams of the crowd and the necessity of looking at the criminal are prerequisites for social harmony, as the need to express anger at a class divided against itself which privileges murder over marriage is the ultimate confirmation of the justice of

capital punishment. Dickens writes that, on perceiving Sikes'
inability to escape, the crowd 'raised a cry of triumphant execration'
so loud that 'it seemed as though the whole city had poured its
population out to curse him' (p.327). This urgent desire to view the
body, the fact that the crowd are 'all panting with impatience [...] to
look upon the criminal' suggests that they make no distinction
between live and dead bodies, that the hanged body and the arrested
criminal merge into one as the sign of their anger and excitement
(p.329). It also testifies to the power of the criminal body as a sign,
where its inability to escape the public gaze is part of the
punishment for murder.

In its description of the mob's behaviour whilst awaiting
Greenacre's appearance, *The Times* listed the same set of criteria for
registering intense disapproval:

> It was then evident that there was a feeling in that
> numerous assembly which would express itself in
> clamorous exultation as soon as ever he appeared to
> atone for the blood which he had shed so unrelentingly;
> and no sooner did those officers, who usually precede the
> criminal to the place of execution, become visible than it
> burst forth in a loud, deep, and sullen shout of execration
> against Greenacre, even before that miserable man came
> under the terrible ordeal of their indignant glance.[28]

When the execution of the criminal atoned for spilt blood, the
exultation the event inspired denied the erotic appeal of the
murderer at the same time that it placed him within the same league
as Jack Sheppard. I would suggest that it became increasingly
difficult to distinguish between admiration and hatred as the
ambiguous nature of the cheers and desire to look on the criminal
meant that the crowd's feelings could be made to fit the line of

argument of newspaper or novel. Descriptions of the hanging of Greenacre drew attention to the power of the gaze of the female spectator, as illustrated in this extract from the *Morning Chronicle*:

> As the body hung quivering in mortal agonies, the eyes of the assembled thousands were rivetted upon the swaying corpse with a kind of satisfaction [...] The crowd seemed as if they never could satisfy themselves with gazing at the hanging murderer. The women were, if possible, more ruthless than the men.[29]

The peculiar satisfaction that springs from the enjoyment of a good hanging is here associated with the feminine, as if the very act of 'ruthless gazing' endows women with a certain status that merges with the thrills they may experience. Although Sikes seems 'thoroughly quelled by the ferocity of the crowd' he also responds to their cries as he is 'roused into new strength and energy' exhibiting both sides of the coin of masculine norms (pp.328, 329). At one point Dickens classifies the cries of the crowd in these terms, noting that 'some spent their breath in impotent curses and execrations' as if the contest for true masculinity continues in their reactions (p.326). A mass of contradictory messages about manhood, punishment and murder, the scene condenses the variety of responses to the body of the soon-to-be-hanged man and implies that they might be mutually dependent.

The overlaps between sexual inadequacy and the victimisation of the lower classes are exhibited in the hanged body of Sikes and its uncertain meanings. Dickens emphasises the orgasmic nature of his fall, leaving the contest between impotence and virility in the site of his body unresolved:

> He fell for five-and-thirty feet. There was a sudden jerk, a
> terrific convulsion of the limbs; and there he hung, with
> the open knife clenched in his stiffening hand.
> The old chimney quivered with the shock, but stood it
> bravely. The murderer swung lifeless against the wall;
> and the boy, thrusting aside the dangling body which
> obscured his view, called to the people to come and take
> him out, for God's sake. (p.328)

The bodily reactions of sexual excitement - the sudden jerk, terrific
convulsion, the stiffening and the quivering - conflict with the
corporeal stillness which heralds the onset of death. Sikes' body can
now be 'thrust aside' and carted away, as it is no longer the object
of the crowd's gaze, but something which obscures the view. The
present participle 'dangling' is a favourite Dickensian gloss for the
helplessness of dead men, used in Fagin's vision of the men hanged
before him and in his memories of the Mannings hanging side by
side on the roof of Newgate. Here it is used to differentiate the
hanged bodies of men and women:

> those two forms dangling on the top of the entrance
> gateway - the man's, a limp, loose suit of clothes as if the
> man had gone out of them; the woman's, a fine shape, so
> elaborately corseted and artfully dressed, that it was quite
> unchanged in its trim appearance as it slowly swung from
> side to side.[30]

Confirming the aspersions cast on Mr Manning's masculinity by his
nervousness prior to execution, the word 'dangling' is linked to
limpness and loss of manhood, as the physical appearance of the
hanged man seems shapeless in comparison to the 'fine shape' of his
wife's corpse.[31] Militating against such an interpretation of Sikes'
body are the syntactic connections between the knife and the

'stiffening' of his hand. Whilst this underlines the eroticised nature of murderous violence, this violence cannot be separated from the rigor mortis of an untimely death, nor from the satisfactions of the crowd. The warning to the lower classes his body should signify then rebounds on the middle classes as a threat of unabated violence, and the continuation of political aggression. His corpse then demonstrates the political power that can be annexed to the sexual shortcomings of working-class men, as their refusal to channel their sexual impulses into marriage carries untold dangers to social harmony.

'The perverted curiosity which executions never fail to excite' was fuelled by the Newgate novel and its insistent focus on the dangerous attractions of male, working-class sexuality.[32] I would suggest that readers of the Newgate text simulated the erotic engagement of the execution crowd, as the novels confirmed the sexual subtexts to murder and judicial punishment. I have argued that the increased focus on male murderers in the Newgate novel considerably deglamorised their representations of criminals, as admiration of the 'fine young chap' was tempered by an awareness of his unchecked violence. Whilst novels by Ainsworth and Lytton celebrated the young criminal's triumph over a cruel social system by lingering on the pleasures of the muscular body, Dickens was to subvert generic conventions by positing a more malevolent version of working-class masculinity. The sexual and social inadequacies of working-class men which the spectacle of the gallows lamented were later harnessed to uncontrollable violence towards women, which altered the female reader's/spectator's eroticisation of the hanged body. However, there were underlying fears that murderers' bodies aroused stronger feelings and provoked more intense erotic responses. It became virtually impossible to deny the pornographic aspects of public executions and the 'disgusting levity' they produced, which is one of the reasons why they were abolished in 1868.[33]

[1] Lynne Segal, *Slow Motion: Changing Masculinities, Changing Men* (London: Virago, 1990), p.264.

[2] John Tosh, 'What should Historians do with Masculinity? Reflections on Nineteenth-Century Britain', *History Workshop Journal*, 38 (1994), 179-202 (p.181).

[3] *Manful Assertions: Masculinities in Britain since 1800*, ed. by Michael Roper and John Tosh (London: Routledge, 1991), p.18.

[4] Segal, p.265.

[5] V. A. C. Gatrell, *The Hanging Tree: Execution and the English People, 1770-1868* (Oxford: Oxford University Press, 1994), p.30.

[6] 'Execution of the Denver Murderers, and their Confessions', *The Times*, 1 May 1837, p.3.

[7] This phrase was used in the report of the execution of the murderer Lightband to heighten the poignancy of his early death. Although he was being punished for murder, the reporter seemed more concerned with the physical appearance of this 'unfortunate man' and his struggles to maintain his hold on his manhood. He describes the contradiction between his physicality and his anxiety: 'He was originally a man of very muscular make, but confinement and, what was worse, mental agony, had made considerable inroads on his person'. See 'Execution of Lightband the Murderer', *The Times*, 27 March 1837, p.6.

[8] Gatrell, p.266. He usefully juxtaposes both men's admiration of the 'fine' figures of the hanged women, as the tightness of their clothes allowed them to retain their womanly shapes after death.

[9] He comments particularly on the 'debauched crew' of women prostitutes 'giggling, drinking and romping' around the scaffold, whilst also suggesting that a 'vigorous, orderly good sense' prevailed among the people. The blend of contrasting forms of classed behaviour added to the difficulties of interpreting the event. See [W.M. Thackeray], 'Going to see a Man Hanged', *Fraser's Magazine*, 22, (August 1840), pp.153, 154.

[10] 'Execution of Bishop and Williams for the Murder of the Italian Boy', *The Times*, 6 December 1831, p.3.

[11] Gatrell, p.38. He also notes the tendency for the body to expel urine and faeces at the moment of death.

[12]Leading article, *The Times*, 14 January 1824, p.2.

[13]References to the works of Henry Fielding and John Gay's *The Beggar's Opera* abounded in reviews of the genre, linking the novelists to the tradition of male picaresque. This unfavourable comparison was used to emphasise the lack of morality in Victorian representations of criminals. One reviewer noted that 'In looking back on the Newgate scenes of Fielding and Gay [...] the first thing which recurs to memory is the noble purpose to which they are directed', whilst *Fraser's Magazine* lashed out at those readers duped into enjoying accounts of criminal life: 'In [Fielding's] dreadful satire of Jonathan Wild, no reader is so dull as to make the mistake of admiring, and can overlook the grand and hearty contempt of the author for the character he has described'. See Review of *Jack Sheppard, Athenaeum*, p.804 and Ikey Solomons (Thackeray), remarks following *Catherine: A Story, Fraser's Magazine*, 21 (February 1840), p.210.

[14]All quotations are taken from Right. Hon Lord Lytton, *Paul Clifford* (1830; London: George Routledge and Sons, 1874).

[15]All quotations are taken from W. Harrison Ainsworth, *Jack Sheppard: A Romance* (1839; London: George Routledge and Sons, [n.d.]).

[16]Gatrell, p.8.

[17]'William Ainsworth and Jack Sheppard', p.228. See also Keith Hollingsworth, *The Newgate Novel 1830-1847: Bulwer, Ainsworth, Dickens and Thackeray* (Detroit: Wayne State University Press, 1963) p.141 for his discussion of this phenomenon. He claims that 'if Jack himself was not quite everybody's darling, Sheppardism was not merely a working-class epidemic'.

[18]'Execution of William Howell for Murder', *The Times*, 27 January 1845, p.7.

[19]'Execution of Michael Slattery', *The Times*, 15 April 1839, p.6.

[20]'Execution of Michael Slattery', p.6.

[21]All quotations are taken from Right. Hon Lord Lytton, *Eugene Aram - A Tale* (1832; London: George Routledge, 1888).

[22]'Murder', *The Times*, 2 January 1832, p.4.

[23]He maintains that 'When the condemned felon played to the approbation of his fellows and mocked the hangman, he was calling on the last, only, and narrow resource available to him with which to anaethetize mortal fear'. See Gatrell, p.40.

[24]Cheering was not necessarily to be associated with good feeling towards the condemned and regret for his death, but could signify the crowd's appreciation of the workings of justice. At the hanging of the infamous Burke in 1829, condemned for murdering thirteen poor people in order to sell their bodies to the anatomy schools, cheering and 'huzzaing' were much in evidence. Vilified as 'the worst of murderers', Burke's convulsions were met with loud huzzas from the contemptuous crowd, who used their cries as a signifier of execration: 'the crowd evinced their abhorrence of the monster Burke [...] by three tremendous cheers'. See 'Execution of Burke', *Manchester Guardian*, 21 January 1829, p.3.

[25]All quotations are taken from Charles Dickens, *Oliver Twist* ed. by Kathleen Tillotson (1837; Oxford: Oxford University Press, 1966).

[26]*The Times*, 13 November 1849, p.6.

[27]*The Times*, 13 November 1849, p.6.

[28]'Execution of Greenacre', *The Times*, 3 May 1837, p.4.

[29]*Morning Chronicle*, 3 May 1837. Quoted in Gatrell, p.69.

[30]'Lying Awake', *Household Words*, 30 October 1852. Quoted in Philip Collins, *Dickens and Crime* (1962; London: Macmillan, 1994), p.240. Collins has a fascinating collection of snippets from Dickens' letters and lesser-known writings in his book. He also suggests that for Dickens, 'murderers were always wholly vile, never pitiful; one of his main objections to capital punishment, and later to public executions, was indeed that hanging a man made him too much an object for sympathy'. See p.254.

[31]Popular disappointment with criminals who failed to live up to ideals of dominant manhood was evidenced in the reporting of the trial and execution of the Mannings in 1849. They were a husband and wife murdering duo; the woman took the leading role in the murder and then upstaged her husband by her calmness on the day of execution. The reporter's withering summary of him as 'the thing that was her husband, but not a man' demonstrates the way in which men can be emasculated by refusing to perform the role of murderer. See *The Times*, 14 November 1849, p.3.

[32]'Execution of the Mannings', *The Times*, 13 November 1849, p.4.

[33]'Execution of the Mannings', p.4.

3

'FIENDS INSTEAD OF MEN': SARAH ELLIS, ANNE BRONTË, AND THE ECLIPSE OF THE EARLY-VICTORIAN MASCULINE IDEAL

When the gender ideologues of the early Victorian era granted man absolute power over the family, they did so on the grounds that he was not only stronger, but also nobler than woman: he could rule the home with wisdom, benevolence, and compassion. However, when they came to give woman a compensatory role, a somewhat different idea of man was required, and his vital nobility became only too fallible in order that it should need his mate's moral care. Thus a masculinity which was far from noble was generated. With reference to the work of Sarah Ellis, one of the most widely-read conduct writers of the period, I hope to demonstrate that this masculinity spiralled out of the control not only of their watchful figure of woman, but also of the ideologues themselves, supplanting their initial model of man and so discrediting male ascendancy.[1] I also hope to demonstrate that this inadvertent conclusion was deliberately dramatized in the novels of Anne Brontë, who depicts households made hellish by demonic male rule precisely to point up the danger of the power imbalance in the domestic sphere. In her progressive vision the failure of redemptive feminine influence – a notion she seizes upon and radicalizes as a reason for woman's equality with man – is attributed to female subservience, which is shown to encourage corruption of women's moral sense and to render them liable to foster rather than to check their menfolk's brutal masculinity. Ultimately Brontë reformulates the domestic paradigm by situating the sexes in a relation of parity and cooperation: only when women enjoy such liberty, she suggests, can they function as moral guides and so realize something approaching the period's masculine ideal in man. But her heroes do not embody this ideal as fully as we might expect; as I will argue, the monstrous masculinity in her novels proves to be as tenacious as that which usurps the schema in Ellis's writings.

'Spots in the Sun': Sarah Ellis's Representations of Men

The official message of the immensely popular series of conduct books which Ellis wrote in the late 1830s and early 1840s for bourgeois women is neatly encapsulated in the following sentence from the text which is addressed to young wives: 'The love of woman appears to have been created solely to minister; that of man, to be ministered unto'.[2] For Ellis, woman's 'love' or greatest desire is realized in ensuring the domestic peace and comfort of her mate; his 'love' is realized in sustaining the home, a responsibility requiring private governance as well as public labour. These very different roles are legitimate, Ellis declares, not only because women are 'inferior in mental power, in the same proportion that [they] are inferior in bodily strength', but also because they do not possess the moral capacity of men.[3] With the kind of reverential awe which she hopes to inspire in her female readers, Ellis writes of

> that great leading peculiarity in man's character – his nobility, or, in other words, his exemption from those innumerable littlenesses which obscure the beauty and sully the integrity of woman's life. From all their underhand contrivances, their secret envyings, and petty spite, man is exempt; so much so, that the mere contemplation of the broad clear basis of his moral character, his open truth, his singleness of aim, and, above all, his dignified forbearance under provocation, might often put the weaker sex to shame. (pp.85-86)

Here the virtues of fairness, frankness, diligence, and restraint are articulated as the natural traits of men – Ellis invokes them in her definition of 'nobility', 'that great leading peculiarity in man's character' – and ranged against the 'innumerable littlenesses' of women, who are enjoined to position themselves as unworthy venerators of their menfolk. Indeed, Ellis goes on to imply that the disparity between the sexes is akin to that subsisting between the human and the divine. Man takes on the character of a guardian angel as she declares,

> And a sacred and ennobling trust it is for woman to have the happiness of such a being committed to her charge – a holy privilege to be the chosen companion of his lot – to come with her helplessness and weakness to find safety under his protection, and to repose her own perturbed and troubled mind beneath the shelter of his love. (pp.86-87)

Ellis's vision of the sexes begins to fragment when she mobilizes the discourse of what was often termed 'woman's influence'. Produced in order to reconcile woman to the stark inequality of her position, this actually worked to destabilize the gender status quo by introducing serious contradictions into the subjectivities of both sexes.[4] In brief, it averred that only woman had the moral purity, precisely because of her cocooned and selfless existence, to awaken and sustain man's 'nobility', the quality upon which rested the health not only of the home, but also of the nation. Without her tutelage man was deemed unable to prevent his arduous public life from activating and propelling into dangerous ascendancy a very much darker aspect of his nature. Thus the discourse effected a striking switching of roles, woman becoming the wise parent to man's unprincipled child. This reversal can be seen in Ellis's work time and again: in the first clause of the sentence just quoted, for instance, woman has the 'sacred and ennobling trust' not merely of her mate's physical well-being but rather of his happiness; by the third clause, however, Ellis has her central thesis in mind and man is the protecting guide while woman is a distinctly ignoble figure of 'helplessness and weakness'. The initial ramifications of the discourse for man are clearly crystallized in the following passage from the first of Ellis's texts:

> How often has man returned to his home with a mind confused by the many voices, which in the mart, the exchange, or the public assembly, have addressed themselves to his inborn selfishness, or his worldly pride; and while his integrity was shaken, and his resolution gave way beneath the pressure of apparent necessity, or the insidious pretenses of expediency, he has stood corrected before the clear eye of woman, as it looked directly to the naked truth, and detected the lurking evil of the specious act he was about to commit.[5]

Suddenly Ellis's angelic man is not beyond temptation and righteous chastisement. His 'integrity' is preserved here but, like 'the specious act he was about to commit', his new masculinity is a 'lurking evil' only too evident: stemming from 'inborn selfishness', it perpetually drives him to the brink of ruthless self-aggrandizement.

Elsewhere it succeeds in driving him over the brink. Ellis's warning that 'all women should [...] be prepared for discovering faults in men, as they are for beholding spots in the sun, or clouds in the summer sky' does not prepare the reader, to appropriate her metaphors, for the total eclipsing or utter washing away of the shining masculine ideal which occurs repeatedly in her books, usually in close proximity to the official model (p.67). Perhaps the most striking manifestation of this problem is that which erupts in the chapter ominously entitled 'Trials of Married Life' from *The Wives of England*. It is with reference to this piece of writing, therefore, that I will examine the way in which Ellis and her figure of woman lose control of man's 'lurking evil'.

The chapter begins with the observation that 'men, with all their dignified and noble attributes, are sometimes, though often unconsciously, indescribably provoking' (p.170). Here Ellis invokes her masculine ideal as she intends it to be constituted after the insertion of the fallibility necessary for the notion of woman's corrective influence. Man's 'dignified and noble attributes' are clearly dominant, his flaws manifesting themselves only 'sometimes' and 'often unconsciously'. Women must keep watch, then, but their task is a very manageable one. However, there is a sign of the distinctly unmanageable masculinity that is soon to rise from these flaws in the fact that, far from being minor in nature, they are 'indescribably provoking'. From Ellis's point of view this description is amply justified during what follows: the flaws proceed to take the place of the 'dignified and noble attributes' as the natural, defining characteristics of man. Indeed, at one point Ellis so far forgets her original formulation that she makes this usurpation explicit:

> these offences against temper and patience originate in one of those peculiarities in the character of man [...] the incapability under which he labours, of placing himself in idea in the situation of another person, so as to identify his feelings with their's [*sic*], and thus to enter into what they suffer and enjoy, as if the feeling were his own. (p.177)

The 'peculiarity' identified here is a world away from the 'nobility' celebrated earlier in the text. What is more, it not only supplants the latter quality, it also cancels the possibility of it: woman can do nothing against a biological 'incapability under which [man] labours'. Indeed, this redundancy is stressed time and again as the 'offences against temper and patience' springing from man's profound egoism are detailed. We hear, for instance, that woman 'might as well "go kindle fire with snow" as attempt to rouse' a man from idleness, that she 'has abundant need for supplies of strength and patience beyond what any earthly source can afford' when married to one who has 'the ruinous propensity' to gamble, and that 'As well might the mourner weeping for the dead expect by tears and lamentations to reanimate the lifeless form, as the unloved wife to recall the affection of her [unfaithful] husband' (pp.172, 200-01). What these examples demonstrate, of course, is that Ellis was inadvertently but quite spectacularly undermining the doctrine of male supremacy: her catalogue of man's potential and ineradicable 'offences', which also includes his being 'inconsiderate and cruel to animals', relishing 'the feeling of power and decision', and abusing alcohol, decisively casts him not as an admirable angel but as a contemptible devil, irredeemably fleshly, reckless, barbaric, and tyrannical (pp.172, 176, 186-89). To be sure, it seems as if Ellis was vaguely aware of what she was doing, for the chapter is almost hysterically eager to maintain woman's subordination. It knocks her off her implicit pedestal as many times as it places her upon it, demanding of her at one point, 'Have you yourself no personal peculiarities exactly opposed to your husband's notions of what is agreeable?', a question it proceeds to answer at length in the affirmative (p.179).[6] Also, the chapter reminds her that when a woman 'chooses to marry, she places herself under a moral obligation to make her husband's home as pleasant to him as she can', the implication being that the obligation obtains no matter how appalling his character (p.181).

I will be arguing that for Brontë it is precisely woman's stagnation under this 'moral obligation' that perpetuates man's viciousness. While Ellis ends up implying that women can do nothing but accept their unhappy condition, male depravity being intractable, Brontë maintains that if they are rejuvenated and elevated man can be redeemed. The radical nature of Brontë's position is made clear when we compare it to that of one of the period's feminist activists.[7] In a letter to *Howitt's Journal* in 1847, the year in which *Agnes Grey*, Brontë's first novel, was published, this 'staunch advocate' articulated exactly the same interpretation of woman's role as 'a domestic drudge or convenience' and of 'man's insatiable passions, vices, and propensities *the most base*':

> Alas! *who* can wonder at the *debased* state of *man*, when
> we look at *woman's state*! – she whose mission is from
> above, whose love is next to that of the Saviour, whose
> immense influence is destined to regenerate the world; and
> thus, by nature so peculiar and sweet, *so pure and so
> noble*, to prove herself *not a slave*, but *man's friend,
> companion, and adviser* [...] be assured, that so long as
> *she* is debased and enslaved, so long shall we, as men, be
> like brutes, subservient to our passions, and they
> predominant over reason, thus making us into a
> degenerated and demoralized race.[8]

Anne Brontë's Fiends

In one of the most despairing of Brontë's poems about Gondal, the imaginary kingdom which she created with her sister Emily, an incarcerated woman tells of her vain attempts to escape her misery in sleep: 'I dream about the world, but then/I dream of fiends instead of men'.[9] The metaphor and the speaker's momentary joy upon waking and finding herself abandoned and alone are not surprising: in Gondal Brontë rehearsed the brutal masculinity that she stages in her novels. The poem 'Z—'s Dream' is particularly prophetic in this respect.[10] Brontë forcefully evokes the danger of removing women's power to check man's huge egoism – which, like Ellis, she identifies as the source of terrible destructiveness – in a narrative where they are not merely peripheral but absent: the latent 'nobility' of two young male friends is tragically consumed by a competitiveness which proceeds to render them warring soldiers and finally one another's prospective assassin. The inevitability of the womanless boys' dark trajectory is emphasized: near the beginning of the poem the speaker, the elder of the two, links the pain, bitterness, and obsessive violence of his 'latter years' with the 'hate that grew with growing strength', and later he attributes the fact that 'both were changed' from friends to foes in part simply to time.[11] But his claim that a dream of a boyhood walk over the mountains with his then best friend replayed a period when 'My present heart and soul were not' is not entirely ironic; the dream sequence does conjure a powerful sense of the tragically neglected gentle natures of both boys (p.136). Although the younger boy's competitiveness and the speaker's 'not over soft or kind' heart show that the children were the fathers of the men, their enjoyment of and alignment with the 'breezy, sunny day' and the beautiful landscape and, more importantly, their deep affection for one another suggest subjectivities that might have been (pp.136-37). Brontë's portrayal of the moment of connection between the boys is rendered all the more moving by its brevity:

> I could have kissed his forehead fair;
> I could have clasped him to my heart;
> But tenderness with me was rare,

And I must take a rougher part. (p.137)

The potential for renunciation of self that is inherent in love for another is inconsistent with the egoism that defines the speaker's ascendant masculine nature; as a result, the looming physical contact is realized not as a uniting embrace but as a divisive struggle for self-aggrandizement: 'grappling, strength for strength we strove' (p.137). Inevitably, the moment of harmony which follows this contest is fleeting; shadowed by the speaker's sense that 'a change were nigh', it serves only to remind us of what will henceforth be alien to the now fully-fledged combatants (p.138). When the dream gives way to the speaker's present reality we are immediately confronted with what *did* constitute the legacy of the struggle – estrangement, hatred, and then death:

> This heart had thirsted for his blood;
> > This hand had allayed that thirst!
> These eyes had watched, without a tear,
> > His dying agony;
> These ears, unmoved, had heard his prayer;
> This tongue had cursed him suffering there,
> > And mocked him bitterly! (p.138)

By detailing the complicity of each of these parts of the speaker's physical and metaphysical beings in the horrific destruction of his former friend, Brontë skilfully conveys the completeness both of his consumption by, and realization of, an egoism that, having expanded to its logical extreme, demands not merely the mastering but the erasure of competitors. The speaker's experience of a moment of remorse in the next stanza serves to underline his abandonment to his fiendish masculine identity, but his interpretation of the occurrence ironically suggests, for others, an escape route from this possession:

> Unwonted weakness o'er me crept;
> I sighed – nay, weaker still – *I wept*!
> Wept, like a woman o'er the deed
>   I had been proud to do. (p.138)

The speaker's contempt for the 'weakness' occasioned by his disorientation upon waking constitutes Brontë's most effective way of affirming that man should feel 'like a woman'; in order to hammer home her message she stresses what succeeds the imperative 'Back foolish tears!', the rest of the poem consisting of the speaker's manic justification of the 'strife/ [...] blood and death' he perpetrates (pp.138, 139). Clearly, his distance from and disdain for woman – the lines quoted above contain the only explicit reference to her in the poem – have brought hell upon earth.

It is precisely this positioning of man in relation to woman that brings hell into the households of Brontë's two novels. I will discuss the consequence before the cause, however, since the sheer horror of many of Brontë's male characters is surely one of the first things to strike her readers. The Gondal soldier's counterparts in *Agnes Grey* and *The Tenant of Wildfell Hall* may not commit murder – upon humans at any rate – but their brutality is different only in degree, not in kind; they realize the same radically self-aggrandizing masculinity that he does, producing a hell that comprises the effects of rampant despotism, temerity, and sensuality. As Brontë details the careers of these characters it seems as if she is staging the very representation of man that rises inadvertently to ascendancy in Ellis's chapter on the 'Trials of Married Life'; they each sustain one, some, or all of the 'offences' that *Agnes Grey*'s unfortunate Lady Ashby discovers constitute the chief exertions of her new husband:

> And then he must needs have me down in the country, to
> lead the life of a nun, lest I should dishonour him or bring
> him to ruin; as if he had not been ten times worse every
> way, with his betting-book, and his gaming-table, and his
> opera-girls, and his Lady This and Mrs That – yes, and
> his bottles of wine, and glasses of brandy and water too![12]

While Ellis's vision of man's depravity snowballs beyond her
control, however, Brontë's is very carefully crafted in order to
render her depiction of his unfitness for domestic dominance as
effective as possible. Hence her deployment of the powerful
metaphor of the devouring predator, which emphasizes the
ravenous, destructive, and remorseless egoism of her many Ashbys.

On one level this metaphor is manifested in direct relation to the
animal kingdom. Invoking an 'offence' listed by Ellis but not by
Lady Ashby, Brontë repeatedly constructs men as beasts preying
upon beasts. She does so most elaborately when the eponymous
heroine of her first novel is governess to the Bloomfield children at
the ironically named Wellwood House. Agnes reports that on the
day of her arrival Tom, her seven-year-old charge, made her 'stand
for ten minutes, watching how manfully he used his whip and spurs'
upon his rocking-horse:

> I told Mr Tom [...] I hoped he would not use his whip and
> spurs so much when he rode a real pony.
>   'Oh, yes, I will!' said he, laying on with
> redoubled ardour. 'I'll cut into him like smoke! Eeh! my
> word! but he shall sweat for it'. (p.15)

Here Brontë explicitly links the boy's ideal of masculine behaviour –

Agnes, of course, applies the terms 'manfully', 'little hero', and 'little gentleman' to him with cutting irony – to a hunting animal's aggression. Though the rocking-horse display of this 'tiger's cub' is ludicrous, it shows only too well that in order to feed his ego he will inflict invasive violence upon an animate creature (p.33). Subsequently this dark forecast is reiterated in literal terms as the boy tells Agnes that he wants finally to consume the next bird that he tortures: 'I mean to roast [it] alive', he says, '[...] first, to see how long it will live – and then, to see what it will taste like' (p.16). Perhaps it is not surprising that after he justifies his cruelty to the birds he captures with the words 'I can't feel what I do to them', the hellish character of his egoism is specified: Agnes invokes the ultimate destination of those who can reason thus. From here Brontë moves quickly to evince that Tom's shocking predatory propensity is not peculiar to him; on the contrary, it is characteristic, as she will show again and again, of *all* abandoned males. Tom tells the horrified Agnes,

> Papa knows how I treat them [the birds], and he never blames me for it: he says it is just what *he* used to do when *he* was a boy. Last summer he gave me a nest full of young sparrows, and he saw me pulling off their legs and wings, and heads, and never said anything; [...] Uncle Robson was there too, and he laughed, and said I was a fine boy. (pp.16-17)

Robson demonstrates his endorsement of the boy's budding masculinity by giving him another nest of fledgings that he can 'wallop': thus both he and his brother-in-law behave like a beast of prey preparing its young for the hunt (p.37). Not surprisingly, Robson pursues gratification at the expense of what Agnes no doubt

ironically calls 'the lower creation' as energetically as his nephew
does: we are told that he brutalizes his favourite dogs. Indeed, he is
a particularly dangerous predator since he is camouflaged by 'the
foppery of stays' (p.36). Affectation is no more of a barrier to this
masculine behaviour than is age. Nor, it is stressed, is class: the
Wellwood men's barbarity cannot be attributed to the fact that they
are, as Mrs Grey puts it, 'purse-proud tradespeople and arrogant
upstarts' for when Agnes arrives at Horton Lodge, the Murray
residence, where she hopes to find thorough-bred, 'genuine gentry',
she learns that the Squire is a devoted fox-hunter, and that his sons
enjoy 'setting their dogs at' cats (pp.44, 46, 84).

Brontë also uses the predator metaphor to realize her male
characters' pursuit of pleasure and power in the human world,
emphasizing that the way in which they treat animals parallels the
way in which they treat people. She does so with particular force in
that portion of *The Tenant of Wildfell Hall* consisting of the heroine
Helen's diary, which tells the story of her disastrous marriage to the
dissolute aristocrat Arthur Huntingdon. Here this character is the
first to be cast explicitly as a predator; significantly, the metaphor
follows closely upon the infatuated Helen's remark that escaping
from the company of the vain and arrogant Wilmot to his 'was like
turning from some purgatorial fiend to an angel of light, come to
announce that the season of torment was past'.[13] Thus we are soon
made to sense that Helen's judgment was awry. When Arthur
springs through the window of the room in which she is painting, a
display symbolic of invasive assertion, he is hardly an image of gentle
selflessness (p.150). During what ensues he emerges as a fiend, a
predator intent upon Helen's pain. Justifying his surname, he hunts
for her sketches of him, manifestations of her secret desire which he
has already rendered, as she laments, 'an eternal monument to his
pride and my humiliation!' (p.148). What he is and what he is

capable of are made clear when he snatches Helen's pictures against
her will: '"Let me have its bowels then," said he; and just as I
wrenched the portfolio from his hand, he deftly abstracted the
greater part of its contents' (p.151). Arthur's feral violence and
exaction will win him several such kills in the course of Helen's
entrapment as Mrs Huntingdon; his success here – Helen's 'distress'
drives her to destroy a miniature over which she had taken 'great
pains and care' – is emphasized shortly afterwards when he returns
from a literal hunt 'stained with the blood of his prey' (p.152).
Arthur, however, is neither the only nor the most formidable
predator that Helen is pursued by; his companion Hargrave
endeavours to satisfy his ego upon her not merely by tormenting her,
but by possessing her, body and soul. Hargrave is particularly
dangerous because, as Margaret Smith points out, 'with Rochester-
like plausibility, [he] presents his seduction as morally justified. He
will rescue Helen from ignoble bondage and restore her and her son
to a loving and civilized environment'.[14] But he intends to devour
Helen's integrity in the process. We are made as acutely aware of his
nature as she is during their gripping chess game, Brontë's most
powerful articulation of the hunt motif. The language of 'the
combat' speaks for itself. Hargrave is 'keen, crafty, bold, and almost
impudent', a 'dog' who looks 'as keen and cruel as if he would drain
her heart's blood'; Helen 'struggle[s] hard against him' only to fall
'inextricably entangled in the snare': '"Check,"' – cried he: I sought
in agony some means of escape – "mate!" he added, quietly but with
evident delight' (pp.288-89). Hargrave's 'exultation' simply serves
to confirm Helen's belief that he sees his kill on the chessboard as a
portent of his success in securing her spiritual death beyond it (it is
no accident that his surname sounds similar to 'her grave'). The
monstrous egoism of Hargrave, Arthur, and the other 'human
brutes' is further underlined by their propensity to turn upon each

other (p.335). In many of the 'hunting' episodes at Grassdale we see the sheer and brutal anarchy that male abandon inevitably leads to. Hattersley's onslaught is typical. Cast explicitly as the behaviour of what the coquette Annabella calls 'a bold, manly spirit' – Hattersley endeavours to render her conscience-stricken husband Lord Lowborough, whom she has implied is unmanly, such a spirit – it shows only how very far from the period's masculine ideal both Hattersley and her conception are (pp.259, 265). Appropriately 'roaring like a wild beast' and '[s]wearing and cursing like a maniac', Hattersley not only engages Lowborough in 'a disgraceful contest' and sets about 'remorselessly crushing [his wife's] slight arms', he also deals Hargrave 'a violent blow' and 'rush[es] upon [Arthur] in a phrensy' (pp.265-68).

Helen's horror at the masculinity which is realized by her husband and his set is by no means representative of the reaction of Brontë's female characters. On the contrary, Annabella's endorsement is typical. Time and again we see and hear of mothers who entertain and encourage her idea of 'a bold, manly spirit'. Mrs Bloomfield, for instance, believes that her son Tom is 'a generous, noble-spirited boy' and reveals that she condones his repulsive cruelty to birds: 'I think,' she tells the shocked Agnes, 'a child's amusement is scarcely to be weighed against the welfare of a soulless brute' (pp.13, 39). Needless to say, the irony is that 'a soulless brute' is exactly what Tom is becoming. The culpability of the mother whose son develops in this way is stressed emphatically in *The Tenant of Wildfell Hall*: Helen describes Arthur's 'foolish mother' as having 'indulged him to the top of his bent' and done 'her utmost to encourage those germs of folly and vice it was her duty to suppress'; indeed, Helen goes on to rail against the woman's *crime* of over indulgence – I can hardly give it a milder name when I think of the evils it brings' (pp.165-66, 214). What Arthur's mother has done, then, amounts to much more than simply neglecting 'her duty'; she has actually worked to force the 'germs' of her son's vicious masculinity. Thus Brontë offers a dramatic interpretation of the failure of 'woman's influence' in texts such as Ellis's. What is more, the novelist locates the source of this 'crime of over indulgence' in the crime, of which Ellis is guilty, of imposing inferiority upon women. In *Agnes Grey* Brontë shows that in a patriarchy women are morally corrupted and brought to respect monstrous male behaviour from a very early age. The violence that is done to young girls is appropriately symbolized during Agnes's first experience of the Bloomfield children: she sees Tom raise his fist to his sister Mary Ann and learns that he strikes her 'now and then to keep her in order' (p.15). A little later we perceive in what Priscilla Costello calls Robson's 'encouraging of the worst sexist extremes' in the children, the thorough degradation of the girls.[15] This 'scorner of the female sex' not only prizes Mary Ann's affectation, he also instils in his nieces as well as in his nephew the manliness of male brutality (p.36). Anticipating Annabella's definition, Robson avers that by indulging his propensities to recklessness and bullying Tom 'manifested his bold and manly spirit, and rose superior to his sisters' (pp.37, 38). The success of Robson's teaching is evident in Tom's despotic 'set[ting] up as ruler' in the nursery and in his sisters' desire to serve him in spite of – indeed, *because* of – his abominable character (p.21). In one remarkable scene Tom wages war upon Agnes without lifting a finger:

> 'Burn it [her work-bag], Fanny!' cried Tom; and *this* command she hastened to obey. I sprang to snatch it from the fire [...] 'Mary Ann, throw her desk out of the window!' cried he: and my precious desk [...] was about to be precipitated from the three-storey window. (pp.29-30)

Brontë shows the esteem of young girls raised in patriarchal environments for the dark masculinity of their masters nowhere more strikingly than in the 'veritable hoyden' Matilda, one of Agnes's teenage charges at Horton Lodge (p.54). Matilda's pride in her father leads her to emulate his behaviour, but, though accurate, her shocking language, 'reckless, headstrong, violent' temper, and ability to delight in the fact that her dog made a leveret '[cry] out just like a child' constitute no very flattering reflection (pp.55, 128-29).

Contrary to Terry Eagleton's belief that Brontë's novels 'do not find morality in the least problematical', neither of her 'pious' heroines entirely escapes the contamination that is only too evident in Matilda.[16] Brontë's contention that women who do have the capacity and the desire to exercise their influence aright will find their exertions utterly fruitless in an environment where woman is merely, as Arthur believes, 'a thing [...] to wait upon her husband, and amuse him and minister to his comfort in every possible way', is forceful enough (p.233). Helen's conclusion that 'God might awaken that heart supine and stupified with self-indulgence, and remove the film of sensual darkness from his eyes, but I could not' constitutes a bold exposure of the Ellisian notion that in such unequal circumstances woman has power over man, as Helen puts it in her ignorance, 'to recall him to the path of virtue' (pp.248, 142). But Brontë's demonstration of the evil of male-dominated households is rendered even more compelling by its insightful suggestion that virtuous women suffer more than straightforward defeat in them: we are shown that they come to display characteristics of the masculinity they despise. This corruption is rendered all the more shocking by its insidious nature: paradoxically, it manifests itself under moral outrage. For instance, Agnes's longing 'to see one of [Robson's dogs] bite him' comes from disgust at his

violence toward them and her crushing of the nestlings is the result
of revulsion at Tom's plans for their destruction (pp.37, 38).
Similarly, Helen, who laments her 'masculinization' explicitly ('I so
identify myself with him, that I feel his degradation, his failings, and
transgressions as my own') evinces vengeful aggression in
endeavouring to persuade her husband to renounce his London
dissipation: '"I shall never live to do it again, if you treat me so
savagely," replied he, pushing me from him. "You've nearly
squeezed the breath out of my body"' (pp.250, 246). Arthur actually
likens Helen's behaviour to that of a 'she tiger'; this may reflect his
desire to level her more than it does the truth, but the very fact that
he can make the accusation points to a certain loss of distance from
the riot of predation on her part. In the end, of course, Agnes and
Helen avoid complete absorption: the former, at the very moment
she fears that her integrity is rotting ('I seemed to feel my intellect
deteriorating, my heart petrifying, my soul contracting'), is, as we
shall see, saved by the curate Weston; the latter courageously severs
herself from the sphere of contagion (p.82). However, judging from
Helen's case at least, it seems that recovery does not prevent
reinfection. When Helen returns to Grassdale to tend the dying
Arthur (whose final 'miseries, bodily and mental' constitute a
harrowing conclusion to his cautionary tale) she finds that even from
his deathbed 'he would make a complete slave of' her (pp.431, 417).
It is perhaps not surprising, then, that in spite of her ostensible
'actuat[ion] by the best and noblest motives' she comes to look
vengeful once again (p.415). Indeed, as she regiments, withholds her
son from, and, in Laura Berry's words, 'virtually proselytizes him to
death', we cannot help but sympathize with her bewildered patient's
cry, 'I am in hell, already!' – however just it is that he should end up
suffering something of the experience of the hunted (p.411).[17]

Anne Brontë's Noble Men

If Brontë seems to take up Ellis's unofficial position in showing that women are rendered impotent in the shadow of male tyranny, she clearly transcends the ideologue's pessimism by going on to portray their power beyond that shadow. When women are liberated, Brontë affirms, they are able to prevent and even to chasten man's brutal masculinity, raising instead the 'nobility' also inherent – but dormant – in his nature. We see the rejuvenated Helen doing this twice in *The Tenant of Wildfell Hall*: she redeems not only her little son, but also the novel's unlikely hero Gilbert Markham.

Significantly, the rebirth of the Helen who can perform these tasks occurs when she has 'got rid of Mr. Huntingdon for a season', shortly before she flees with little Arthur. The mood is one of emancipation and health ('the moment he was gone, I breathed again, and felt my vital energy return'), qualities which are associated with the boy's fate in his mother's hands: 'I exerted all my powers to eradicate the weeds that had been fostered in his infant mind, and sow again the good seed they had rendered unproductive' (p.354). This horticultural imagery effectively conveys the choking, barren nature of the masculinity that has been reared in the boy by his father – whose scheme to 'make a man of him' consisted of prompting him 'to tipple wine like papa, to swear like Mr. Hattersley, and to have his own way like a man, and [send] mamma to the devil when she tried to prevent him' – and the tender, beneficial nature of the masculinity that will grow under his mother's care. Ironically, Helen's nurturing of the boy – which includes constant vigilance and the literal rendering of wine as poison – is attacked by the 'civilized' circle at Linden-car as precisely the way to prevent him from 'walk[ing] honourably through the world': 'you'll spoil his spirit, and make a mere Miss Nancy of him', Mrs Markham protests (pp.25, 28, 29). But what Helen knows and what the reader will see – not only in her diary – is that their model of male development, which leaves boys to learn by experience alone, cannot realize the masculine ideal: 'for fifty – or five hundred men that have yielded to temptation,' Helen boldly declares, 'shew me one that has had virtue to resist' (p.28). In the end Helen's practice is vindicated not only by the fact that her son becomes 'a fine young man' who makes a happy marriage, but also by the fact that *she* brings Mrs Markham's eldest son to a more honourable stride (p.469).

Though Gilbert and his mother would object to the observation, it is clear that, as N.M. Jacobs points out, the novel 'approach[es] a pervasively violent private reality through a narrator who embodies an ideology that justifies the violence'.[18] While the young Gilbert of the initial narrative clearly believes that his masculinity is approximate to the ideal, his behaviour often evinces a 'manliness' that is in fact perilously close to that of Arthur and his companions. This disjunction is sharply evoked in an episode that stresses both Mrs Markham's cosseting of her son and his consequent sexism: having come home late for supper, complained of 'the overdrawn tea', and allowed his sister to brew him a fresh pot, Gilbert remonstrates that through his mother's running of the house according to 'what's agreeable to the gentlemen' he 'might sink into the grossest condition of self-indulgence and carelessness about the wants of others' (p.53). Elsewhere we see that if he has not sunk completely, he is certainly wallowing dangerously. He expects all women to gratify him and when they refuse to do so he is given to viciousness, both verbal and, more sinisterly, physical. After Helen refuses to submit to his opinion during the debate over children's education, for instance, he implies that she is bigoted and gives her hand 'a spiteful squeeze' (p.32). Egoism, irrationality, and violence come to be prominent features of his early passion for Helen. Again showing the gulf that can subsist between his conduct and his conception of himself, he allows hearsay to persuade him that Lawrence is her lover – he had said, 'I should be unworthy the name of a man, if I could believe anything that was said against her, unless I heard it from her own lips' – and he horsewhips his supposed rival, declaring, astonishingly, that 'it would teach him better manners in future' (pp.89, 109). Appropriately, then, the male predation that pervades Helen's diary is explicitly anticipated in Gilbert, who characterizes his state just before he receives the text thus: 'I felt disposed to dally with my victim like a cat' (p.118).

Nevertheless, it must be emphasized that Gilbert is not as abandoned as Arthur will be shown to be. The fact that Gilbert harbours a correct idea of the masculine ideal suggests that Mrs Markham's intimation that she has not been 'slaving to indulge his follies and caprices' bears some truth (p.29). What is more, he does on occasion behave in direct contrast to Arthur: his affection for little Arthur is genuine and beneficial, he encourages Helen's love of books, and he is not averse to labour, sometimes appearing at work in the fields of his farm. Indeed, these signs of a struggling 'nobility' are strong enough to interest Helen in his salvation. In her preface Brontë wrote that she 'wished to tell the truth, for truth always conveys its own moral to those who are able to receive it' (p.3). Helen's diary 'tells the truth' about the masculinity Gilbert is in danger of being consumed by; the fact that Helen gives the document to him demonstrates her faith in his 'ability to receive' its moral. Officially, of course, he does so and fully; he recognizes the legitimacy of Helen's 'prejudice against [him], and her hard thoughts of our sex in general', and he strikingly likens her purifying effect upon him to that of a solar epiphany:

> this chaos of thoughts and passions cleared away, giving

> place to two distinct emotions: joy unspeakable that my
> adored Helen [...] shone bright, and clear, and stainless as
> that sun I could not bear to look on; and shame and deep
> remorse for my own conduct. (pp.380, 382)

Gilbert's shedding of his egoistic masculinity is also conveyed on a structural level. In the third narrative he allows Helen to share the storytelling, to speak for herself: we read her letters to Lawrence about Arthur's decline in Gilbert's to Halford about his and Helen's gradual coming together. What this technique forecasts for Helen's second marriage is that her powerful newfound liberty will be accepted: she will at last enjoy a union based on equality and cooperation.

Agnes, of course, enjoys such a marriage with her first choice: 'I defy anybody to blame him as a pastor, a husband, or a father' she declares at the end of her narrative (p.164). The excellence of her spouse comes as no surprise since he has consistently constituted Brontë's most distinct reproduction of the period's masculine ideal. Looking remarkably like a novelistic realization of Ellis's divine man, Edward Weston comes to Agnes already purified (it is stressed that his mother was 'the dearest of his early friends'), a saviour who will purge her of corruption:

> The gross vapours of earth were gathering around me,
> and closing in upon my inward heaven; and thus it was
> that Mr Weston rose at length upon me, appearing like the
> morning-star in my horizon, to save me from the fear of
> utter darkness. (pp.82, 91)

As 'the splendid sunset' which illuminates his cliff-top proposal to Agnes emphasizes, Weston will continue to bring divine light into her life (pp.163-64). And not only into hers: it is made clear that he is a beacon for all of his flock. The old cottager Nancy, for instance, tells Agnes that as he removed her spiritual anxiety 'a new light broke in on my soul' (p.79). Exactly what makes Weston's masculinity so refulgent is effectively conveyed as the curate takes shape in opposition to the rector Hatfield; in every respect they are, as Inga-Stina Ewbank puts it, 'as antithetical as the Bad Angel and the Good'.[19] Hatfield is the man that Weston could have been, an ecclesiastical predator who abuses his power to torment those parishioners he can hurt with impunity. In the metaphoric scheme of the novel his brutalizing of the cottagers' animals signals his like treatment of their souls: thus he kicks Nancy's cat as he does her hope of Heaven (pp.75-76). The monstrousness of his ego is underlined as he justifies this behaviour by appropriating a jealous God: Hatfield's sermons, Agnes protests, '[represent] the Deity as a terrible task-master, rather than a benevolent father' (p.69). The first confirmation of Weston's divergent masculinity comes with his subversion of this teaching. 'God is LOVE' he tells Nancy (p.78). The curate's ensuing career – which forecasts the 'strenuous exertions' he will undertake as a *model* rector – shows that he is love too: he is *kind* to animals, he sows peace and charity among the cottagers, and he supplies the material wants of the needy out of the 'little as he has' (pp.164, 81). The beauty and beneficence of Weston's actions are touchingly symbolized in the 'lovely primroses' he picks for Agnes, who 'long[s] intensely for some familiar flower' to ease her homesickness (pp.88-89).

Brontë's vision of man, then, is not a relentlessly pessimistic one. But the fact that Weston is the only 'noble' man in *Agnes Grey* (Agnes's father disqualifies himself by committing the 'offences' of gambling and then idleness), and the fact that until the reformed Gilbert appears in the last third of *The Tenant of Wildfell Hall* there are but faint traces of the ideal (Richard Wilson being self-absorbed and Lawrence at best a marginal figure), should alert us to the danger of overemphasizing the point. Indeed, as we read beyond the official characters of the 'noble' men we are presented with, we begin to perceive another and more subtle eclipsing of the masculine ideal: both Weston and the post-diary Gilbert emerge as rather less distinct from their ignoble brethren than they at first appeared.

If Weston's initial manifestations are characterized by moral brilliance, they are not remarkable for their warm emotion. Nancy notes that he looked 'a bit crossish' and Agnes goes so far as to say that he 'did not impress me with the idea [...] of such an individual as the cottagers described him' (pp.77, 83). Though these comments are immediately qualified, Weston's 'crossish' demeanour persists: when he does smile, for instance, Agnes asserts that the moment is 'too transient' (p.99). This demeanour is significant since it lends a hardness to Weston which intensifies the distinct sense that some of his behaviour toward Agnes is insensitive and even cruel. On the walk home from church, for instance, he will allow the coquette Rosalie to '[engross] him entirely' and drive Agnes, to her misery, from the conversation (pp.109-10). Again, he does not contrive to see Agnes after her father dies, actually making her think, 'he does not care for you', and he lets her leave Horton Lodge with only the briefest and most cryptic intimation of his affection for her (pp.135, 138). His ensuing period of silence serves to reduce her to self-depreciation and then physical illness ('I never saw you look so wretched' her mother remarks); thus he can even be seen as augmenting the novel's evocation of self-serving man's detrimental effect upon woman (pp.139-41, 141). When he does eventually seek her out he tells her:

> You must have known that it was not my way to flatter
> and talk soft nonsense, or even to speak the admiration

> that I felt; and that a single word or glance of mine meant
> more than the honied phrases and fervent protestations of
> most other men. (p.163)

Even if we overlook the rather arrogant tone of this explanation it is hardly satisfactory. Although cast as a frank and therefore truly manly utterance, it in fact attempts to justify hurtful reserve: we have seen only too well that Agnes needed very much more than 'a single word or glance' from him.

In Gilbert's case the problem of the receding masculine ideal is evinced not by unamiable reserve but by unamiable candour. On several occasions after his officially chastening experience of the diary Gilbert expresses himself in a way which suggests that he has not learned the text's lessons as fully as Helen would hope.[20] Indeed, aspects of his behaviour in the third narrative recall the Huntingdon set just as aspects of his behaviour in the first narrative anticipate them. He confesses to Halford at the start of the final instalment, for instance, that while reading Helen's diary he 'felt a kind of selfish gratification in watching her husband's gradual decline in her good graces, and seeing how completely he extinguished all her affection at last' (p.381). Thus Helen's second lover feeds his ego upon her pain much as her first did while courting her: there is a difference only of degree, not of kind, between Gilbert's 'gratification' in her diary and Arthur's in her portfolio. Again, on the very morning that succeeds his reading of the diary we see Gilbert harrassing Helen in the Hargrave mode ('that man is *not* your husband'), the evil of which is amply registered in Helen's horror: 'For God's sake, don't *you* attempt these arguments! No *fiend* could torture me like this!' (pp.384, 385). And, as if he is not forgetting the third member of Grassdale's hellish trinity, Gilbert manifests his irritation with Eliza as Hattersley might: 'I seized her arm and gave it, I think, a pretty

severe squeeze, for she shrank into herself with a faint cry of pain or
terror' (p.444). Gilbert's continuing capacity for such behaviour is
evident even when he is officially at his most 'noble'. The proposal
scene, for instance, presents him, as Elizabeth Langland argues, as 'a
man without arrogance'.[21] But it can also be read as evincing exactly
the opposite. Gilbert's failure to interpret Helen's offering of the
rose could signify his failure to comprehend her desire for equality
with him: it is significant that, after a display of assertiveness which
recalls Arthur's before the portfolio episode (he leaps through the
window for the discarded flower), Gilbert appropriates the marriage
proposal and renders it conventional (p.444).

Ultimately, then, Brontë proves no more able than Ellis to contain
the egoistic masculinity she unleashes. In her novels as in the
ideologue's conduct books it erupts where it is not meant to, and
works to destabilize their official projects. For what she ends up
implying is that the corruption of men is a symptom not of an
undesirable mode of masculinity, but of the condition of maleness
itself.

[1]Writers who produced texts very similar to Ellis's include Elizabeth
Sandford and Sarah Lewis. All three are referred to in Joan Perkin,
Victorian Women (London: John Murray, 1993).

[2]Sarah Stickney Ellis, *The Wives of England: Their Relative Duties,
Domestic Influence, & Social Obligations* (London: Fisher, Son & Co,
1843), p.76.

[3]Ellis, *The Daughters of England: Their Position in Society, Character, &
Responsibilities* (London: Fisher, Son, & Co, 1842), p.3. Further references
are given after quotations in the text.

[4]For a discussion of the discourse's modification and problematization of
woman's role see Catherine Hall, 'The Early Formation of Victorian
Domestic Ideology' (1979), in *White, Male, and Middle Class: Explorations*

in Feminism and History (Cambridge: Polity Press, 1992). pp.75-93 (pp.86-87).

[5]Ellis, *The Women of England: Their Social Duties and Domestic Habits* (London: Fisher, Son, & Co, 1838), pp.51-52.

[6]'I would ask,' Ellis begins, 'if you have never treasured up against your husband some standing cause of complaint, to be thrown at him when an opportunity is offered by the presence of a friend, or a stranger, for discharging this weapon from the household quiver with perfect safety to yourself?' (pp.179-80). Ellis certainly cannot be accused of painting a rosy picture of the marital institution which she strives to reproduce.

[7]The agitation for women's rights was intensifying in the late 1840s. Organized feminism was only a few years away: in 1855 Barbara Leigh Smith campaigned for the introduction of a Parliamentary Bill granting women the right to hold and acquire property after marriage.

[8]A.W., 'Improvement of the Social Condition of Women', *Howitt's Journal* 1 (1847), p.29. The radicalization of the idea of woman's 'immense influence' was to be a feature of the feminist campaigns of the next few decades. As Philippa Levine puts it in *Victorian Feminism 1850-1900*, 'Feminists took hold of the position to which they were limited by Victorian ideology and inverted its precepts, turning the duties of moral guardianship into a crusade which castigated the laxity and degradation of precisely those who ascribed to them that role' (London: Hutchinson, 1987), p.133.

[9]Anne Brontë, 'A Voice from the Dungeon' (1837), in *The Poems of Anne Brontë*, ed. by Edward Chitham (Hampshire and London: Macmillan, 1979), pp.60-61 (p.60).

[10]For a discussion of 'Z—'s Dream' and other relevant Gondal poems, which explores their manifestation of Brontë's belief that 'the man who hates his brother is unlikely to remain in tune with nature', see Enid L. Duthie, *The Brontës and Nature* (Hampshire and London: Macmillan, 1986), pp.76-78 (p.78).

[11]Brontë, 'Z—'s Dream' (1846), in Chitham, pp.136-39 (p.136, p.139).

[12]Brontë, *Agnes Grey* (1847; London: Everyman, 1991), p.152.

[13]Brontë, *The Tenant of Wildfell Hall* (1848; Oxford: World's Classics,

1993), p.137.

[14]Margaret Smith, 'Introduction' to *The Tenant of Wildfell Hall*, p.xxiii.

[15]Priscilla H. Costello, 'A New Reading of Anne Brontë's *Agnes Grey*', *Brontë Society Transactions* 19 (1987), 113-18 (p.116).

[16] Terry Eagleton, *Myths of Power: A Marxist Study of the Brontës* (London: Macmillan, 1975), p.123.

[17] Laura C. Berry, 'Acts of Custody and Incarceration in *Wuthering Heights* and *The Tenant of Wildfell Hall*', *Novel* 30 (1996), 32-55 (p.44).

[18]N. M. Jacobs, 'Gender and Layered Narrative in *Wuthering Heights* and *The Tenant of Wildfell Hall*', *Journal of Narrative Technique* 16 (1986), 204-19 (p.213). *The Tenant of Wildfell Hall* is presented as a series of papers written and arranged by Gilbert in 1847. He tells the story of his courtship of Helen twenty years before, inserting in the middle the diary that she wrote from 1821-27 while married to Huntingdon and then the letters that she wrote to her brother detailing her brief return to Grassdale.

[19]Inga-Stina Ewbank, *Their Proper Sphere: A Study of the Brontë Sisters as Early-Victorian Female Novelists* (London: Edward Arnold, 1966), p.64.

[20]Critics have tended to see the post-diary Gilbert as either reformed – see, for instance, Jacobs, p.213, Elizabeth Hollis Berry, *Anne Brontë's Radical Vision: Structures of Consciousness* (Victoria, B.C.: English Literary Studies, 1994), pp.103-6, and Elizabeth Langland, *Anne Brontë: The Other One* (Hampshire and London: Macmillan, 1989), p.58, pp.134-37 – or unregenerate – see, for instance, Eagleton, p.135, and Ewbank, p.83.   I argue that he is both, albeit on different levels.

[21]Langland, p.137.

4

'A MAN OF HIS DAY': LITERARY EVOLUTION AND MASCULINITY IN GEORGE GISSING'S *NEW GRUB STREET*

New Grub Street, George Gissing's best-known novel, is often viewed by critics simply as an illustration of the Victorian literary world.[1] However, this is a severely limited perspective in that the novel aims to do something other than provide an accurate portrayal of an existing situation. A cogent reason for the novel's success is that in it Gissing confronts and conflates topical contemporary issues: the future of authorship, the future of mankind, and, within both, the future of masculinity. In this essay I wish to explore Gissing's project of conflation as a spur to his literary development and a reassurance of his masculinity, to ascertain how far he was in sympathy with the contemporary climate, and to examine his construction of masculinity within his own life and within *New Grub Street*.

The novel's picture of the literary world is incomplete. It shows an almost exclusively male Grub Street of writers struggling to survive, a hive of competitiveness spurred by evolutionary fear. This masculine world fosters a vicious circle; success indicates masculinity, and masculinity indicates success. Failure is due to weakness, to not being a 'proper man', and the outward representation or appearance of masculinity is the most important thing. The characters constantly judge themselves in comparison with their male contemporaries, to see who is most likely to succeed. This stance reflects Gissing's own literary world, in itself a version of the dominant masculinised ideology of authorship.

New Grub Street is very much a novel of its day in its anxiety about gender. Pioneering women campaigned for the traditionally male privilege of working, and condemned the sexual and moral double standards still largely in place. It was suggested in fiction that women would select partners according to their reproductive fitness, while in 'real life' the New Woman was accused of 'peopling the world with stunted and hydrocephalic children' to cause 'ultimate extinction of the race'.[2] In this climate of change, the position of men and masculinity was necessarily under review, if not direct attack. Gissing himself was already committed to a masculine world of literature, of books for 'thinking and struggling men', and married his second wife Edith Underwood, seemingly from a combination of sexual and literary frustration, in the early stages of writing *New Grub Street*.[3] He was in a position to be acutely affected by the threatened shift in the balance of power, whatever his attitude towards it.

A starting point for many of these anxieties was the work of Charles Darwin, which originated the concept of natural selection and provided a strongly-gendered analysis of sexual selection. Darwin notes in *The Origin of Species* that the struggle for a partner is exclusively male, while in *The Descent of Man* he states explicitly that the male is modified in the process of sexual selection, while the female chooses her male partner.[4] Darwin's work inspired several eugenic theories. In 1852 Herbert Spencer argued that excess fertility causes evolution since the weak will die leaving the strong to continue the race, positing an optimistic, automatically regulated improvement of mankind.[5] By 1894, though, Francis Galton pronounced 'a serious necessity to better the breed of the human race';[6] his degenerative pessimism requires special efforts of selection and breeding. Both, though, are already considering the future of humanity.

These claims, hypotheses and suggestions are illustrated by information drawn from animals, human breeding being discussed in the most remote and impersonal terms. Darwin and his successors may have felt that emphasising gender roles with regard to humans was indelicate, yet there is also the possibility that they did not wish to emphasise the concept of female choice and male struggles to be chosen when convention implied the opposite. In addition, there is the suggestion that the future of the race lies with women. The hint of a certain unease on the part of these male theorists is inescapable.

The literary milieu, both in Gissing's view and in actuality, partly sidestepped gender relations in being divided by gender. Gissing's literary realm was almost exclusively male in its composition, consisting of encounters in the masculine domain of the club, with subsequent dinners and visits. Gissing himself seems to have accepted this division as perfectly normal, since he never refers to it. Elaine Showalter writes of 'a developing Female Aesthetic' of feminine 'difference'; this suggests that women authors perceived themselves as a separate branch of literary history outside male bastions.[7] But Showalter does not state whether this was from choice or necessity.

This division, accepted or not, fuelled Gissing's anxieties about literary identity. He writes to his brother, commenting on Carlyle's death:

> Does it not seem now as if all our really great men were leaving us, and, what is worse, without much prospect as yet of any to take their place. Where are the novelists to succeed Thackeray, Dickens, George Eliot? What poets will follow upon Tennyson and Browning when they, as must shortly be the case, leave their places empty?[8]

This male-oriented view may be influenced by the memory of Carlyle, champion of 'great men'; yet the inclusion of George Eliot in his list suggests that Gissing's use of the word 'men' is not meant to imply female inferiority. As a man he is concerned with his place in literature among (English)men; his view of the literary scene is exclusively male and English. Gissing is both optimistic and pessimistic; he sees the end of a literary era, but at this point he had published just one novel, *Workers in the Dawn*, so that his letter serves partly as self-reassurance. He is not ready to fill the place of a great man in modern literature, but neither is anyone else. Indeed, the idea of writers occupying a place left vacant at their deaths suggests specific niches in which the next generation can establish themselves, in a process of natural succession.

Other literary figures were less ambivalent about the future of literature. A. J. Balfour prophesied a bleak future at the Royal Literary Fund's annual dinner in 1893: 'I do not know that any of us can see around us the men springing up who are to occupy the thrones thus left vacant'.[9] But H. G. Wells saw the passing of the 'great Victorians' as a good thing:

> The last decade of the nineteenth century was an extraordinarily favourable time for new writers and my individual good luck was set in the luck of a whole generation of aspirants. Quite a lot of us from nowhere were 'getting on' [...] every weed and sapling had its chance, provided only that it was of a different species from its predecessors.[10]

Both opinions come from men sufficiently established to be able to pronounce on the future of literature with authority. Wells, confident in his modernity and retrospectively certain of his success, uses optimistic evolutionary language, while Balfour, designating thrones of literary achievement unfilled by the present generation, hints at degeneration. In each case the certainty of the men's positions determines their opinion of the strength of contemporary literature.

But other problematic changes were happening in the literary market. Nigel Cross notes a 'gradual shift of power from paternalist libraries to childish readers' as the public demanded lighter fiction and the circulating libraries lost power (p.216). 'Paternalist' and 'childish' suggest a radical transformation in the relationship between author and market, and in writers' attitudes to the reader whose literary tastes were revealed. They also imply, in the power shift from authoritative, masculinised libraries to weak, feminised readers, an irresponsibility towards literature. The new-found public ability to exercise choice meant that a division began to form between 'the serious novel' and 'the bestseller'. Writers started to divide or be divided into 'tradesmen' and 'artists'.[11] However, the gendering of this division is unclear; an implication of being an 'artist' is a manly striving for the best, and yet the point of a 'tradesman' doing a job of work is that he is by definition a man, since women were generally perceived as not working. The masculinist ideology excludes women entirely from a legitimate literary world, while being unable to establish its own masculine credentials.[12]

Gissing placed himself overtly on the side of the artists, describing a Society of Authors banquet as 'a mere gathering of tradesmen'.[13] But he also wrote stories for Clement Shorter for two guineas per 1000 words; this is unequivocally the action of a 'tradesman', albeit one whose paid hack-work allowed him to produce his 'serious novels'. The uncertainty of Gissing's literary position leads him to be peculiarly aggressive in self-defence, engaging in desperate rivalry with any other writer encroaching on his specific field (or alternatively, usurping his throne). He

genuinely admires Charlotte Brontë and George Eliot, and
foreign writers such as Daudet, Dostoevsky, and even Conrad,
but can barely praise a fellow male English author:

> A paper on Stevenson I cannot read; my prejudice
> against the man is insuperable, inexplicable, painful; I
> hate to see his name, and certainly shall never bring
> myself to read one of his books. Don't quite
> understand the source of this feeling.[14]

Gissing's groundless dislike probably springs from Stevenson's
enviable success as an adventure story writer, ensuring a
distinctly male literary identity.

Gissing's unstable position as a writer led him to stake out his
territory by adopting an established 'great man', first as a model,
then as a literary ancestor. He chose Charles Dickens, and begins
in unmixed admiration: 'Dickens could not even write the
shortest note without some admirable fun in it. What a man he
was!'[15] However, in Gissing's later writings on Dickens he is
sometimes severely critical or patronising, as in his preface to
Barnaby Rudge:

> By endeavouring to fit his original work into an old-
> fashioned frame, he merely encumbered himself, and
> showed at a disadvantage in comparison with writers
> far below him.[16]

Gissing unfairly reads him according to the literary standards and
fashions of his own day; he needs to see Dickens as a man of a
past time to reduce him to a manageable size. In seeing Dickens'
faults as well as acknowledging his virtues, Gissing establishes
himself as a fellow master. He also manages to compare himself

favourably with Dickens and thus assure himself that he is the more masculine and the more 'successful'.

Gissing is torn between his wish to succeed Dickens and to follow his own path. An early letter to his brother documents this struggle:

> Certainly I have struck out this path for myself in fiction, for one cannot, of course, compare my methods and aims with those of Dickens. I mean to bring home to people the ghastly condition (material, mental and moral) of our poor classes.[17]

Gissing begins by defensively asserting that he is doing original work, then modestly rejecting a comparison with Dickens. But his next sentence suggests that he is undertaking something which the earlier writer neglected or failed to do, and proving his superior masculinity in facing what Dickens would or could not.[18]

When Gissing was an established author, he at last identified Dickens definitively as his literary father, recalling in 1901 his sight as a child of the woodcut commemorating Dickens' death, 'The Empty Chair':

> Not without awe did I see the picture of the room which now was tenantless [...] and I began to ask myself how books were written, and how the men lived who wrote them. It is my last glimpse of childhood. Six months later there was an empty chair in my own home, and the tenor of my life was broken.[19]

Perhaps the title of the woodcut first suggested to Gissing that writers occupy distinct places in the literary world. At any rate, the empty chair and 'tenantless' room suggest a vacuum needing to be filled, and Gissing delineates his first tentative thoughts about stepping into the breach. 'My last glimpse of childhood' links the death of Gissing's father with that of Dickens, who implicitly is cast as a replacement, literary father. Gissing becomes Dickens' son, and thus in succession lived as the men who wrote books did.

Yet despite Gissing's explicit self-styling as the heir of Dickens, his work more closely resembles Thomas Hardy's, particularly in their later books. In terms of influence, Hardy is perhaps a literary elder brother; by the time Gissing has found his feet as a writer Hardy is both established and contemporary. Gissing's rivalry towards Hardy is encapsulated in his diary description of *The Hand of Ethelberta* as 'surely old Hardy's poorest book' (p.236). 'Poorest' implies low literary and monetary value, and thus low success and, implicitly, failed masculinity, while 'old Hardy' is both familiar and contemptuous; he would be impotent and weak, unlike the young, virile Gissing.

But Gissing also notes snippets of information about Hardy, as in this diary entry from 1892:

> See it mentioned in a paper today that Hardy writes in copying ink, and thus supplies himself with a duplicate. Think I must do the same, to avoid the fearful possibility of lost MS. (p.280)

While this is undoubtedly a handy hint, Gissing seems inclined to take it up simply because Hardy does it. This is vaguely superstitious, as if imitating Hardy's writing methods, down to the ink he uses, will guarantee successful writing. Despite his carping, Gissing has identified Hardy as one of the fittest, and aims to evolve into a similar but superior version by the talismanic power of copying-ink.

In his personal writings Gissing shows contradictory attitudes towards literary evolution and the contemporary literary climate. On one hand he fears the implications of change; will he survive as a writer at all, will he become a tradesman satisfying a childish public, will this somehow feminise his work and him, will literature itself change beyond recognition? On the other he attempts self-establishment as a successor, suggesting his belief in a system of natural selection in a male-oriented world. Gissing has already seen that much as he might wish the old order to persist he needs to understand the new one, but he wishes to fit into and succeed in the new literary world rather than change it further. *New Grub Street* shows Gissing taking the first steps in that direction. He creates a fictional analogue to his perceived literary world, in which he can chart the destiny of various authorial types, to create solutions for his own dilemmas about writing, inheritance, and masculinity.

Gissing read widely in contemporary science; he had certainly read Ribot's *Hérédité* and *The Origin of Species*, and probably *The Descent of Man*, by the time of writing *New Grub Street*. He ascribes a similar degree of knowledge to one of his protagonists, who is much more optimistic about applying its theories to himself. The novel opens with Jasper Milvain, a confident aspiring writer, indulging in favourable comparisons, explicitly identifying himself as one of 'the fittest' and characterising his friend Edwin Reardon, an actual novelist, as the reverse:

> 'But just understand the difference between a man like Reardon and a man like me. He is the old type of unpractical artist; I am the literary man of 1883. He won't make concessions, or rather, he can't make them; he can't supply the market [...] he's behind his age'.[20]

In Jasper's eyes, Reardon is a different (and less advanced) species or variation; he is an artist who 'can't', and is, implicitly, unsuccessful, limited, over-refined, weak and feminised, while Jasper is this year's model of the literary man. At first sight the heading of this chapter, 'A Man of His Day', refers to Jasper, the modern literary businessman. Yet it also refers to Reardon as the man of a day which has passed, emphasising the transience of modernity. Jasper's boasts of his own (untested) literary prowess and Reardon's imminent failure almost invite fate to reverse his prophecy. But this does not happen; Jasper's power of display, his male signals, reinforce other characters' belief in him - apart from his sisters, who are proof to his partly sexual self-promotion. Jasper begins to perform his mating dance even before suitable partners arrive; a sign of confidence, and also an indication that to him the dance is as important as its objective, that the promise of success is as good as success.

In terms of evolutionary characteristics, Jasper is bound to succeed and Reardon to fail. Jasper's father was a thriving veterinary surgeon (which could account for Jasper's interest in Darwinian theory), while Reardon's pursued many occupations unsuccessfully. Notably, Gissing makes this divergence occur in the male line. Jasper, explicitly, has a superstition which 'forbids me to take a step backward'; quite literally, he is determined to progress, to become as highly evolved a man of letters as he can (p.421). His singlemindedness is a typically masculine trait. Reardon, though, is willing to go backwards, to return to his employment as a clerk, and longs to retreat to the decayed empire of Ancient Greece.

Jasper and Reardon are depicted as chiefly separated by their attitude to writing, appearing to replicate the 'artist/tradesman' division current in 'real life' literary circles. Reardon is shown as an amateur artist, while Jasper regards literature as a trade; his judgement that Reardon's last novel failed rests on terms of sales, not merit. Jasper equates quality and marketability. Yet the money he makes is less important to him than his identity as a successful literary man. This ambition of Jasper's exposes the false opposition set up for the reader. If Jasper were the businessman he claims to be, he would choose a different trade altogether, or at least a more remunerative field. But his literary ambitions are at least as strong as Reardon's, and not entirely dissimilar.

Reardon is fixed from the start as a failing writer whose practical wife will not sympathise with his failure. His strength declines from a zenith occurring before the novel begins, the publication of *On Neutral Ground*. Even here, the non-aggressive, unambitious picture this title conjures up suggests that Reardon is incapable of being a successful author, in worldly or artistic terms, because he does not possess the traditionally masculine characteristics. The two writers compete because they want to occupy the same ground - there is no neutral ground at all, and Jasper is better able to choose, win and defend his territory than Reardon is. John Gross remarks that Reardon makes a career of preserving his professional honour and what he writes is less important; indeed, Reardon is more theoretical than actual novelist.[21] He is presented as a perfectionist frustrated by the necessity of earning a living. Significantly, Gissing rewrites two of his own experiences with Reardon as protagonist. Reardon's encounter with a famous novelist whose lifestyle encourages him to write replicates Gissing's encounter with the engraving of Dickens' house, 'The Empty Chair', while his struggle to write *Margaret Home* mirrors Gissing's diary entries on writing *New Grub Street*.[22] However, Reardon is portrayed as out of touch, programmed to fail, contrasting with Gissing's already achieved success. By putting Reardon through the same ordeals and writing his failure, Gissing makes another comparison of masculinity favourable to himself.

And Reardon is not a pure artist; he is first shown grinding away at a pot-boiler for cash, presumably intended for female or feminised readers. Paradoxically, Jasper's willingness to sacrifice his sisters' comfort to his career suggests a more conventional artistic temperament. He may encourage his sisters to write, but their work is for children; there is no question of them writing on the same terms.[23] John Goode states that 'Reardon's whole story depends on his tacit acquiescence in Milvain's world view'.[24] But Reardon's struggle for money is more than a tacit acquiescence. Reardon can be seen as a less successful Milvain, in the sense that all the writers in *New Grub Street* are assessed by Gissing as more or less successful men. Gissing's own competitive ambivalence towards Dickens, Hardy and Stevenson, men at a level of success to which he can only aspire at present, supports this hypothesis. At bottom, the novel implies that one's status as tradesman or artist is less important than success in either sphere, proving one's manhood.

Goode also argues that Gissing makes Biffen, the 'real hero', commit suicide in order to suppress his literary approach as an alternative to Milvain's (pp.136-39). However, Biffen exists in isolation. He needs no public, no competition or comparison, and in this satisfaction he is both more and less than the novel's masculine standard. He is an alternative approach, certainly, but also functions at another, extreme level of success and masculinity. When Biffen is forced, in loving Amy Reardon, to compare himself to other men, he loses his isolation, needs to relate to others, and is unable to do so. Biffen's inability to realise himself fully as a man, his vision of where he falls short, leads to literary impotence, and then to suicide. Two types of the successful man are presented, successful in love or successful in writing, and Biffen's realisation that he cannot be successful in love makes him unable to write at all. Pure artistry is presented as incompatible with male sexual fulfilment.

Noticeably, neither Reardon nor Jasper are concerned about children; Jasper never wishes for them, while Reardon dislikes his small son. Their literary productions are their children, and their pride in them reflects back on themselves, in a dead-end process. Implicitly, writing is anti-evolutionary; both authors are too busy propagating themselves by means of their work to produce children. Jasper's evolutionary ambitions are about evolving himself - he is concerned for his own good, not the good of the race. In this respect they are almost ungendered; their maleness is diverted to another cause.

The novel makes all success dependent on a strong gender identity. Being a successful 'serious' writer is an affirmation of masculinity in the novel, and being a successful non-serious writer is an affirmation of femininity; Reardon wins Amy once he has produced a successful book, and Dora, writer of children's books, is the most conventionally appealing female character in the novel. Anything else produces an indeterminacy of gender, which appears as a disadvantage, and a sign of failure. Reardon's masculinity is affirmed by Amy only before their marriage, during the flashback to his previous life. He continually struggles and fails to keep some sense of himself as a 'literary man', unable to produce the great, famous novel which would prove his manhood.

Marian Yule is Edwin Reardon's female counterpart. But her state seems more volatile than Reardon's; she is less obviously doomed to failure. Her appearance suggests that she is repressed and sexually undeveloped, and she sends out confused gender signals:

> [...] a girl of perhaps two-and-twenty, in a slate-coloured dress with very little ornament, and a yellow straw hat of the shape originally appropriated to males; her dark hair was cut short, and lay in innumerable crisp curls. (p.15)

The plainness of Marian's dress, her hat and short hair suggest a masculine nature, but her curls imply an innate femininity on which outside influences have imposed. It is never made clear whether Marian deliberately dresses as bluestocking or New Woman, or whether it is all she can afford. Similarly, her involvement in the literary world suggests force, coupled with a lack of femininity; but she is actually employed as her father's unpaid and uncredited research assistant. Marian is good at her job, but her very proficiency leads Alfred Yule to regard her as an employee rather than as a daughter, or indeed a woman. Neither Marian's career nor her sexuality is permitted to develop, and when her inheritance falls through she becomes a library assistant. In a world where men write and women read, she is an unsexed servant. The general tone of the novel implies that in Marian's indeterminacy and failure to assert herself, a self implicitly bound up with her femaleness, she is more to be pitied than feared. But unlike Reardon and Biffen, Marian's story does not reach a definitive end; as she is female, Gissing does not seem to need to evaluate and pass judgement on her in the same way.

The two most successful characters are Amy and Jasper. They are also the two characters whose gender is defined most strongly. Amy is generally acknowledged as beautiful, and is devoted to her child. Paradoxically, the clarity of these feminine attributes gives her a masculine air, which is reinforced by Gissing's presentation. Amy is a strong woman, and on occasion a fierce mother; Reardon castigates her mentally for attending to the demands of their son rather than his own. In Reardon's view, through which Amy is shown, men are strong, active and definite, while women are weak, passive and nebulous; he cannot recognise the neutral ground between his self-defined oppositions. Though Amy is a recognisable feminine type, it is not one which Reardon or the narrator acknowledges. In addition, in *New Grub Street* success is almost by definition a masculine attribute. Marian Yule is more typically feminine, but her comparative weakness means that her femininity is constantly threatened. Similarly, Jasper Milvain, complementing Amy, shows plenty of masculine aggression in backing himself against Reardon as a successful author.

An essential correspondence between the pair, though, is that they are aware of themselves as mutable. Gissing's language in describing Amy's reaction to Reardon's proposed re-employment as a clerk is suggestive: 'she glared like the animal that defends itself with tooth and claw' (p.228). The echo of *In Memoriam* aligns Amy with Nature herself, implying that her brutish reaction to Reardon's regression is natural; notably, Reardon understands it not as natural, but low. Similarly, Jasper knows that his moral nature is too weak to survive without money; he congratulates himself on obtaining money and thus saving himself: 'I have much of the weakness that might become viciousness, but I am now far from the possibility of becoming vicious' (p.514). Amy and Jasper are evolutionarily favoured in that they are aware of the optimum conditions for their prosperity and will make other sacrifices to attain them. They show the conventional attributes of the opposing gender, 'masculine' fierceness for Amy, 'feminine' hesitation for Jasper, to ensure the final attainment of suitably strongly-gendered positions in society.

At the end of the novel, though, the pair become comparatively sexless. Jasper is shown as an uncritical, passive, ideologically feminised consumer, dreaming while Amy plays the piano for him. He has changed in appearance: he looks older than he is, with thinning hair, wrinkles, careful dress, and a softer, firmer voice (p.511). These changes suggest that Jasper's struggle to attain literary eminence has aged him and diminished his masculinity; but they also imply that, having attained that position, he can allow himself to relax into a less masculine, more assured role than that of the aggressive boastful bachelor of his former days. Amy has also changed, in that 'that suspicion of masculinity observable in her when she became Reardon's wife impressed one now only as the consummate grace of a perfectly-built woman' (p.511). This, despite the narrator's assumption of her greater femininity, suggests rather that Amy can now be comparatively passive - her femininity has changed in type. But 'perfectly-built' implies that Amy's new femininity, conscious or not, is partly a self-constructed society role.

Amy and Jasper's marriage appears to be a partnership of equals, neither partner claiming more power, both free to be creator or consumer. Yet their indeterminacy of gender (despite the claims about Amy's new-found womanliness) leaves the relationship with little sexual charge. They embrace and gaze into each other's eyes, but this is an expression of affection and pleasure in each other's achievements. Sexuality is a symptom of incompleteness in *New Grub Street*, in that it is relinquished on achieving a successful position. Notably, the conventional Victorian novelistic sign of a successful marriage, a child either present or on the way, is absent. Since for Jasper and Amy literary success equals material, social and sexual success, they no longer have to occupy conventional gender roles. They can literally afford to cease their gender anxieties.

However, Jasper, having reached the top of the literary heap, is now past his peak. He has been transformed from the aggressive male fighting to gain territory to the elder statesman defending it. Instead of the Oedipal warfare which Harold Bloom suggests as a model for literary influence, the writers in *New Grub Street* suffer from a Laius complex - they all fear the literary successor who will kill their reputation. Jasper, having 'killed off' Reardon as competition, and then married his wife, should be aware of the dangers. Paradoxically, he has lost by winning - Jasper was at his best as a male animal when he was pronouncing his powers, doing his mating dance. On attaining a position, his limitations become visible and his potential decreases. Gissing makes it clear that Jasper loses as well as gains in his rise to the top.

While a strong gender identity is essential for success in the world which Gissing presents, masculinity is ephemeral. Once Jasper has achieved success, he relaxes into a less masculine role; is masculinity an individual construct which can be abandoned once it has been proved? Alternatively, is it a resource which has to be husbanded carefully and which Jasper has exhausted? Gissing does not reach a satisfactory conclusion about masculinity in the novel, and no absolutely masculine character exists. Reardon and Biffen die, while Jasper and Whelpdale are successful, but in succeeding become elderly, established, no longer interesting. They are momentarily the men of their day, before their day passes just as Reardon's did; and with the death of masculinity comes the death of literature. Aggressive masculinity favours a standard of marketability, succeeds by it, eradicates the unmarketable, and then is eradicated by success. Implicitly Gissing argues that literature is an outdated form killed by a masculine drive for material success; but this remains a hidden conclusion.

New Grub Street is ruled by an interventionist, annoyingly omniscient, and distinctly male, narrator. This assumed didactic narration suggests an author asserting his authority, trying to regenerate an audience of feminised, passive consumers. In dramatising this power shift between writer and reader as part of the novel rather than confronting it privately, Gissing explores the topic partly in order to establish his own relationship to it. The narrator's masculine voice almost passes unnoticed in a text where active characters and serious writers are men. Indeed, the narrator agrees with the ideology that masculinity equals success, while disapproving of it. The reader is meant to choose his story in a process analogous to an evolutionary sexual selection; the active male narrator shows his decisiveness and secures the feminised, passive reader. But despite the reader's conventional passivity, the reader is also the newly empowered public whom the author must satisfy

Ultimately the narrator's heroes, Reardon, Biffen and Marian, are overthrown by the stronger characters, Jasper and Amy, as these characters prevail in the narrative. By personifying his fears about not being a man of his day in the form of the outdated didactic narrator, then confirming his distance from that figure by ensuring his defeat, Gissing asserts his evolutionary superiority, his ability to struggle and succeed (in both senses of the word). Similarly, the versions of authorship which Gissing presents fail, or if successful are presented as fundamentally flawed, as he justifies his chosen path to himself. It is clear from his personal writings that Gissing felt both threatened and stimulated by masculine ideologies of dominance and superiority which were at least partly his own creation. *New Grub Street* allowed Gissing to be at ease with his literary position by delineating, comparing and rejecting all others.

Ironically, *New Grub Street* proved to be a successful literary three-volume novel about the end of literature and three-volume novels. It made Gissing's reputation, particularly because it was acclaimed by fellow authors.[25] Gissing entered a sphere of interviews, photographs, literary clubs and socialising; the sphere of an established writer. After *New Grub Street* Gissing continued to deal with the issues of gender identity and success, but there were no more books specifically about authors and authorship, or so exclusively about men and masculinity. Perhaps, having written the novel in pursuit of answers to his own literary and personal dilemmas, the lack of any final answers acted as a catharsis. At any rate, by writing *New Grub Street* and keeping one step ahead of the literary game, Gissing secured, at least for the moment, his own position as a man of his day.

[1]Nigel Cross, *The Common Writer* (Cambridge: Cambridge University Press, 1985); John Gross, *The Rise and Fall of the Man of Letters* (London: Weidenfeld & Nicolson, 1969).

[2]Ménie Muriel Dowie, *Gallia*, 1895, ed. Helen Small (London: Everyman, 1995); Charles G. Harper, *Revolted Woman: Past, Present and to Come* (London: Elkin Matthews, 1894), p.27, quoted in Sally Ledger, 'The New Woman and the crisis of Victorianism', in *Cultural Politics at the Fin de Siècle*, eds. Sally Ledger, Scott McCracken (Cambridge: Cambridge University Press, 1995), pp.22-44 (p.31).

[3]George Gissing, *Letters to Members of His Family*, collected and arranged by Algernon and Ellen Gissing (London: Constable, 1927), p.74. Gissing's diary powerfully suggests the connection for him between sex and writing: 'Tuesd. Sept. 16. Strayed about, and thought of a new story. Feel like a madman at times. I know that I shall never do any more good work until I am married.' 'Wed. Sept. 24. Oxford [Music Hall] - E[dith] U[nderwood]' (*London and the Life of Literature in Late Victorian England: The Diary of George Gissing, Novelist*, ed. Pierre Coustillas [Brighton: Harvester, 1978], p.226).

[4]Charles Darwin, *The Origin of Species*, 1859, ed. and introd. J. W. Burrow (Harmondsworth: Penguin, 1987), p.136; Charles Darwin, *The Descent of Man*, 1871 (Princeton: Princeton University Press, 1981), vol. 1, pp.272-73.

[5]Herbert Spencer, 'Human Population in the Future' (*Westminster Review*, April 1852), reprinted in *The Principles of Biology* (London: Williams & Norgate, 1884), vol. 2, pp.499-501.

[6]Francis Galton, *Natural Inheritance* (London: Macmillan, 1889), p.198. Galton, Darwin's cousin, had the reassurance of knowing that he was descended from 'good stock' (see *Hereditary Genius* [London: Macmillan, 1925], pp.202-3); Francis Galton, *National Review*, August 1894, quoted in Allan Chase, *The Legacy of Malthus* (Urbana: University of Illinois Press, 1980), p.101.

[7]Elaine Showalter, *Sexual Anarchy: Gender and Culture at the Fin de Siècle* (London: Bloomsbury, 1991), p.64.

[8]Gissing, *Letters to Members of His Family*, p.92.

[9]A. J. Balfour, speech to Royal Literary Fund, 1893, quoted in Cross, p.214.

[10]H. G. Wells, *Experiment in Autobiography* (1934), quoted in Cross, pp.212-13.

[11]Anthony Trollope's cheerful exposition of his work ethic, seemingly indicative of his position as a tradesman, horrified many readers: 'It had at this time become my custom [...] to write with my watch before me, and to require from myself 250 words every quarter of an hour' (*An Autobiography*, 1883 [London: Williams & Norgate, 1946], p.241).

[12]Christine Battersby argues in *Gender and Genius* (London: The Women's Press, 1989) that genius itself was presented as male from pre-Romantic times. However, there are no geniuses at all in *New Grub Street*.

[13]Gross, p.200.

[14]Coustillas, p.33. In 1902 Gissing appended: 'Was this mere jealousy? Of course I have long since ceased to be capable of such feeling.' His complacency seems to have come with his success. On Brontë to his sister Margaret: 'She is the greatest English woman after Mrs. Browning. [...] she wrote a style such as you find in no other writer' (*Letters to Members of His Family*, p.191). Here Gissing first posits a separate female literary canon, and then an integrated one. Interestingly, the two female novelists Gissing most admired both used male pseudonyms.

[15]Gissing, *Letters to Members of His Family*, p.55.

[16]George Gissing, *The Immortal Dickens* (London: n. publ., 1925), pp.173-74.

[17]Gissing, *Letters to Members of His Family*, p.83.

[18]This is closely related to Harold Bloom's suggestion of the relation between new poems and existing ones: 'Every poem is a misinterpretation of a parent poem. A poem is not an overcoming of anxiety, but is that anxiety' (*The Anxiety of Influence* [Oxford: Oxford University Press, 1973], p.94). In *The Political Unconscious* Fredric Jameson undermines Bloom's theory of anxiety, commenting that 'A book such as Gissing's early *Nether World* is as Dickensian as one likes, provided it is understood that the hold of Dickensian paradigms over Gissing is not the result of some charismatic power of a temperamental or artistic sort, but rather testimony for the fact that these paradigms offered objective 'solutions' (or imaginary resolutions) to equally objective ideological problems confronted by the younger writer' (Fredric Jameson, *The Political Unconscious* [London: Methuen, 1981], pp.185-6). Jameson presents Dickens as a benign ancestor instead of Bloom's archetypal oppressor, implying that Gissing has no Oedipal compulsion, but Dickens seems to exist in both capacities for Gissing, hence his ambivalence towards him. *The Nether World* and *In The Year of Jubilee* can be read as rewriting aspects of *Bleak House* and *Our Mutual Friend*; their similar themes have a different tone, and resolutions which almost parody the originals. Gissing's 'rewrites' are not misinterpretations of Dickens, but in their change of tone they show a degree of tension towards him. However, Gissing's private comments to his brother are more aggressive than his actual artistic method, and it is difficult for even Gissing to be very aggressive and competitive towards a dead author, by implication already succeeded.

[19]Gissing, *The Immortal Dickens*, pp.6-7.

[20]George Gissing, *New Grub Street*, 1891, ed. and introd. John Goode (Oxford: Oxford University Press, 1993), pp.8-9.

[21]Gross, p.215.

[22]Coustillas, pp.213-31.

[23]As a Darwinian, Jasper may also have subscribed to the view that women were simply not as good at writing as men; Darwin stated that 'higher eminence' was achieved by men in activities 'requiring deep thought, reason, or imagination' (*The Descent of Man*, p.858, quoted in Battersby, p.118).

[24] John Goode, *George Gissing: Ideology and Fiction* (London: Vision Press, 1978), p.116.
[25] Cross, p.225.

5

'I AM THE LOVER AND THE LOVED- I HAVE LOST AND FOUND MY IDENTITY': EDWARD CARPENTER AND *FIN-DE-SIÈCLE* MASCULINITIES

Situating Edward Carpenter within a history of modern masculinities is not an easy task. His rugged, outdoors version of a homosexual lifestyle appears unfamiliar in the context of the late nineteenth century. After the trial of Oscar Wilde in 1895, the dominant public perception of the homosexual was as an effeminate aristocrat. In our own time, the post-Stonewall period has seen such a proliferation of gay identities that Carpenter's 'Uranian' hardly appears distinctive. If Carpenter had a historical moment in recent times it was probably the early seventies. Speaking at a History Workshop conference in 1991, Alan Sinfield identified the brief revival in interest in Carpenter's life and work at that time with the need within the early gay liberation movement to find positive alternatives to the effeminate stereotype. Carpenter's masculine homosexuality provided that alternative, but the moment and the need have passed. Consequently, any attempt to understand his definition of the 'Uranian' as part of a tradition within gay history is probably doomed to failure. Instead, it makes more sense to understand it as part of the constellation of new, emergent identities that characterised the English *fin de siècle*. These would include the New Woman and the Wildean aesthete, but the Uranian also bears an important relation to such apparently opposed figures as George Gissing's embittered, conservative male subjects, William Morris's socialist masculinity of the future, and the lonely imperialist heroes of Conrad's modernist romances.

Carpenter was a utopian socialist whose ideas spanned many of the radical movements of the late nineteenth and early twentieth century. A man who made his own sandals (he even sent out a pair

to Olive Schreiner in South Africa, where they must have been
more suitable than in the North of England), he might have been the
original of George Orwell's crank socialist: the 'fruit-juice drinker,
nudist, sandal-wearer, sex-maniac, Quaker, "Nature cure" quack,
pacifist and feminist'.[1] He resigned a fellowship at Cambridge to
attempt a 'simple' life in Derbyshire. Cynically, one might say that
this was a less than heroic attempt by a single middle-class man to
live without servants; such cynicism seems to be borne out by
reports that his working-class lovers did the housework.
Nonetheless, his example offered a powerful alternative to
bourgeois norms of masculine behaviour. In addition, he was an
active member of the Sheffield Socialist Society, and helped to fund
socialist newspapers like the Social Democratic Federation's
Justice. His long poem *Towards Democracy* was heavily dependent
on Walt Whitman's *Leaves of Grass*, but, in contrast to the latter's
deliberate ambiguity, *Towards Democracy* was openly homoerotic.
By the early twentieth century, Carpenter's ideas about sexual and
social relations had influenced radical thought on both sides of the
Atlantic, and were influencing German sexual radicalism,
Bloomsbury and Greenwich Village. One might say that what he
has missed in becoming a well-known historical figure, he made up
for as a pervasive medium for progressive ideas.

Carpenter's revolt was, from the first, against the norms of
English, Victorian society. The title of his early collection of essays,
Civilization, Its Cause and Cure, signalled a counter-enlightenment
project. This was true both in the sense described by E. P.
Thompson in his discussion of William Blake, and in the sense
explored by T. W. Adorno and Max Horkheimer in *The Dialectic
of the Enlightenment*.[2] Thompson writes of the 'counter-
enlightenment resistance' practised by Blake against the Age of
Reason.[3] Carpenter's critique of civilisation was in that tradition,

but in the second half of the nineteenth century it was the determinist narratives of evolutionism that legislated against dissident desires. Civilisation for Carpenter had the same negative charge it acquired for William Morris. Both writers set themselves against the Victorian idea of progress, and were opposed to the Fabian version of that narrative later displayed in the writings of George Bernard Shaw and H. G. Wells. The title of Carpenter's volume effectively inverted the medicalisation of moral discourse current in the 1880s, suggesting a dialectic of enlightenment where the scientific rationalism that would heal was actually the cause of the wound. Civilisation brought about the psychic divisions that create a disassociation between love and desire in 'the vast system of commercial love', while the body itself becomes fetishised: 'Man [...] abandons his true Self for his organs'.[4] Opposed to the dominant interpretative framework of the period, social Darwinism, where Carpenter did engage with evolutionist ideas, he developed a quasi-Lamarckian approach that stressed the importance of a radical will.

Against evolutionism as an objective and irrevocable force, Carpenter posited an idea of willed evolution he called 'exfoliation'. Where evolutionism in its social Darwinist mode provided narratives which shored up the dominant gender identities of the Victorian age, exfoliation stressed the potential for self-definition: 'Desire, or inward change, comes first, action follows, and organisation or outward structure is the result'.[5] This radical desire defined the identity of Carpenter's 'Uranian' against the determinist narratives of social Darwinism. Such narratives were, potentially, open to a pluralist reading of infinite variation.[6] However, in practice, they perceived same sex desires at best as a product of what John Addington Symonds, in a letter to the sexologist Havelock Ellis, called aberrant 'sports'.[7] The term 'Uranian' was appropriated by a number of artists and poets in the late nineteenth century as positive identification with love between men. In Greek mythology Uranus is the personification of the heavens, and in Plato's *Symposium* 'Uranian' signifies a heavenly love, above vulgar, earthly desires. For Carpenter and Symonds the example of Ancient Greece and what Symonds called 'the imaginative basis of desire' were crucial elements in an argument against medical science. Following Rita Felski's book, *The Gender of Modernity*, we can see the Uranian as one of the subaltern identities that emerges both within and against modernity. Felski argues that it is too simplistic to see modernity as irredeemably masculine (and, by implication, heterosexual):

> For every account of the modern era which emphasises the domination of masculine qualities of rationalization, productivity, and repression, one can find another which points - whether approvingly or censoriously - to the feminization of Western society, as evidenced in the passive, hedonistic, and decentred nature of modern subjectivity.[8]

Carpenter's Uranian represents one sexual identity amongst the competing versions that emerged in the late nineteenth century The construction of the Uranian as outside the dominant gendered positions of the late-Victorian period permitted a critical response to those positions, and in his visionary work of sexual liberation, *Love's Coming of Age*, Carpenter was able to analyse masculinity in relation to both dominant and emergent sexual identities. Formulated against the scientific rationalism of the age, his definition of the Uranian provided the starting point for a critique of middle-class masculinity from within. In his best-known work he

described a notion of identity that eschewed binary oppositions. He
described 'the planetary law of distances in relation of people one
to another', an understanding of his reformulation of masculinity is
best achieved in terms of a number of different elements, none of
which can be reduced to a single or unilateral cause.[9] He analysed
Victorian masculinity in a section of *Love's Coming of Age* called
'Man the Ungrown'. Here he mapped out the kind of constellation
that made up an immature, middle-class, masculine identity.

> This ungrown, half-baked sort of character is
> conspicuous in the class of men of the English-speaking
> well-to-do class. The boy of this class begins life at
> public school. He does not learn much from the masters;
> but he knocks about among his fellows in cricket and
> football and athletics, and turns out with an excellent
> organising capacity and a tolerably firm grip on the
> practical and material side of life - qualities which are of
> first rate importance, and which give the English ruling
> classes a similar mission in the world to the Romans of
> the early empire.[10]

The most interesting aspect of this description is its understanding
of middle-class masculinity as formed through a relationship
between men. Carpenter's focus on all male institutions, the 'Law
or Army or Church or Civil Service or Commerce' prefigured Eve
Kosofsky Sedgwick's thesis of the importance of homosocial desire
in the formation of male dominance.[11] Sedgwick argues that the
codes of behaviour signifying middle-class masculinity in
nineteenth-century England were governed by what she calls 'male
homosocial desire'. Middle-class men socialised in all-male
institutions like public schools, Parliament, the army and the
Church. Strong bonds were established between them, excluding

women, and those men deemed less than masculine. Yet the nature
of these bonds was contradictory. Despite their overt
heterosexuality, a covert homoeroticism characterised men's
relationships with one another. The organisation of power along
class and gendered lines was reinforced by male homosocial desire.
Sedgwick's thesis demonstrates the way in which a particular form
of social organisation derives some of its power through sexual
relations, even when sexuality is not seen by the actors themselves
as an important determinant of their behaviour. Carpenter's
understanding already included this observation.[12] He described
how women and working-class men were given subordinate
positions in a constellation that privileges the homosocial bond.
Although, unsurprisingly, he was less egalitarian than today's queer
theorists, assuming a continuing leadership role for middle-class
men:

> In many respects the newer Women and the Workmen
> resemble each other. Both have been bullied and sat upon
> from time immemorial, and are beginning to revolt; both are
> good at detailed and set or customary work, both are bad at
> organisation; both are stronger on the emotional than on the
> intellectual side; and both have an ideal of better things, but
> do not quite see their way to carry it out. Their best hope
> perhaps lies in getting hold of the Well-to-do Man and
> thumping him on each side till they get him to organise the
> world for them.[13]

This assumption was widely held, and is treated with bitter irony in
Gissing's anti-feminist novel, *The Odd Women*. In answer to a question
about the Dandyish Everard Barfoot, 'But what can a man do, unless
he has genius?', the feminist Rhoda Nunn replies (without irony)

'There's the emancipation of the working classes'.[14] If Carpenter was more forward-looking than the reactionary Gissing, then he still (and with some approval) saw middle-class masculinity as central to a future constellation of class, gender, and (implicitly in his reference to the empire) 'race'. The difference between the two *fin de siècle* writers resided in their understanding of history. Gissing's masculine protagonists hardened their identities against an onslaught of historical forces, a process that culminated in his last novel in a retreat to the countryside with a very different purpose to Carpenter's own retreat to the Derbyshire village of Millthorpe in 1881. Where Carpenter attempted a life of manual labour working a small-holding, and wished to challenge gendered roles, the protagonist of Gissing's last novel, *The Private Papers of Henry Ryecroft*, attempts to escape labour altogether with the help of a female servant. Ryecroft, after years of a poverty-stricken life as a moderately successful writer in London, gains a legacy of £300 per annum and retreats to the countryside. There he is able to cultivate a masculine identity there that was no longer possible in the city:

> London is the antithesis of the domestic ideal; a social reformer would not even glance in that direction, but would turn all his zeal upon small towns and country districts, where blight may perhaps be arrested, and whence, some day a reconstituted national life may act upon the great centre of corruption.[15]

Nothing demonstrates the gendered co-ordinates of this masculine space better than Ryecroft's carefully constructed domestic environment, and the position of his housekeeper:

> My house is perfect. By great good fortune I have found a housekeeper no less to my mind, a low-voiced, light-

> footed woman of discreet age, strong and deft enough to
> render me all the service I require, and not afraid of
> solitude. She rises very early. By my breakfast-time there
> remains little to be done under the roof save dressing of
> meals. Very rarely do I hear even a clink of crockery;
> never the closing of a door or window. Oh, blessed
> silence! (pp.12-13)

This flight to domesticity is a step beyond the domestic hearth of
the Victorian novel. Rather than advocating a return to the family,
marriage is always a source of conflict in Gissing's novels. In the
context of the New Woman's 'invasion' of the public sphere, he
constructed a new individualised masculinity against the social. In
Henry Ryecroft, the silence of the retreat is striking: the absence of
other voices that might challenge a carefully reconstructed identity.
The housekeeper can only just read and write; she lacks (or rather
is denied) a consciousness that would pose a threat to Ryecroft.
Instead, she is seen going to church, establishing a pattern and an
order into which he can fit: 'All the tranquillity of life depends upon
the honest care of this woman who lives and works unseen' (p.60).

In contrast, while Carpenter shared some of the gendered
presumptions of his age, he resisted any concept of identity as a fixed
constellation of gender or class. He was always concerned with its
potential transformation, writing of what he called 'the amazement of
expanded identity'.[16] He described that vision in the last chapter of
Love's Coming of Age:

> the idea of terrestrial society for which we naturally strive is
> that which would embody best these enduring and deep
> seated relations of human souls; and that every society, as far
> as it is human and capable of holding together is in its degree
> a reflection of the celestial City. Never is the essential real

> Society quite embodied in any mundane Utopia but ever
> through human history is it working unconsciously in the
> midst of mortal affairs and impelling towards an expression
> of itself.[17]

For Carpenter, the utopian impulse was an essential element in the
process of exfoliation. He belonged to the group 'The Fellowship of
the New Life', which was later to develop into the Fabian Society, and
he understood the 'new life' to be in tune with history, which is
evolving towards the point where a full expression of utopia will be
possible. The seeds of a new utopian constellation, the new relations
'of human souls', were already present in the Victorian configuration of
masculinity. If his belief in 'the essential real Society' still reflected the
teleological bias of the Victorian age, then the 'amazement of expanded
identity' was nonetheless a radical proposition, which was developed
more fully in his long poem, *Towards Democracy*. The force of
democracy was liberatory for all, and its aim was an equality that
would override previous distinctions:

> Not as in a dream. The earth remains and daily life
> remains, and the scrubbing of doorsteps, and the
> house and the care of the house remains; but Joy fills
> it, fills the house full and swells to the sky and reaches
> the stars: all Joy! (p.14)

Nonetheless, even in *Towards Democracy* an emancipatory spirit
conflicted with the continuing centrality of a privileged masculine
subject. The poem exemplified Carpenter's counter-enlightenment
project. Utopia emerges from the wreckage of civilisation. This is
expressed most clearly in Part 3, titled 'After Civilization'. The new life
arises out of the debris of modernity:

There, in vision, out of the wreck of cities and
civilizations,
    I saw a new life arise.

    Slowly out of the ruins of the past - like a young fern-
frond uncurling out of its own brown litter-
    Out of the litter of a decaying society, out of the
confused mass of broken down creeds, customs, ideals,
    Out of distrust and unbelief and dishonesty, and Fear,
meanest of all (the stronger in the panic trampling the weaker
underfoot);
    Out of the miserable rows of brick tenements with their
cheapjack interiors, their glances of suspicion, and doors
locked against each other;
    Out of the cant of Commerce - buying cheap and selling
dear - the crocodile sympathy of nations with nation,
    The smug merchant posing as a benefactor of his kind,
the parasite parsons and scientists;
    The cant of Sex, the impure hush clouding the deepest
instincts of boy and girl, woman and man; (p.215)

The wreckage after civilisation might be compared with Benjamin's
interpretation of Klee's Angelus Novus, irresistibly propelled by a
storm 'into a future to which his back is turned, while the pile of debris
before him grows skyward. This storm is what we call progress'.[18]
Carpenter's lengthy, broken lines list the fragments of a decaying
culture; yet it is this fragmentation of culture which permits the 'new
life' to appear. There is a view of completed labours in Carpenter's
poem that is not present in Benjamin's 'Theses on the Philosophy of
History'. In lines that can be compared with Morris' News from
Nowhere, simplification and collectivity provide the solutions to decay:

> The few needs, the exhilarated radiant life [...]
> The plentiful common halls stored with the products of
> Art and History and Science to supplement the simple
> household accommodations;
> The sweet and necessary labor of the day;
> All these I saw - for man the companion of Nature.
> (p.217)

'After Civilization' might be interpreted as a utopian imagining of the dissolution of the relations that make up the constellation of Victorian masculinity. In their place emerges the new utopian identity of the 'I' ('All these I saw') which is not bound by the same repression of nature that characterises Victorian culture. *Toward Democracy* represents a progressive attempt by Carpenter to break out of the limits of late-Victorian masculine identity, and to assert the transcendent 'I' of democracy that provides the point of democratic mediation for all other subjectivities. In the true state of democracy, that which Carpenter calls the 'free society' in *Love's Coming of Age*, there should be no differentiation between subjects; all would be part of the transcendent 'I'.

> Joy, joy arises - I arise. The sun darts overpowering piercing rays of joy through me, the night radiates it from me.
> I take wings through the night and pass through all the wildernesses of the worlds, and the old dark holds of tears and death - and return with laughter, laughter, laughter
> (p. 14)

Central to his critique is a transformation of the homosocial bond through explicit desire. In the poem, 'As a Woman of a Man', a sexual love between men undoes the repressive constellation of Victorianism to permit the emergence of a new identity, the Uranian:

> Come! who art no longer a name:
> Gigantic Thou, with head aureoled by the sun - wild among the mountains-
> Thy huge limbs naked and stalwart erected member,
> Thy lawless gait and rank untameable laughter,
> Thy heaven-licking wildfire thoughts and passions-
> I desire. (p.141)

A comparison with perhaps the best-known utopian text of the *fin de siècle* is striking here. In William Morris' *News from Nowhere* the male body acts as a signifier of the dignity of labour in a socialist society. Reading Morris against Carpenter brings out the subtext of homoeroticism that was an implicit part of that image. *News from Nowhere* can be understood as a homosocial discourse that attempted to create bonds of comradeship between men. Its central section, which takes up approximately one third of the text, is a dialogue between the narrator, Will, and old Hammond, a conversation from man to man that establishes the historical events that have established socialism. In contrast with socialist man, the women of the future are problematic figures: both Clara and Ellen represent different versions of New Women, and perplex the male characters. A good example of the text's writing of desire occurs when Will and his guide Dick come across a scene that is reminiscent of Ford Madox Brown's painting, 'Work':

> We came just here on a gang of men road-mending, which delayed us for a little [...] There were about a dozen of them, strong young men, looking much like a boating party at Oxford would have looked in the days I remembered, and not more troubled by their work; their outer raiment lay on the

> road-side in an orderly pile under the guardianship of a six-
> year-old boy, who had his arm thrown over the neck of a big
> mastiff, who was as happily lazy as if the summer day had
> been made for him alone.[19]

The economy of desire in the passage is interesting. The gang of men is being observed by a group of women, but Will watches both men and women:

> a half-dozen of young women stood by watching the work
> of the workers, both of which were worth watching, for
> the latter smote great strokes and were very deft in their
> labour, and as handsome clean-built fellows as you might
> find a dozen of in a summer day. (p.228)

The passage is ambiguous. '[B]oth' appears at first to refer to the men and the women, splitting his masculine gaze between two gendered objects of desire. It is only later that it becomes clear that it is the work and the workers that are 'worth watching'; this clarification routes Will's desiring gaze (or what we might call Will's will) through the women's eyes. They mediate same-sex desire between men so that the erotic pull of the socialist brotherhood is displaced. Part of Carpenter's contribution to late nineteenth-century English socialism was to a more direct exploration of the homoerotics of masculine labour. Much of the original shock value of his work came from his sexualised identification with male workers. Developing the hints contained in the poetry of Walt Whitman, *Towards Democracy* exploited the ambiguity of a language of secret glances between men in public places. In poems like the 'The Carter' and 'The Stone-Cutter' young men are brought to an enlightenment that is explicitly a consciousness of Democracy, and implicitly sexual.

> So in the dirt, amid the filthy smoke and insensate din of
> the great city,
>   Into my attic came my friend the carter and sat with me for
> a while.
>   Young and worn, these are the words he said:
>   "Never before could I have believed it, but I see it all now;
>   There is nothing like it - no happiness - when you have
> clean dropped thinking about yourself.
>   But you must not do it by halves - while ever there is the
> least grain of self left it will spoil all;
>   You must leave all behind - and yourself be the same as
> others. (pp.266-67)

However, the representation of working-class men as objects of desire in *Towards Democracy* is problematic. The imagined constellation that Democracy brings is expressed by the carter, but his vision is framed by the superior knowledge of the poet-narrator, who already knows what he comes to tell. In the final lines of the poem, the carter's experience is universalised by the narrator, in a way that transforms difference into unity.

> Thus in the din and dirt of the city, as over the mountains
> tops and in the far forests alone with Nature,
>   I saw the unimaginable form dwelling, whom no mortal eye
> may see,
>   The unimaginable form of Man, tenant of the earth from
> far ages, seen of the wise in all times -
>   Dwelling also in the youthful carter. (p. 267)

The poem is saved by the indeterminacy of the utopian future, the 'unimaginable form of Man'. Carpenter's new subjects teeter on the edge of the new world of what Ernst Bloch calls the 'Not-Yet-

Become'.[20] They occupy a marginal position where the new constellations they might form are not yet clear, but this vision of an excess beyond the actually existing is constantly threatened by a safer universality, which would already fix the positions from which they speak.

Carpenter's utopian 'I' performed the function of undoing the relationship between the masculine identity principle, and the collective other. However, while *Towards Democracy* was successful in imagining the dissolution of the dominant form of masculine identity, it was less clear about the exact nature of the new identity that will replace it. Carpenter oscillated between his critique of Victorian masculinity, which expressed a yearning for the free society, and an attempt to envisage that society, which inevitably refixed the boundaries of possibility. This is an inherent problem with utopianism. As that most rigorous critic of Victorian mores, Oscar Wilde, put it, utopia is 'the one country at which Humanity is always landing. And when Humanity lands there, it looks out, and, seeing a better country, sets sail'.[21] For Carpenter, the discovery of that country was the 'disclosure within of a region transcending in some sense the ordinary bounds of personality' which exists 'equally (though not always equally *consciously*) in others'.[22] The problem with the poems of *Towards Democracy* was that while the fragmentation of Victorian culture was successfully represented by the poetic form, the utopian solution to the disintegration transcended the masculine principle of identity by expansion and inclusion rather than through a recognition of difference. Utopia, according to T. W. Adorno, 'rattles the chains of identity'.[23] While Carpenter's transcendent utopianism did indeed rattle the chains of identity, it went on to construct new fetters. This was expressed in one of Carpenter's most powerful inclusive statements in *Towards Democracy*: 'I am the lover and the loved- I have lost and found my identity' (p.244). The primacy of the middle-class, masculine subject that Carpenter retained in his critique of Victorian masculinity persists in *Towards Democracy*. In this respect the transcendent 'I' reproduces some of the forms of the original constellation of middle-class masculinity in its relations of class, gender and 'race'. In particular, it preserves the hierarchy of conscious subjectivities over more 'natural' beings.

These limitations are most clear in the relationship between the transcendent 'I', and other, still subordinate identities: working-class men, women, and the 'racial' other; those who share in the transcendent region of the utopian 'I', but not yet 'equally *consciously*'. *Towards Democracy* constructs a vision that transforms from the position of power, endowed by his further sight. This is perhaps most clear in relation to gender relations, where the 'New Woman' of the late nineteenth century is recognised as part of the potential of Democracy, but the way she is incorporated into Carpenter's naturalism does little to challenge the conventional association of women with nature:

> I see the noble and natural women of all the Earth; I see their well-formed feet and fearless ample stride, their supple strong frames, and attitudes well-braced and beautiful;
> On those that are with them long Love and Wisdom descend; everything that is near them seems to be in its place; they do not pass by little things nor are afraid of big things; but they love the open air and the sight of the sky in the early morning.
> Blessed of such women are the children: and blessed are they in childbirth. The open air and the sun and the moon and the running streams they love all the more passionately for the sake of that which lies sleeping in them. (p. 81)

The New Woman is represented as closer to nature because of her biological function as mother. The new constellation that is achieved here certainly privileges nature over culture, but a nature that already functions to privilege a masculine perspective. To point this out is not to criticise Carpenter for gratuitous biologism - many of the New Women themselves made similar appeals to nature to define an independent femininity - but to recognise how the limits of his utopianism affect the character of the cultural transformation in which he is both agent and participant. In this respect, the shape of the new utopian constellation does little to change the fact that the masculine subject is privileged, even if Carpenter's Uranian identity is clearly different from conventional Victorian masculinity.

The danger of universalising is perhaps most obvious in the treatment of the colonial or 'racial' other:

> I dream the dream: I dream the dream of the soul's slow dis-entanglement.
>
> Where you bend ankle-deep in mud all day in the rice plantations for a few half-pence; and the sun sails on - slow, slow - over the steamy land [...]
> Where you recline by your camp-fire in the African wild, watching the moonlight dances of the natives - the fantastic leaps of the dancer, the rhythmical hand-clapping of the spectators;
> Where you drop down the river in the sun, past the dreaded mud-banks and wildernesses of mangroves;
> I dream the dream. (p.75)

Here, Carpenter's use of the colonial other to break out of the straitjacket of the sexual relations of the bourgeois family has a contradictory effect. On the one hand, the exotic other signified through class and 'racial' definitions does provide a world of utopian possibility and freedom. On the other, there is the danger that the discourses are used simply to reinforce those definitions. In the above passage, the subjects of the dream appear to move ambivalently between 'native' and European spectator. Again the sense of a shifting constellation of subject positions operates a dialectic between possibility and the frame of 'the dream', which fixes the constellation as part of the imagination of the eurocentric dreamer.

Perhaps surprisingly, Carpenter's orientalist dreams offer a comparison with Joseph Conrad's imperialist romances. The early modernist's impressionism often created a similar dreamscape, and, as I have argued elsewhere, Conrad's modernism can be read as a direct response to the emergent identities of the *fin de siècle*.[24] His heroes retreat into subjectivity much as Henry Ryecroft retreats from the confusing world of the late nineteenth-century city; but where Ryecroft's escape was a kind of defeat, Conrad was able to rewrite masculine subjectivity as a new kind of aesthetic strategy.

Three paradigmatic definitions of the term 'inwardness' used, by men, in that watershed year of the *fin de siècle*, 1895, demonstrate how Conrad's modernism emerged in reaction to the cultural politics of that decade. In June 1895, the critic Hugh Stutfield used the term 'inwardness'[25] in a pejorative sense in an article in *Blackwoods Magazine* entitled 'Tommyrotics'. The article was an attack on George Egerton's two collections of 'New Woman' short stories, *Keynotes* and *Discords*, which shocked the public in the decadent 90s before the Wilde Trial. Stutfield, reflecting back on the trial as part of his condemnation of decadence remarked that it 'must surely have opened the eyes even of those who have hitherto been blind to the true inwardness of modern aesthetic Hellenism.'[26] Edward Carpenter used the term 'inwardness' with a different inflection in November of the same year. Writing to Havelock Ellis, who was writing a book on what he called 'sexual inversion', Carpenter used the word positively to describe his own homosexuality against Ellis's medical definitions. He wrote: 'I doubt whether you can *quite* appreciate the true inwardness of this kind of love'.[27] At the beginning of the same month, Conrad had also used the term in a positive light about his approach to writing. In a letter to Edward Noble, he wrote:

> When I speak about writing from an inward point of view - I mean from the depth of my own inwardness. Lay bare your own heart, and people will listen to you for that, - and only that is interesting.
> Everyone must walk in the light of his own heart's gospel. No man's light is good to any of his fellows. That's my creed from beginning to end. That's my view of of life, - a view that rejects all formulas, dogmas and principles of other people's making. These are only a web of illusions. We are too varied. Another man's truth is only a dismal lie to me.[28]

At a time when Stutfield is repelled by writing subjectively, and by Wilde's living example of subjective desire, Conrad applauded it. In 1895, Conrad had just started his writing career; *Almayer's Folly* was published in the first half of that year. He was certainly not sympathetic to women's fiction.[29] However, the concept of inwardness allowed him to write a new masculine subjectivity. Conrad's late novel *Victory* might be understood as the end point in the process, which began in the 1890s. In *Victory*, Axel Heyst attempts a life which is, or ought to be, a 'masterpiece of aloofness', a retreat in order to reconquer the world with a Schopenhaurian belief in the supremacy of consciousness and a pessimistic denial of the will to live. Heyst's attempt is not successful. He fails to reconcile himself to his island retreat in the South Seas and he fails to detach himself from social ties or give up desire. Instead, his repressed attachments return, at first in the form of a woman, and then as three 'desperadoes' who invade the island, breaking down the layers of his isolation. Nonetheless, Heyst's failure does not prevent Conrad from rewriting masculine subjectivity as an aesthetic ideal, a victory, where to Gissing it had appeared as a defeat. The following passage gives a taste of the novel's aestheticism:

> The islands are very quiet. One sees them lying about, clothed in their dark garments of leaves, in a great hush of silver and azure, where the sea without murmurs meets the sky in a ring of magic stillness. A sort of smiling somnolence broods over them; the very voices of their people are soft and subdued, as if afraid to break some protecting spell.
>
> Perhaps, this was the very spell which had enchanted Heyst in the early days. For him, however, that was broken. He was no longer enchanted, though he was still a captive of the islands.[30]

The silence is significant. It provides the opportunity for a new subjective masculine voice to become dominant. In one way this might be taken as yet another reason to reflect on the failure of Carpenter's project. Conrad's work operates to silence the voices with which Carpenter wishes to engage. However, Conrad's selective use of a subjective masculinism should not be allowed to detract from the genuine transformation of masculine identity Carpenter's utopianism achieves. It is possible to read Carpenter's utopian, transcendent 'I' as a real attempt to go beyond the limits of the time. His critique of Victorian masculinity and his vision of what might replace it has a vital place in our understanding of the work of better known writers like Gissing, Morris, Wilde and Conrad. His work is a vital key to the constellation of *fin de siècle* masculinities. It is important because he pioneered an early attempt to show how identity is made up of a combination of different elements. Despite its shortcomings, his counter-enlightenment project is part of a tradition that remains central to the critique of modern masculinities.

[1] George Orwell, *The Road to Wigan Pier* (Harmondsworth: Penguin, 1962), p.152.

[2] E. P. Thompson, *Witness Against the Beast: William Blake and the moral law* (Cambridge: Cambridge University Press, 1993); Theodor Adorno and Max Horkheimer *The Dialectic of the Enlightenment* (London: Verso, 1979).

[3] E. P. Thompson, p.86.

[4] Edward Carpenter, *Civilization Its Cause and Its Cure* (London: Swan Sonnenschein, 1889), pp.26, 28.

[5] Edward Carpenter, *Civilization*, p.133.

[6] Gillian Beer, *Darwin's Plots* (London: Routledge, 1983).

[7] John Addington Symonds, *The Letters of John Addington Symonds*, Vol.III, ed. by Herbert M. Schüller and Robert L. Peters (Detroit: Wayne State University Press, 1967-69), p.787.

[8] Rita Felski, *The Gender of Modernity* (Cambridge, Mass: Harvard University Press, 1995), p.4.

[9] Edward Carpenter 'Love's Coming of Age' in *Selected Writings, Volume 1: Sex* (London: Gay Men's Press, 1984), p.174.

[10] Carpenter, 'Love's Coming of Age', p.110.

[11] Eve Kosofsky Sedgwick, *Between Men* (Baltimore: John Hopkins University Press, 1985).

[12] Sedgwick discusses Carpenter in her final chapter on 'English Readers of Whitman' in *Between Men*.

[13] Carpenter, 'Love's Coming of Age', p.112.

[14] George Gissing, *The Odd Women* (London: Virago, 1980), p.87.

[15] George Gissing, *The Private Papers of Henry Ryecroft* (Oxford: Oxford University Press, 1987), p.153 (hereafter page numbers in text).

[16] Edward Carpenter, *Towards Democracy* (London: Gay Men's Press, 1985), p.133 (hereafter page numbers in text).

[17] Carpenter 'Love's Coming of Age', p.176.

[18]Walter Benjamin, 'Theses on the Philosophy of History', in *Illuminations*, trans. by Harry Zohn (London: Jonathan Cape, 1970 [1955]), p.260.
[19]William Morris, 'News from Nowhere', in *Three Works by William Morris* (London: Lawrence and Wishart), pp.227-228 (hereafter page numbers in text).
[20]In Bloch's *The Principle of Hope*, the concepts of the 'Not-Yet-Conscious' and the 'Not-Yet-Become' seek to tease out future potential from the present conditions of possibility (Oxford: Basil Blackwell, 1986 [1959]), pp.8-9.
[21]Oscar Wilde, 'The Soul of Man Under Socialism', in *De Profundis and Other Writings* (Harmondsworth: Penguin, 1987), p.34.
[22]Edward Carpenter 'A Note on "Towards Democracy"', in *Towards Democracy* (London: Gay Men's Press, 1985), p.410.
[23]*'Vielmehr rüttelt Utopia an den Ketten der Identität: sie wittert in ihr das Unrecht, gerade dieser zu sein und nur dieser'*, from Theodor Adorno, 'Spuren', in *Gesammelte Schriften* 11 (Frankfurt am Main: Suhrkamp Verlag, 1974), p.238. See *Notes to Literature*, trans. by Shierry Weber Nicholson (New York: Columbia University Press, 1992 [1961]), p.205. But Nicholsen translates *'Ketten'* as cage.
[24]Scott McCracken, 'A Hard and Absolute Condition of Existence: Reading Masculinity in *Lord Jim*', in *The Conradian*, 17: 2 (Spring 1993), pp.17-38; Scott McCracken, 'Postmodernism a *Chance* to Reread?', in *Cultural Politics at the Fin de Siècle*, ed. by Sally Ledger and Scott McCracken (Cambridge: Cambridge University Press, 1995), pp.267-89.
[25]The *OED* definitions of 'inwardness' include: '2. The inward or intrinsic quality of a thing; the inner nature, essence or meaning [...] 5a. Depth or intensity of feeling or thought; subjectivity' (2nd ed.).
[26]Hugh Stutfield, 'Tommyrotics', *Blackwoods Magazine* 157 (June 1895), p.835.
[27]Carpenter to Ellis, 28 November 1895, quoted in Grosskurth, *Havelock Ellis* (London: Allen Lane, 1980), p.183.
[28]Conrad to Noble, 2 November 1895, in *Joseph Conrad: Selected Literary Criticism and The Shadow Line* (London: Methuen, 1986), pp.30-31.
[29]Which is not to say that he was not influenced by women writers. Susan Jones argues that 'between 1890-95 one of the most significant relationships of his early literary life had been with a [...] woman', Marguerite Poradowska, and

that Conrad appropriated her romantic representations of women. See Susan
Jones, 'Representing Women: Conrad, Marguerite Poradowska, and *Chance*',
in *Conrad and Gender*, ed. by Andrew Michael Roberts (Amsterdam: Rodopi
Press, 1993).
[30]Joseph Conrad, *Victory* (Harmondsworth: Penguin, 1963), p.68.

6

'COMING ON STRONG': THE ABJECTION OF
PORNOGRAPHY

In 1980, Julia Kristeva published *Pouvoirs de l'horreur*, in which she articulated her theory of abjection. Just a year earlier, Andrea Dworkin published *Pornography: Men Possessing Women.* Both these books received great praise (as well as great condemnation), and both have achieved a privileged status among academics. Very crudely, Kristeva proposed that our bodily excretions - tears, faeces, sperm - are a permanent threat to our psychic health. Equally as crudely, Dworkin proposed that pornography enslaves women within masculinist ideologies which use the penis as a weapon, and sperm as part of its artillery. Although not directly related to issues of pornography, Kristeva's notion of abjection has profound implications for an analysis such as Dworkin's.

Analysing the relationship between pornography and attitudes to women has long been a main-stay of feminist thought.[1] Indeed, there have been few arguments more bitter between feminists than those revolving around the influence that porn has on men and their resulting behaviour towards women. It is always easier to prove one's point by going to extremes, but two examples of feminist argument surrounding pornography should illustrate the depth of feeling aroused by the subject. The first is from Dworkin's book:

> A saber penetrating a vagina is a weapon; so is the camera or pen that renders it; so is the penis for which it substitutes (vagina literally means 'sheath'). The persons who produce the image are also weapons as men deployed in war become in their persons weapons.[2]

The second is a response to this by lesbian sado-masochist Pat Califia:

> Never mind that the term 'pornography' was coined by Victorians, not by the ancient Greeks [...] Never mind that the anti-porn movement has done at least as much damage as 'the male system' to make 'whores' seem vile in the popular imagination. This book is available to anyone, male or female, who can pay for it or steal it. It will certainly seem vile to many people. Therefore this book is a whore.[3]

Between the anti-porn evangelist and the macho slut, there are many shades of feeling, styles of rhetoric, exhortations and counter-exhortations. Compare this to the amount of time spent by men's studies on the issue of pornography and the difference is striking. Admittedly, men's studies is comparatively new, has had to define its methodological limits, propose areas of study hitherto under-represented by female gender studies, and so on. But, even so, the lack of writing on pornography is noticeable, not least because so much of the anti-porn feminist assault has been predicated on the notion articulated by MacKinnon that:

> the sexualized subordination of women to men *is* the sex-gender system. In a dual motion, gender becomes sexual as sexuality is gendered, and pornography is central to the process through which this occurs.[4]

The extent to which pornography is central to this 'dual motion' will form a substantial part of the present chapter. Linked to this theme will be the importance of Kristeva's notion of abjection, and its relevance to the complex and contradictory position of pornography in relation to masculinity.

For Julia Kristeva, abjection is primarily a mode of disgust, a bewildering and terrible threat that is inescapable because it is bound up in our own bodies. It is the pre-condition of subjectivity but also a permanent and inescapable threat to that subjectivity. During the pre-Oedipal phase (0-6 months) the child begins a process of self-recognition which is the dawn of abjection. The recognition is more of a negative understanding of its own objectal limits rather than any form of autonomous assertion. Through the flow of bodily excretions - tears, urine, faeces, mucus etc. - the solid border of the body becomes recognised as being indeterminate and mutable. The expelled 'objects', though, do not form a clear and easily limited boundary between inside and outside (subject as defined corporeally and object as defined as anything extra-corporeal), but are a sort of indistinct hinge, located at rims. These rims are the folds of skin, crevices and holes from where the objects are expelled - eyes, nose, mouth, anus, genitals. A rim is the space which ruptures the continuity of a body, but which also guarantees the body's wholeness (the anus or nostril, for example), and the traversal of this space through expulsion or intrusion creates erotic objects. Because these objects are perceived as exterior to the subject (in other words, objects for the subject) but nevertheless created from within the subject, they come to be seen as 'detachable'.

These rims assume a significance for the subject and are inextricably bound up in the three categories of abjection which Kristeva identifies: food, waste, and the signs of sexual difference. The three categories of abjection transgress in ways specific to the particular subject or culture what the subject or culture considers to be the *corps propre*, or 'one's own clean and proper body'.[5] This relates physically to such apparently mundane examples as the skin of milk which, through morphological resemblance ignites the nervous system, sparking spasms of disgust in the stomach, gagging. The skin of the milk is a border, a film, which covers over and contains the liquid beneath; to touch it, to take it into one's mouth is to drink oneself as metaphor and to recognise oneself as decay. Abjection also swaggers to the very borders of life:

> A wound with blood and pus, or the sickly acrid smell of sweat, of decay, does not signify death. In the presence of signified death - a flat encepholograph, for instance - I would understand, react, or accept. No, as in true theater, without makeup or masks, refuse and corpses show me what I permanently thrust aside in order to live.[6]

Bodily fluids, the 'refuse' of our 'selves', mark us as subjects while highlighting our fragility. Our tears express us in pain or joy at the same time as washing us away. Our faeces extract from us that which we had assumed was our nourishment. Our mucus dribbles out of us, imploring us to breathe while clogging us up. Sperm promises a life other than our own while draining men of their vitality; it augments masculinity while proclaiming males' eventual death and succession, making them abject.

Socially, as well, as part of society's 'clean and proper body' the abject - that which 'does not respect borders, positions, rules' - causes reactions of disgust, rejection and bewilderment.[7] This is particularly the case when a person appears to betray a tacit social contract which binds them to a specific identity. Kristeva provides a list of social abjects:

The traitor, the liar, the criminal with a good conscience,
the shameless rapist, the killer who claims he is a saviour
[...][8]

And perhaps one could add the pornographer who claims he is a
moralist.

An important consideration before progressing any further is
how pornography is to be defined in this essay. For Andrea
Dworkin, pornography is as pornography does and is a non-
contradictory 'genre'.[9] It is a genre which, furthermore, according
to Dworkin's partner John Stoltenberg 'tells lies about women. But
[...] tells the truth about men'.[10] Scott Tucker, in response to
Stoltenberg's book, presents the reader with two images. Both are
descriptions of porno calendars. One,

is open to April: a close-up photo of a leather-vested,
bare-breasted woman whose hand is gloved in another
woman's ass, her cunt also visible with two rings through
the labia.[11]

The other,

a photo of myself in boots, harness, and a leather jock
taken in 1986, the year I won the International Mr.
Leather contest. No genitals in view, no fucking, but my
ass is bare and the props and regalia are redolent with
perversion.[12]

Quite where Stoltenberg's truth and falsehood are to be found in
these images is a mystery. Pornography is heterogeneous, with
genres within genres, variations in quality, market, distribution and

production. And none of it can be reduced to a single, easily definable target group, as Pat Califia points out:

> Many people do not fantasize about the kind of sex they actually have. Fantasy is a realm in which we can embrace pleasures that we may have very good reasons to deny ourselves in real life...[13]

What, then, is the relationship between a certain male-centred pornography and masculinity? Initially, it is essential that attention be drawn to the terms 'male' and 'masculine'. Sex and gender are distinct categories, contrary to MacKinnon's insistence on 'the sex-gender system' quoted above. To differentiate so severely between the categories requires the acceptance of a strong cultural influence on constructions of identity, where the latter is understood as a tentative and mutable composite of a multiplicity of subject positions at any one time. Sex is one of the subject positions, sexuality is another, gender is another, to mention nothing about class, ethnicity, physical ability or occupation. As each one of these subject positions is alterable at any time (or at least open to alteration) identity can never be securely fixed.

If the choice of subject positions is limited by the casual elision of two distinct categories, for example sex and gender, then the individual's potential to mediate their own contradictions is severely limited. Without this mediative safeguard, contradictions *between* subject positions can appear as contradictions *within* a single subject position, leading to a sense of social disorientation and psychic collapse. The sex and gender distinction, while providing a sophisticated theory of identity, has the difficulty of trying to engage with biology. A theory of gender which refuses the biological runs the risk of simplification and willed ignorance. The implications of a biological determination in behaviour could be worrying and allow for conservative justifications of genuinely socially-constructed symbolic categories. However, to recognise biology as part of behaviour - the importance of testosterone and its relationship with aggressivity, for example - is a far cry from implying that 'humans are captives of their physiology' [14]

To keep sex and gender as distinct analytic categories is a vital part of gender research. This need not, however, negate the relationship between certain sex-features (primary and secondary sexual characteristics, hormone levels) and the mutation of these into gender-features. Sex, then, can be seen as one of the signs of gender, distinct from but implicated in the construction of masculinity:

> Masculinity as signs contributes as much to the reality of gender differences as do the physical differences that have led traditional researchers to ascribe 'masculinity' to men and 'femininity' to women. [15]

Diana Saco's essay 'Masculinity as Signs' rigorously explores the notion of a masculinity as defined through the interplay of competing sign systems, and studies the effect of cinematic representations of (and on) masculinity. The term 'representation' is one of the most important in the whole debate about masculinity and pornography. Teresa de Lauretis, talking generally about the construction of gender identity, asserts that, 'The construction of gender is both the product and the process of its representation', with this representation 'convey[ing] the idea that gender is constructed through the media (presented) as if it were direct knowledge of real objects (as if it were representation)'. [16]

Versions of masculinity, therefore, are created through pornography which itself implies a masculinity which precedes the image. To suggest that the inescapable terror of male supremacy *is* the pornographic function, as Dworkin and MacKinnon do, is problematized by the more sophisticated theoretical framework offered by Saco. This framework does not allow for the easy repudiation of images; nor does it assume an unambiguous correlation between image and viewer, insisting as Saco does on concentrating on issues of address, decoding and intersubjective mediations.

Saco's interrogation of these concepts can be used in verbal as well as visual media. Arguing against Laura Mulvey's seminal article 'Visual Pleasure and Narrative Cinema', Saco proposes the possibility of 'multiple forms of address and the concomitant multiple subject positions into which spectators can be hailed', as opposed to the determined masculine subject position of Mulvey.[17] By emphasising the interpellative process of address, Mulvey ignores, according to Saco, 'the possibility for interventions by the spectator', a possibility which is essential for Mulvey's reading to have been an option in the first place.[18]

The reader/viewer, occupying one of the possible subject positions open to her/him, is now able to code their particular reading, adopting codes which adhere to conventional types or which act oppositionally. The degree to which the particular coded readings are individual choices requires, again, the understanding that gender construction is both the process and the product of its representation. And part of the process is necessarily the reception which demands a receptor who is already marked as occupying a variety of subject positions in the construction of his/her identity. These multiple subject positions, or 'intersubjectivities', carry with them beliefs, desires and *investments* which precede the reception of an image and prejudice that reception while still being open to that image's influence. Saco explains it thus:

> Investment in a particular discourse implies also
> investment in a particular way of reading and
> understanding the things we experience. Consequently,
> our investments may militate against our being
> subjectified by a dominant mode of textual address, but
> they also limit the number of ways in which we can read
> a text.[19]

In response to the notion that pornography is reducible to the sex-
gender system, a system which implies a non-contradictory
alignment of gender and sexuality within a single subject position,
Saco takes issue with MacKinnon's notion of gendermarked
sexuality. Lesbian sado-masochism, while apparently replaying
masculine sexual practices through acts of dominance and
submission

> constitute[s] a significantly different social identity with
> demonstrably little investment in dominant discourses of
> gender and (hetero)sexuality.[20]

Lesbian pornography (a term which is itself fraught with
contradiction and debate) - if one accommodates issues of address,
decoding and intersubjective mediation - is a distinct discursive
formulation from that which is male-centred, penetrative, straight
pornography.[21]

A dominant feature of the type of pornography which I am
discussing and which I have rather cumbersomely called 'male-
centred, penetrative, straight' is its emphasis on ejaculation, and
could therefore better be called 'ejaculocentric'.[22] A couple of
quotations should serve to illustrate the point:

> He lay discharging until a flood of thick sperm deluged
> my interior [...] I raised myself on my cushions. I dipped
> my handkerchief into the cool sea-water and sopped up
> all I could of the tremendous overflow I had received.[23]

> Sabine watches the ejaculation with curiosity, her fingers
> holding his penis as the milky fluid gushes out.[24]

> While I felt his gland throb in my entrails and inundate
> me with his voluptuous liquid...[25]

The language here (and a host of other quotations would have
served equally as well) is one of plenitude, abundance and vigour.
The men in these quotations are not marked as particularly
exceptional in the texts, yet their ejaculations are practically mythic.
A sex-sign (sperm) has become gendered (like facial hair) and,
again like facial hair, or penis size, it is an exaggeration of the sex-
sign which marks its genderedness.

For Dworkin these images of male penetration/ejaculation are
uncomplicatedly of the type where women are presented as
permanently sexually available, as 'Whores [who] exist to serve
men sexually'.[26] The fact that it is women who are ostensibly the
subjects of the books does little to deny the fact that the mode of
address is predominantly masculine. This, it can be argued,
facilitates for the male viewer/reader a process of identification with
the male characters in the text. The male reader is therefore
addressed as an adjunct of the text, someone who is not identical
with the man in the book, but who could be so. The male reader
becomes a part of phallic power and domination, actively
contributing - through his pornographic relationship with women -
to a social relationship of subjugation. However, address is mutable
as Saco has demonstrated, so that subversive decodings predicated

on intersubjective mediation disavow the monologic imperative that Dworkin claims. It is indeed possible that this style of pornography allows masculine identification, but it is as likely that:

> The text constantly reminds the reader of his own troubling self, his own reality - and the limitation of that reality since, however much he wants to fuck the willing women or men in his story, he cannot do so but must be content with some form of substitute activity.[27]

Pornography's pre-condition (from a particular feminist analysis) is that of a hierarchized social-sexual order where masculine dominates feminine, and this pre-condition is central to the representations offered for consumption. These representations, though, also serve as presentations - constructions - which may be viewed/read as

> affectively and effectively addressing the boundaries and limitations of the male body and extending and complicating the peremptory simplicity of male sexual experience.[28]

In other words, watching or reading male exploits which inevitably end in floods of cum is, or can be, an abject experience.

As a social phenomenon pornography does not respect borders, positions or rules. In displaying images of male supremacy, it can be seen as being commensurate with prevailing ideologies, as Dworkin powerfully asserts:

> In pornography, his sense of purpose is fully realized.
> She is the pinup, the centrefold. The poster, the postcard,

> the dirty picture, naked, half-dressed, laid out, legs
> spread, breast or ass protruding. She is the thing she is
> supposed to be: the thing that makes him erect. In literary
> and cinematic pornography, she is taught to be that
> thing...[29]

Again, however, one must take into account notions of address,
decoding and intersubjective mediation, and also posit those aspects
of pornography which challenge those aspects of a patriarchal
society that a monolithic masculinist reading of pornography would
have to deny. The representation of guiltless, non-marital, non-
monogomous sexual activity (which is effectively the staple diet of
most of the novels of the sort being discussed in this essay)
transgresses codes and conventions which attempt to fix a social
body that is clean and proper. If masculinist ideologies are the pre-
condition of the type of pornorahy being discussed here, and if
masculinist ideologies are also the pre-condition of patriarchy (Law
of the Father/Symbolic Order) then pornography is its abjection, it
is

> the underside of the symbolic. It is what the symbolic
> must reject, cover over and contain. The symbolic
> requires that a border separate or protect the subject from
> the abyss which beckons and haunts it: the abject entices
> and attracts the subject ever closer to its edge.[30]

Pornography is the 'object' expelled by a society. It marks
sexual difference/hierarchy while threatening that very hierarchy
through excess, transgression and explicitness. The viewer/reader is
thus rejuvenated, subjectively reinforced as, in the very act of
transgression, the boundaries being traversed are reaffirmed.

Simultaneously, however, he is threatened as the borders of the social body, its very constructedness, are represented, and he recognises himself as complicit with the transgression: he is both inside and outside of society's clean and proper body; abjected. This also has consequences for the assumption of subject positions as he occupies both the pre-existing social formulations for the socialised and the asocial, creating intersubjective tension and contradiction.

Not only is the very act of pornography a state of abjection, but within this the male viewer/reader is presented with further reminders of his own borders, his own decay, his own death. For all the power, vigour and 'manliness' that the characters in porn display, they cannot escape the fact that the symbol of their masculinity (their sperm) is also the threat to their subjectivity, is an 'overflowing' of their corporeality.[31] In a very literal way, sperm

> signals the precarious grasp the subject has over its own identity and bodily boundaries, the possibility of sliding back into the chaos out of which it emerged.[32]

This fear of return to chaos (to the semiotic, or non-symbolic state of pre-Oedipality, pre-ego - maternal engulfment) identifies the abject as 'a rare avowal of the death drive'. The now commonplace association between sex and death can, therefore, be seen as yet a further complication in the pornographic representation of masculinity. The exaggerated amount of sperm in pornography heightens notions of sexual difference, and opens the way for a gendered sex-sign. This sperm, however, is a category of abjection (both as expulsion and as a form of sexual difference), and thus threatens the precarious identity of the male at the same time as rejuvenating his masculinity.

This would appear to present us with a contradiction. If the representation of masculinity in pornography, particularly with reference to sperm, is so soaked in abjection and death drives, then why is it so popular? Kristeva asserts the socially and individually specific nature of abjection, while still insisting on its general articulation as a valid thesis. It could, therefore, simply be the case that men who read pornography just find abjection elsewhere and are undaunted by semen. It could also be the case that despite pornography's transgressing of the clean and proper social body, that body can withstand this transgression because porn does supplement the sex-gender system with enough vigour to counteract its negative abject implications.

It is entirely probable that pornography's popularity is due to a perceived lack in male sexual fulfilment, that it is 'some form of substitute activity' which, while being temporarily enjoyable, does cause the male to address 'the boundaries and limitations of the male body', therefore contemplating the abject. Abjection, in its general sense, does not require a totalized theory of the psyche. In its specific demonstrations - the skin of the milk, the wound, the corpse, menstrual blood, sperm - it can be read as the abjection of a specific subjectivity. In reading pornography, then, the reader is able to choose his position of address and code of reading, and assume these choices through a sophisticated mediation of his intersubjectivities, attempting to produce an identity with as much to invest and as little to lose as possible. In this way his masculinity is perhaps briefly bolstered, as Dworkin would assert, as he occupies a prescribed, pro-patriarchal subject position. The intersubjective mediations are necessarily prey to their specific abjections, however, and the potential for images of his own mortality (the abject being a rare avowal of the death-drive) cannot be kept at bay. Because of this, he should not be surprised if the moment of ultra-masculinity is also the moment when his self-hood dribbles abjectly onto the sheets.

[1]See Lynne Segal, *Slow Motion: Changing Masculinities, Changing Men* (London: Virago, 1990), p.222.
[2]Andrea Dworkin, *Pornography: Men Possessing Women* (Reading: The Woman's Press, 1981), p.25.
[3]Pat Califia, *Macho Sluts* (Boston: Alyson Publications, 1988), p.18.
[4]Catherine MacKinnon, 'A feminist/political approach: "pleasures under patriarchy"', in *Theories of Human Sexuality*, ed. by James H. Geer and William T. O'Donohue (New York: Plenum, 1987), p. 81.
[5]This is the phrase used throughout Leon Roudiez's translation of Julia Kristeva's *Powers of Horror: An Essay on Abjection* (New York: Columbia University Press, 1982).
[6]Kristeva, p.3.
[7]Kristeva, p.4.
[8]Kristeva, p.4.
[9]Dworkin, p.25.
[10]John Stoltenberg, *Refusing to be a Man: Essays on Sex and Justice*, quoted in Scott Tucker, 'Gender, Fucking and Utopia: An essay in response to John Stoltenberg's *Refusing to be a Man*', *Social Text 27* (1990), p.3.
[11]Tucker, p.3.
[12]Tucker, p.5.
[13]Califia, p.16.
[14]Perry Treadwell 'Biologic Influences on Masculinity', in *The Making of Masculinities: The New Men's Studies*, ed. by Harry Brod (Boston: Allen and Unwin, 1987), p.284.
[15]Diana Saco, 'Masculinity as Signs: Poststructuralist Feminist Approaches to the Study of Gender', in *Men, Masculinity and the Media*, ed. by Stephen Craig (London: SAGE Publications, 1992), p.23.
[16]Teresa de Lauretis, 'The Technology of Gender', qu. by Saco, p.26; Saco, p.25.
[17]Saco, p.29.
[18]Saco, p.30.
[19]Saco, p.35.
[20]Saco, p.37.

[21]See, for example, Pat Califia's desire for more lesbian pornography that allows representations of straight female and male, and gay male sexuality in *Macho Sluts* (p.16). This, inevitably, raises questions about the nature of what 'lesbian' pornography consists in: is it pornography that depicts lesbian activity but which could easily be written by a straight man; is it pornography written by a lesbian but which, like Califia's work, features straight or gay male sex? The same questions, of course, can be asked of 'straight' pornography.

[22]I would like to thank Mark Robson of the University of Leeds for providing me with this term.

[23]Anonymous, *Eveline* (London: Headline, 1991), p.147.

[24]Anonymous, *Sabine* (Reading: Nexus, 1989), p.120.

[25]E. K., *Regine* (London: Star, 1987), p.148.

[26]Dworkin, p.200.

[27]Angela Carter, *The Sadeian Woman* (London: Virago, 1979), p.14.

[28]Saco, p.38.

[29]Dworkin, p.128.

[30]Kristeva's notion of the 'maternal' is not biologically bound and cannot be attributed to 'woman', as 'woman' does not exist as a discrete ontological category for her. See Elizabeth Gross, 'Language and the limits of the body: Kristeva and abjection', in *Futur*Fall: Excursions into Post-Modernity*, ed. by Gross et al. (University of Sydney, 1986), p.111.

[31]*Eveline*, p.147.

[32]Elizabeth Gross, 'The Body of Signification', in *Abjection, Melancholia and Love: The Work of Julia Kristeva*, ed. by John Fletcher and Andrew Benjamin (London: Routledge, 1990), p.101.

7

SEX, DRUGS AND THE ECONOMICS OF MASCULINITY IN WILLIAM GOLDING'S *RITES OF PASSAGE*

William Golding's *To the Ends of the Earth: A Sea Trilogy* is set in the early nineteenth century, aboard a battered old warship making her way from Britain to Australia. It is narrated by men; the ship is a male-dominated environment. An investigation of the text's constructions of masculinity is crucial to any reading. In the first part of the discussion, I wish to focus on the two narrators of the first volume, *Rites of Passage*, with reference to their experience of sexuality, the taking of drugs (opium and alcohol), the act of writing, and the complex economy of desires and restraints which, I shall argue, constitutes them as masculine subjects. In the second part of the chapter, I shall concentrate on the account of *Rites of Passage* given by Valentine Cunningham in his book *In the Reading Gaol: Postmodernity, Texts and History*. His analysis of the novel overlooks the vital economy or trade between repression and desire in the construction of the masculine subject, and between author and reader in the construction of meaning. I will argue that authorial indeterminacy can become a source of pleasure for the reader, and need not be ignored or suppressed. This indeterminacy radically compromises the control over the text which Cunningham associates with Golding's anti-postmodernist, defiant patriarchal authority. Thirdly, I will address the fundamental conflict between the positions taken by Cunningham and Jacques Derrida on the issue of the deconstruction *of* deconstruction. Cunningham claims that in *Rites of Passage* 'Golding has taken a spectacular leaf out [of] Derrida's books. This is the deconstructionist practice turned against deconstructionists'.[1] This has important implications for our construction of the masculine author. I shall argue that 'Golding' is harder to find in the text than Cunningham imagines. Instead of controlling the text, the implied author is feminized, in the sense of being rendered passive, by the indeterminacy and intertextuality which compromise his authority.

The main narrator of *Rites of Passage* is Edmund Talbot, an ambitious young man who hopes to begin a profitable career as a civil servant in the Antipodes. He has one heterosexual encounter on board, and he hears of several others, both heterosexual and homosexual. He is relatively rich and extremely well-connected; this gives him a privileged status on the ship, but also makes him the target of those who seek his money. Throughout the trilogy, he regularly consumes alcohol and occasionally takes opium. During the first part of the voyage, he writes a journal, nominally addressed to his powerful godfather, who is also his patron. The other narrator is Robert James Colley, a parson. Like Talbot, he has one sexual encounter during *Rites of Passage*; he drinks alcohol for the first time and fellates one of the sailors, Billy Rogers. Soon afterwards, he goes to his cabin to lie alone and die.

The central point at which writing, drugs and sexuality meet in *Rites of Passage* is Colley's fellatio. Colley is using a drug he has never taken before, and this gives him the courage, or the recklessness, to express the sexual interest in Rogers which he never admits in his writing; his letter to his sister, found and read by Talbot, refers to Rogers as a prime example of manliness, a sailor hero, rather than as an object of amorous desire. It is left to Talbot to attempt to guess what happened, and to write his speculations in his journal. He concludes that Colley died of shame. It seems that after drunkenly fellating the sailor, Colley knew that he could no longer sublimate his sexual desires into religious feelings about 'that bond between two persons which, Holy Writ directs us, passes the love of women'.[2] If Talbot is right, then Colley dies because a process of exchange can no longer take place; the balance of forces within him, which checked *eros* by sublimating it into spiritual love, no longer holds. Colley's subjectivity is the site of an economy of conflicting impulses, in which his desire for Rogers eventually triumphs when he makes the fatal decision to visit the forecastle (possibly a pun on fuck's'le, or sexual place) where he becomes drunk and fellates the sailor. This economy prevents his manuscript (the never-sent letter to his sister) from becoming either an expression of homosexuality or of spiritual affection; instead, it is both. Colley conceals his sexual love for Rogers beneath and among allusions to his religious love for Christ. Colley is also attracted to a young woman, Zenobia Brocklebank, or so Talbot believes (p.68). The parson is neither a heterosexual nor a homosexual in the twentieth-century sense of a person exclusively attracted to one gender, but is the site of desires and restraints which pull him towards and away from the things he wants.

Although Talbot is apparently less complicated in terms of sexual orientation than Colley, his sexuality is also subject to constraints. He finds himself sexually attracted to Zenobia Brocklebank, but he knows that he cannot be seen to be her lover. He is forced to search for a secret place to have intercourse with her; this search is a difficult and frustrating one. Eventually, he decides upon a location that would normally be too public (his own cabin, whose walls are very thin) but also upon a time that will suit his purpose; that of the on-deck 'entertainment' at the Equator, which will distract the crew and passengers. He is also restricted by the need to keep his own reputation intact; he attempts to withdraw before ejaculation in order to prevent pregnancy. When this attempt fails, he realizes that should Zenobia become pregnant, he might have to marry her off, to avoid rumours about the child's paternity. He even considers Colley as a possible husband for Zenobia, after the parson's flirtatious attention to her earlier on (p.94). He is also aware of the possibility that she is a prostitute, but believes that paying her would be beneath his dignity (p.88). He imagines that she might be seeking an attachment to him in order to use his influence to obtain work for her nominal father, and putative lover, the portrait painter Mr. Brocklebank. Talbot, then, believes in his own masculine sexual and social authority, but also recognizes the economic context out of which it is constructed. His heterosexuality is not, apparently, in doubt, but he cannot simply act upon his desire; instead, he must negotiate the restrictions which society puts upon his sexuality. These restrictions are balanced by permissions and freedoms created by his social status. He may well be able to rape with impunity; he does not take the trouble to confirm that Zenobia is accepting his advances, and claims to his godfather that her struggles were part of 'a nicely calculated exertion of strength that only just failed to resist me' (p.86). Zenobia confesses nothing publicly. Talbot is thus allowed to escape the possible criminal consequences of his act. He is free to seduce, or force himself upon, vulnerable women, but is restricted by the need to keep his escapades private and to silence their repercussions.

The narrators' use of drugs likewise reveals the extent to which their activities and desires are socially restricted. Even before the drunken fellatio, alcohol is linked to Colley's sexual interest in Rogers, when the parson records his admiration for the sailor upon seeing him drink his ration of rum, which he mythologizes as 'flaming ichor' (p.218). Alcohol helps Rogers to appear godlike in Colley's eyes, but it also underlines the social difference between them, and thus the power relations which keep the parson from the object of his desire. The sailor, whose social inferiority is signified by his participation in the rite of the rum ration, is desirable, but is only attainable with disastrous consequences. Ironically, it is Colley's attempt to identify with the crew by sharing their rum which leads to his downfall. Talbot's drug-taking is more extensive and habitual than that of Colley, but can also be seen to compromise his sense of independent control over his circumstances. He initially decides to ration his brandy intake, but finds himself drinking heavily later on (pp.25, 136). His use of opium and brandy makes him dependent upon a socially inferior man: Wheeler, his servant, who sells him the drugs, and who also helps him to bed when he is drunk (p.136). Wheeler, as his name suggests, is the ship's wheeler and dealer; he is the supplier of opium to the passengers, and in the fashion of the stereotypical pusher, he attempts to raise the price, claiming that supplies are running low. Ironically, he uses a 'gentleman' economist as his justification; a male authority figure is cited to support a system of co-dependency in which a working-class man (Wheeler) compromises the independence of his superior (Talbot) by creating a desire for the drug (p.44). Talbot, in this instance, refuses the opium; later in the trilogy, though, he is forced to take it when he goes mad with love, and also takes it for seasickness.[3]

The two narrators' drug habits and sexualities, when examined together, produce a complex picture of masculinity. It is a state which evolves out of a network of social and psychic forces; it cannot be identified with either heterosexuality or homosexuality. It is never autonomous, but emerges from an economy of power relations, in which some men are dominant and other men (and women) dependent, although these roles are fluid. Colley's and Talbot's independence and self-control are compromised by their sexual desires and escapades with drugs; they are not self-determining in their gendered identity, but find that their masculinity is evolved out of a complex system of desires and restraints.

The importance of this economic system is overlooked by Valentine Cunningham in his reading of the novel. He states that opium is 'a drug that is, characteristically of this novel, connected with writing. "I believe there is a gentleman ashore as has wrote a book on it," says Wheeler [...]'.[4] Cunningham fails to realise, or omits to mention, that the 'it' about which the gentleman has written his book is not opium, but the economic law of supply and demand; the gentleman is the economist cited by the servant to justify his increased prices. What Wheeler actually says, according to Talbot, is this:

> [The paregoric] *is* rather strong, sir [...] And of course as he has less left, the purser has to charge more for it. That's quite natural, sir. I believe there is a gentleman ashore as has wrote a book on it.[5] (p.44)

The book is either Adam Smith's *The Wealth of Nations*, published in 1776, or another economic text written from the same *laissez-faire* perspective. In an unregulated market, a scarce item becomes more costly, assuming the same number of people want it as badly as before. Smith himself describes what happens to those who desire a commodity when it becomes scarce:

> Rather than want it altogether, some of them will be willing to give more. A competition will immediately begin among them, and the market price will rise more or less above the natural price, according as either the greatness of the deficiency, or the wealth and wanton luxury of the competitors, happen to animate more or less the eagerness of the competition.[6]

In *Rites of Passage*, pleasure must usually be bought, either for money or at the price of scandal; Colley's death through shame after his drunken fellatio is the most extreme example of this, but Talbot's consideration of the possible consequences of his dalliance with Zenobia, and his dependence on Wheeler's supply of brandy, show that the trade-off is widespread. Pleasure itself becomes a commodity, which is saleable and buyable, being situated amid an economy of competing, desiring masculine subjects, all of whom have differing degrees of eagerness, and deeper or shallower pockets.

Cunningham's reading of the novel, and of Golding's role in the text, does not take this into account. He focuses on the orality of Colley's fellatio:

> [Colley's] particular oral action, his fellatio with Rogers, is what the sailor slangily called 'getting a chew off a parson' [...] The clergyman comes to die of shame essentially because that phrase did not stay just a phrase, a noise in the mouth, but got itself tragically translated into action, in another kind of mouth activity. And in encapsulating all this in a single word, Golding has taken a spectacular leaf out [of] Derrida's books.[7]

Here Cunningham wishes to impose a particular economy upon the text, a system loaded in favour of 'moral, onto-theological' reference where words are less significant than the actions to which they supposedly refer.[8] For him, if 'getting a chew' could remain 'just a phrase', then Colley would not have to die: the action, and not the word, is tragic.[9]

We should look beyond Cunningham's stress on morality, and instead examine the hidden economy of forces which operates not only on the masculine subjects within the text, but on the supposedly authoritative masculine subject lying outside or above it: the implied author. Just as the masculine identity of the narrators evolves economically, so does that of the 'Golding' inferred by the reader. This goes against the position taken by Cunningham, who sees Golding's role in terms of an authority that is, by my reading, patriarchal. He believes that the novel is 'Golding's act of *old man's* defiance' and that it 'comes from *a man* who was no doubt exceedingly fed up over being sniped at for years on end as too traditionalist'.[10]

A reading of a male character or implied author which argues that he is the product of an economy of conflicting restraints and desires implies a very different construction of masculinity from a reading which allows for the direct signification of his desire on the page. Cunningham's interpretation of *Rites of Passage* belongs to the latter type of reading. An important element of it is his connection of *paregoric* (the term for the solution of opium drunk by Talbot) with writing. Cunningham uses this to illustrate Golding's authoritative referential ambition, but also his intense focus on language:

> *paregoric* [...] derives from Greek words for speaking and the public place of speaking, the public assembly of the vocal electorate. *Paregoric* implies, at root, sweet talking, smooth talk. So, in a single word, Golding sums up his textual purposes, encapsulates the overlap he's demonstrating between the inside and the outside reference of words and text: *paregoric*, a word for talk, for words, for what comes out of the mouth; but also a word for the non-verbal, a medicine that comes from the outside, invading the mouth, the domain of words that it will not allow to be occupied only by words.[11]

He believes that this combination of reference and linguistic density is a deliberate attempt by Golding to use 'postmodernist theory' against the postmodernists themselves:

> *Rites of Passage* is evidently the response of a strong old-fashioned moralist fiction-maker to that postmodernist theory which has sought to outlaw realism, parable, fictions about knowable or 'real' persons, novels with moral or theological ambitions, stories keen to make truth-claims about the world and human behaviour - Golding's kind of novel, in other words [...][12]

Cunningham claims that he knows what Golding intends and means; his account implies an authority lying above the text. However, we can, unlike Cunningham, refuse to restrict our reading to an exposition of Golding's alleged intentions. We can instead try to find the 'dissolve' between voices or meanings in instances where the reader cannot determine authorial intent, and where the implied author, as masculine subject, is situated inside a network of forces that both enable and constrain him. The term 'dissolve' comes from Roland Barthes' *The Pleasure of the Text*: 'the seam, the cut, the deflation, the *dissolve* which seizes the subject in the midst of bliss'.[13] Such a dissolution of the authorial subject can be discerned, for example, in the very paragraph which Cunningham uses to support his argument, the instance where Talbot associates opium with writing:

> I have, at a moderate estimate, already written ten thousand words and must limit myself if I am to get our voyage between the luxurious covers of your gift. Can it be that I have evaded the demon opium only to fall victim to the *furor scribendi*? (p.45)

There is certainly, as Cunningham claims, a high degree of lexical trickery here. It is legitimate to suggest that opium is connected to writing; however, the text's play with language does not end here by any means. Talbot claims that he seeks to 'get' the voyage 'between the luxurious covers' of the bound volume presented by his godfather. There is a pun on procreation here, and on the conjugal bed. The white page becomes the blank white sheet on which Talbot will beget the voyage; the book's 'luxurious covers' suggest bed linen. Talbot is ironically portrayed in the paternal role, as the father of the voyage, analogous to a traditional masculine author, possessed of the 'formidable paternity' discussed by Barthes and promoted by Cunningham.[14] However, Talbot's appropriation of this role is compromised. Fertilization will only occur if he limits himself; that is, writes fewer words. It is the *furor scribendi*, the madness of writing, which threatens this self-imposed limitation, and may cause the hoped-for procreation to fail through wasteful excess, thus compromising the intended purpose of Talbot's volume, itself the gift of a patriarchal authority, his godfather. The text does more than simply suggest that writing and opium are analogous; it also implies that they are equally tempting providers of dangerous pleasure. Cunningham's reading overlooks this pleasure; by basing his account of the text on the search for authorial intent, he fails to locate the site of Barthes's 'dissolve'. We cannot determine whether Golding intended the procreative puns, or not; the implied author, as well as Talbot, is subject to dangerous, pleasurable dissolution. The pleasure here also belongs to the reader, who need not necessarily become frustrated by this authorial indeterminacy: on the contrary, he/she can enjoy it, as it intensifies and problematizes his/her search for meaning.

Rites of Passage seems willing to acknowledge such pleasure. It does not suggest that male writing (let alone male sexuality) should be kept within disciplined limits; the tone of the passage is far too playful for that. Talbot puts his worry about the *furor scribendi* in terms of a witty rhetorical question, intended more to amuse his godfather than to suggest a genuine existential threat. Talbot, in fact, has no trouble finding another set of 'covers' beneath which he can continue his attempt to father a narrative. He simply buys another volume from the purser once the first is full. Talbot, unlike Colley, has wealth, and is therefore in a position of relative economic freedom; he can fulfil his desires, and assert his masculinity, more easily as a consequence.

Cunningham shows how the usefulness of Falconer's *Dictionary of the Marine*, an intertext for *Rites of Passage*, 'fades in and out' throughout the novel.[15] Unfortunately, Cunningham does not allow Golding to fade in and out in a similar way, even though the implied author can be shown to be indeterminate. In an economic reading of the text, we can accept that such puns and cruxes as those on 'get' and 'covers' may be either intentional or accidental, and we can therefore claim that the implied author's alleged patriarchal control over the text is compromised by the effects of indeterminacy. If, unlike Cunningham, we read the implied author of *Rites of Passage* as the product of an economy of conflicting forces, then we can see that any desire he may have to control the text, or to express a meaning within it, may well be affected by forces over which he has no control, and which tend to compromise his masculinity by rendering him passive.

One such force is the intertextuality which compromises the text's apparent integrity. A male writer may believe he is transcribing a personal viewpoint into the text, pursuing a desire for meaning in an active, masculine fashion associated with patriarchal authority; but at the same time, he may unconsciously be transcribing a source, and thus revealing his own passivity. In this respect, intertextuality might be seen as a feminizing force, which blurs the authoritarian singularity of male control and gives the implied male author characteristics stereotypically associated with the opposite gender. In his analysis of Plato's *Phaedrus* and the *pharmakon* in *Dissemination*, Jacques Derrida argues that for Socrates writing, unlike speech, can be taken and manipulated or misinterpreted by anyone.[16] Writing is 'a wayward, rebellious son':

> Uprooted, anonymous, unattached to any house or country, this almost insignificant signifier is at everyone's disposal, can be picked up by both the competent and the incompetent, by those who understand and know what to do with it [...] and by those who are completely unconcerned with it, and who, knowing nothing about it, can inflict all manner of impertinence upon it.[17]

Although Derrida concentrates on the relation of father and wayward son implied by Plato, writing could equally, and in this context more usefully, be seen as a wayward daughter, the product of an implied mother. The reader is able to discover intertextual echoes, and thus unearth threats to the author's control, in places where the implied masculine author may well have imagined he was at his most original and independent. When the reader detects intertextuality, the wayward daughter begins to enumerate her possible fathers, and thus to declare her own illegitimacy, placing the implied author in a precisely *maternal* position, as the one parent whose connection with the illegitimate child can be guaranteed, but whose right to a sole claim on that child is negated by its numerous possible paternities, which create a potentially infinite pattern of genetic inheritance. Moreover, not only is writing powerless against the effects of reading, so is the implied subject producing it; the implied author, inferred by the reader from the text, may be configured by the reader at will. Cunningham's own remarks about Golding's anti-postmodernist defiance are examples of one such configuration. This suggests that the implied author can occupy a stereotypically feminine position of passivity and powerlessness, the Other concealed, but nevertheless also implied, by a stereotypically masculine claim to authority.

In practice, however, the implied author will occupy neither of these positions exclusively; any reading of a text will have to negotiate between inferences of either. There is a tension between masculine authority and the feminizing effects of intertextuality which creates an economic balance of forces affecting the implied author; this results in a dialectical relationship between control and passivity.[18] Cunningham has no trouble deciding for himself what Golding's aims were in writing *Rites of Passage*, and where Golding intended specific effects. However, 'Golding' might be somewhat harder to tease out of *Rites of Passage* than Cunningham believes. A whole area of pleasurable engagement exists for the reader here, who must use his/her own imagination and critical faculties to construct his/her own picture of Golding's intent. Like John Fowles's fiction, Golding's text allows for a Barthesian pleasure which is anything but a polemical assertion of authorial selfhood. Lance St John Butler gives a good account of this:

> The 'pleasure of the text', Barthes' explicit connection of the play of fiction with the play of sexual encounter, becomes in Fowles [and, I suggest, in Golding] an elaborate erotics of fiction that takes us well beyond the search for [authorial] authenticity [...] We are not dealing with self-obsession but rather with the position of the Postmodern/Poststructuralist author for whom the

> problem of writing is that he is at once all-powerful (the
> ludic God, the magus) and indeterminable (the blank
> space [...][19]

Cunningham's interpretation of *Rites of Passage* ignores the possibility, outlined by Butler, of a dialectical relationship between authorial self-expression and self-abnegation, between the novelist as 'all-powerful' and as 'indeterminable', as patriarchal, theological authority and as an evasive (non-)entity subject to *différance*, a feminized, passive 'blank space', the mother of the wayward daughter, open to (mis)interpretation from any quarter. Such a relationship would not force the reader to abandon the search for authorial intent. On the contrary, it would encourage this search and allow the reader pleasure in the process.

This pleasurable search need not be incompatible with what Cunningham calls 'the deconstructionist practice'.[20] Despite his claims about Golding's defiant anti-deconstructionist stance, the traditional quest for meaning and reference is not something outlawed or avoided by Derrida and other poststructuralist critics. Cunningham, in fact, admits this, but tries to turn this admission into an attack upon Derrida:

> In seeking to prove that meaning eludes the old fixing
> claims of the dictionary, Derrida is perpetually fixed in a
> quite traditional lexicographical position - the work of
> fixing, establishing meanings, past and present; showing
> how meanings grow and shift; *trading in etymologies*.[21]

Derrida is not trying to evade such affirmations. If anything, his work actively seeks them out, in order to question them. His texts are highly conscious that any language-user is 'trading in etymologies': that is, participating in an economy of exchange, where his/her desires are affected by forces which either make meanings available, or deny them. Derrida's recognition of the importance of economy is clearly outlined in 'Structure, Sign and Play' in the Discourse of the Human Sciences:

> whether he wants to or not - and this does not depend on a decision on his part - the ethnologist accepts into his discourse the premises of ethnocentrism at the very moment when he denounces them. [...] But if no one can escape this necessity, and if no one is therefore responsible for giving in to it, however little he may do so, this does not mean that all the ways of giving in to it are of equal pertinence. [...] It is a question of explicitly and systematically posing the problem of the status of a discourse which borrows from a heritage the resources necessary for the deconstruction of that heritage itself. A problem of *economy* and *strategy*.[22]

There are, Derrida suggests, several 'ways' of giving in to ethnocentrism (or in Cunningham's terms, of assuming a 'traditional lexicographical position'). The fact, then, that the poststructuralist critic may appear to be 'fixed' in such positions does not necessarily invalidate his/her discourse; one can assume these positions in different ways, some of which are more 'pertinent', or fruitful for the critic, than others.

Cunningham's analysis of Golding poses precisely the problem that Derrida wishes to see 'explicitly and systematically' outlined. Cunningham describes *Rites of Passage* as a discourse which borrows from the poststructuralist heritage 'the resources necessary for the deconstruction of that heritage itself'. I quote again his claim that this is exactly what Golding is doing, that *Rites of Passage* is an example of 'the deconstructionist practice turned against deconstructionists'.[23] However, despite the astuteness and sophistication of his reading, Cunningham does not read *Rites of Passage* in terms of 'a problem of *economy* and *strategy*'. Instead, he isolates one possible element of Golding's intent - a desire to respond to accusations of traditionalism - and bases his reading of the novel upon this. His illustration of the complicity of the novel with poststructuralist lexical models is performed 'explicitly', but not 'systematically'. The complicated, problematic economy governing Golding's possible relationships to his readers and critics is ignored. This also applies to Golding's alleged status as a defiant textual authority (or novelistic patriarch). Cunningham does not centre his discussion on gender, but his implied model of authorship is a traditionally masculine one based on notions of independence and control. Deconstruction is a direct threat to this independence, as far as Cunningham is concerned; masculine authority is self-governing rather than economically motivated and restrained.

Despite Cunningham's claim that Golding wrote *Rites of Passage* in order both to copy and to defy the postmodernists who supposedly attacked him, the novel's dense linguistic trickery, and the frequency of its self-conscious puns and allusions, may equally be part of a defensive strategy intended to assert control over the text, and to mask the extent to which Golding, like any other writer, may have borrowed phrases unwittingly, or may have created puns or other linguistic effects without having intended to do so. The text's Barthesian 'dissolves', such as the procreational pun on 'get' and 'covers' cited earlier, would suggest that the implied author's masculine desire to father the text is compromised by a polysemic dissolution of authority which threatens his very status as a source of meaning and textual organization, and thus feminizes him.

There are other, similar examples of the dissolution of the implied author; *Rites of Passage* contains many cruxes, or unsolvable ambiguities, in which authorial intent can neither be proved nor disproved. One can, for example, question the degree of Golding's control over the text's spelling of the term 'paronomasia'; in each case, the word is wrongly spelt as 'paranomasia' (pp.224, 264). This incorrect spelling is left intact in the one-volume edition of the trilogy.[24] Talbot, like Colley, places the word in quotation marks, and mentions to his godfather that Colley used it (p.264). This seems to be an allusion to Colley's pretentiousness; Talbot cites the parson's choice of the Greek term as yet another indication that he was an upstart with ideas above his station. Talbot might also be using the quotation marks to foreground Colley's failure to spell the word properly; however, he never mentions this, and the reader is given no indication that Talbot has noticed the parson's poor spelling as well as his pretension. So the reader cannot even be certain whether Golding himself knew how to spell 'paronomasia'; it is possible that the misspelling was an authorial error, which the editors of *Rites of Passage* and the one-volume trilogy did not notice. The term is spelt correctly in *A Moving Target*, also published by Faber, which may suggest that Golding created Colley's error deliberately.[25] On the basis of *Rites of Passage* alone, though, it is impossible to tell whether Golding intended Talbot and/or Colley to misspell the word or not. The author is indeterminate; he has no paternal authority over the text's language. Like Talbot, he 'gets' the voyage between the covers of the book, but in doing so relinquishes his control over the text.

Cunningham ignores the crux over 'para/paronomasia'; this is ironic, given that he focuses on words beginning with para, and entitles one chapter of his book, 'The Logics of Para'.[26] He uses this chapter to argue that textual and extra-textual phenomena are parasitical upon one another, and that neither one is simply the host, and the other the parasite. I would agree with this, at least as far as *Rites of Passage* is concerned, but on the grounds of the indeterminacy of the text's implied author, rather than on the grounds of his alleged 'old man's defiance' in his rejection of postmodernism and/or deconstructionism as understood by Cunningham.

Cunningham is well aware that there are cruxes in the text, but he neutralizes them by turning them into effects of Golding's alleged plan of authoritarian defiance, thus ignoring the problem that they raise for his interpretation. Cunningham notices that *Rites of Passage* incorporates elements of Falconer's *Dictionary of the Marine* when Talbot recycles its language, but he claims that the dual usefulness and uselessness of Falconer's terminology, and the resultant '*naval cruxes*' are the products of Golding's vision and wisdom:

> The dualism [between meaning/reference and meaninglessness/indeterminacy] becomes in Golding's hands intensely powerful and moving. His manipulation of it is why *Rites of Passage* is a fiction of such extraordinary importance for our lexically sceptical times.[27]

I would argue that the text's cruxes reflect the inevitable inadequacy of definition, or of representation, rather than any 'moving' authorial assertion of a 'dualism' between reference and meaninglessness. For example, Colley's death remains mysterious. *Rites of Passage* knowingly fails either to represent the sexual acts in the cable locker, or to discuss the state of mind which caused Colley to die. The novel alludes to, but does not define, the causes of his death. Talbot only gradually discovers what has happened. He does not know, but only infers, that a fellatio took place in the cable locker, on the basis of hearsay evidence. Much else could have happened also, as Rogers's interview with Talbot, Summers and the Captain implies; Anderson refers to 'buggery', as opposed to fellatio, and Rogers hints that several officers were involved (pp. 254, 255). The full details of what happened, or of Colley's feelings, are never revealed, either in *Rites of Passage* or the rest of the trilogy; Wheeler tells Talbot 'the true story' in *Close Quarters* (the second volume), but Talbot primly refuses to write it down.[28] Thus Colley's sexual encounter becomes something that cannot easily be narrated. This is a highly compromised form of referentiality; the text can refer to the incident, but can never bring it before the reader directly. Instead, it represents its central events by means of mendacious or inadequate secondary discourses, and at the same time, represents its own sources. Through its account of Colley's downfall, it plays with its predecessors, offering a re-enactment of some of the features of *Billy Budd*, *Heart of Darkness* and *The Rime of the Ancient Mariner*, without ever giving the reader a definitive authorial reading of these texts.[29]

Rites of Passage acknowledges its own dependence upon other books, and the feminized, intertextualized status of its implied author. It is not the product of a singular impulse of patriarchal 'defiance' somehow translated onto the printed page, but is the site of continually shifting allusions and puns which frustrate the reader's attempts to draw from the text a simple, knowable meaning. Like Talbot and Colley, Golding is a subject situated in an economy of desires and restrictions; this, not authority, is the basis of his masculinity.

[1]Valentine Cunningham, *In the Reading Gaol: Postmodernity, Texts and History* (Oxford UK, Cambridge USA: Blackwell, 1994), p.194.
[2]William Golding, *Rites of Passage* (London: Faber, 1982), p.214.
[3]William Golding, *Close Quarters* (London: Faber, 1988), pp.134, 184.

[4]Cunningham, p.193.

[5]Emphasis in original.

[6]Adam Smith, *An Inquiry into the Nature and Causes of the Wealth of Nations*, 2 vols., ed. by William Robert Scott (London: G. Bell and Sons, 1921), vol. 1, p. 57.

[7]Cunningham, p.194.

[8]Cunningham, p.192.

[9]A chew of tobacco is another drug; even in death, Colley's reputation is affected by his alleged drug use, as the more moralistic passengers castigate him for such a filthy habit. The parson's tobacco-chewing is a fiction created by Lieutenant Summers in order to obscure Rogers's allusion to the fellatio, which would of course have created a far greater blot on Colley's reputation if publicly known (p.272).

[10]Cunningham, p.192; my emphasis.

[11]Cunningham, p.193.

[12]Cunningham, pp.191-92.

[13]Roland Barthes, *The Pleasure of the Text*, trans. Richard Miller (New York: Hill and Wang, 1975), p.7.

[14]Barthes, p.27.

[15]Cunningham, p.196.

[16]Cunningham makes use of the *pharmakon* in his book, in order to support his argument that the textual and non-textual are parasitic on one another (Cunningham, pp.337-41). Unlike Cunningham, I see the *pharmakon* as a means of showing that the implied author cannot fit into the role of patriarchal controller of the text.

[17]Jacques Derrida, *Dissemination*, trans. Barbara Johnson (London: Athlone Press, 1993), pp.145, 144.

[18]Golding knew that authors may quote unintentionally, and that their claims to absolute control over their texts are thus compromised. In *A Moving Target* (London: Faber 1984, p.161), he describes how he inadvertently lifted a phrase from George Bernard Shaw, and was worried about this, until he discovered the passage from Swift from which Shaw had taken the sentence. Although in the same paragraph he claims that a writer must progress through such unconscious parody in order to discover an original voice, his own confession to having quoted Shaw quoting Swift would suggest that this unconscious parody might be a more persistent phenomenon than he would like.

[19]Lance St John Butler, 'John Fowles and the Fiction of Freedom', in *The British and Irish Novel Since 1960*, ed. by James Acheson (London: Macmillan, 1991), pp.62-77; the citation appears on pp.63-64.

[20]Cunningham, p.194.

[21]Cunningham, p.191; my emphasis.

[22]Jacques Derrida, *Writing and Difference*, trans. Alan Bass (London: Routledge, 1978), p.282; emphases in original.

[23]Cunningham, p.194.

[24]William Golding, *To the Ends of the Earth: A Sea Trilogy* (London: Faber, 1991), pp.192, 227.

[25]Golding, *A Moving Target*, p.160.

[26]Cunningham, pp.337-62.

[27]Golding, *Rites of Passage*, p.259 (emphasis in original); Cunningham, p.197.

[28]Golding, *Close Quarters*, p.221.

[29]There is no room here to explore *Rites of Passage*'s intertextual allusions in any detail. Among the more obvious ones are: Prettiman's design to shoot an albatross in order to disprove the superstition voiced in Coleridge's poem; Billy Rogers's name and station of foretopman, showing that he is an ironic inversion of Melville's Billy Budd; and Talbot's plan to write to Colley's sister with a sanitized account of his death, echoing the lies told by Marlow to Kurtz's intended (pp.73, 252, 277).

8

CLASS AND MASCULINITY IN TONY HARRISON'S 'ME TARZAN' AND 'V'

Commenting on working-class grammar-school boys of the 1950s, Somerset Maugham famously remarked 'They are scum'.[1] He openly panders to class distinctions in which these pupils are denigrated to the status of bacteria invading the grammar school, a supposed preserve of middle and upper-class culture. Judging by the amount of space allocated in his *oeuvre* to his experience as a pupil of Leeds Grammar School (1948-1955), Tony Harrison was affected by decriers such as Maugham, who resented his trespassing into the pedagogical establishment entrenched before the 1944 Education Act. One such critic is the unnamed teacher in one of Harrison's most popular poems, 'Them & [uz]', who forces the youth to learn Received English.[2] This trauma for the pupil is enacted not only in terms of class, as several of Harrison's critics have remarked, but also in terms of gender.[3] By italicising '*He*' (indicating the teacher) in the poem's second stanza, the poet highlights both the class distinction between the pupil and master, and the fact that the linguistic battle is pitched between two males (p.122). 'Them & [uz]' depicts both a middle-class teacher patronising the 'barbaric' pupil from the wastes of south Leeds, and a boy traumatised by his rejection by a male authority figure. A double emasculation ensues: the child is also alienated by the community he grew up in, which regards education as a dangerously feminising force, since it enables him to avoid traditionally male, working-class vocations. Moreover, the pupil even writes poetry, a third emasculation which earns him the label of a cissy in Harrison's poem 'Me Tarzan' (p.116).

Such examples of the links between class and gender have been neglected in recent times by studies of masculinity. Theories surrounding this complex cultural phenomenon often debate the perennial relationship between sex and gender to the detriment of modalities such as class. For example, Roger Horrocks' book *Masculinity in Crisis* is marred by his tendency to transform his chiding of the fact that only a paucity of men exist who consider what it means to be male into a form of scaremongering. Even though he argues that there is indeed a distinction between the poles of sex and gender, the reader is still left with the sense that all Horrocks' patients act similarly simply because they are men, and not because this behaviour is effected by social strata. The totalising, psychoanalytic navel gazing is at work here in the sense that it seems that all men are actually worse off than women due to phallogocentric traditions: they feel 'abused, unrecognised by modern society [...] manhood offers [...] emptiness and despair'.[4] As Lynne Segal succinctly puts it in *Slow Motion*, 'The reality of male power [...] tends to be washed away with the tears shed for men's underlying vulnerability'.[5]

In contrast, in *Between Men*, Eve Kosofsky Sedgwick argues that Lacan

> creates a space in which anatomic sex and cultural gender
> may be distinguished from one another and in which the
> different paths of *men's* relations to male power might be
> explored (e.g. in terms of class).[6]

However, few critics have been attracted to Sedgwick's reading of Lacan in terms of his recognition of the relationship between masculinity and class. And the few that have reacted have usually chosen to focus on bourgeois men.[7] Even Judith Butler's incisive challenge to the reification of the 'ostensible categories of ontology' of 'man' and 'woman', and her emphasis on 'regional modalities of discursively constituted identities', has failed to engage critics in an investigation into the performativity of, for example, the 'working-class male' and the 'middle-class male'.[8] In what sense are working-class males wolfing down Spotted Dick and custard - as opposed to bourgeois men fiddling with their cafétières - performing 'discursively constituted' class and gender identities?[9]

Such correlations between gender and class are depicted throughout Harrison's poetry, as I shall demonstrate in my analyses of the poems 'Me Tarzan' and 'V'. In 'Me Tarzan', Harrison figures himself as an adolescent attempting to come to terms with an apparent opposition between classical (middle and upper-class) and popular (working-class) constructions of masculinity. This split is reflected in the movement of the first stanza. In lines one and two, his friends try to tempt him down from his attic room; in the second half of the quatrain, the narrator refuses the offer, and immerses himself in his Classics' homework. And yet popular versions of masculinity are figured both in the friends' and pupil's cultural references and modes of articulation, which suggests that the supposed binary between the two constructions may actually give way to more complicated instances of agency. For a start, the civilisation/barbarism dialectic, which parallels the classical/popular model in the poem, illustrates that 'civilised' historical figures are just as violent, if not more so, as their 'barbaric' counterparts. Julius Caesar, emperor of the Roman 'civilisation', is figured as a colonialist, whereas the Apache chief Geronimo becomes a symbol of indigenous rebellion against the white settlers in America, rather than a savage element of the 'Wild' West (p.116).

At the beginning of 'Me Tarzan', Harrison depicts the Classics pupil's chance to bond in the predominantly working-class, and (although not, in the late twentieth century, exclusively) male phenomenon of the gang. It is worth pausing to uncover exactly

what, linguistically and politically, he would become involved in if
he chose to join this popular display of masculinity. 'Gang''s
etymology evokes both a subversive and oppressed history.
Referring to a working-class 'company of [...] men', 'Chiefly in a
bad or deprecatory sense [...] associated with criminal societies', it
also meant a company of slaves, and is now linked to left-wing
movements, such as China's Cultural Revolutionary Left accused
after the death of Mao Tse-tung of counter-revolutionary
conspiracy, and the 'Gang of Four' who left the Labour front bench
to form the SDP in 1981.[10] Hence the marginalised and yet
deliberately secretive nature of the Beeston group demands a
particularised mode of articulation. So they adopt a 'whistled gang-
call', devoid of significance to those not part of the gang, and the
melodious yet inarticulate sounds of the yodel (p.116). Tarzan's
hollering is employed particularly, since the Johnny Weissmuller
films were particularly popular in the 1950s.

If he joined this subversive and yet marginalised group of boys,
the pupil would ape a working-class form of masculinity in the
traditional manner, bonding on the street with male members of the
local community. But, as Richard Hoggart writes in *The Uses of
Literacy*, the scholarship boy is more likely to opt for the feminised
space of the home:

> He is [...] likely to be separated from the boys'
> groups outside the home, is no longer a full member
> of the gang which clusters round the lamp-posts in
> the evenings; there is homework to be done. But these
> are the male groups among which others in his
> generation grow up, and his detachment from them is
> emotionally linked with one more aspect of his home
> situation - that he now tends to be closer to the
> women of the house than to the men. This is true,

> even if his father is not the kind who dismisses books
> and reading as 'a woman's game'.[11]

As opposed to Hoggart's anatomical male/female split between the street and home, Harrison presents a classical version of masculinity available within the confines of the attic in 'Me Tarzan'. The pupil is about to go, and, aping Tarzan, swing down on his liana from the attic room to the inviting streets below. But instead of the 'barbaric' ape-man, he adopts the 'civilised' role model of Labienus, Caesar's principal subordinate in Gaul from 58 to 51 BC.[12] And yet both the classic and popular models are textual, and have more in common than the pupil realises. The poet hints at the connections in terms of sexuality: the phallic liana, coupled with its echo of the title of Harrison's first collection *The Loiners*, and all the sexual baggage that the phrase entails, suggest that the school boy fiddles with his tackle in order to eleviate the boredom of the classical text. Masturbation is then paralleled by the comic phallocentricity of the Roman's 'flaming sword' (p.116). Yet in the third stanza, he switches to analysing the emasculatory effects of the Classics in the sense that he is denied access to the gang. This process is figured in terms of an inability to orgasm. 'It's only his jaw muscles that he's tensed' - as opposed to other muscles operating in the lower part of the body during orgasm - 'into an enraged *shit* that he can't go'. Instead of the eruption of adolescent semen as a mark of his untainted working-class masculinity, the narrator ejaculates the signifier of a baby's source of pleasure: faeces.

Whether he joins the gang or not, the pupil will be involved in the self-referential production of male fantasy divorced from any referent of female sexuality. Whether in the company of the boys, Tarzan, Count Basie's orchestra (*'Twelfth Street Rag'*), Labienus

or himself, he is amongst men. Hence the poem's title: 'Me Tarzan'
focuses on the ape-man and pupil's imagined, male subjectivity at
the expense of the other half of the catch-phrase, 'You Jane', and
any notion of the female. Despite the fact that Hoggart argues that
the scholarship boy 'tends to be closer to the women of the house'
than to the bread-winning father in working-class culture, the only
sense we have of the absent mother is contained within abstract
conceptions of femininity.[13] Florence, Harrison's mother, is a
notoriously marginalised figure in the 'School of Eloquence'
sequence as a whole, even if she does get a whole sonnet to herself
with 'The Effort'. The sequence is more concerned with the
genealogical links between the father and son, as figured in poems
such as 'Currants' and 'Continuous'. Perhaps this marks a
departure between Hoggart's sociological study specific to the
Leeds suburb of Holbeck (but falsely generalised into a national
exposition of 'the working class'), and the literary text of 'Me
Tarzan', which may choose to figure the feminine in a different
manner entirely. But this seems unlikely, if considered in the light of
the importance Harrison does occasionally give to his mother in
terms of his literary vocation (for example, in 'Blocks' she teaches
him how to read). By focusing on his relationship with his father,
and marginalising the mother, Harrison exemplifies the perceived
need for working-class sons to bond with the father by, for
example, becoming an apprentice in the same trade, and without
openly admitting mutual ('feminine') affection. The silenced mother
in 'Me Tarzan' thus illustrates the pupil's determination to
construct a purely masculine self. At the same time, his inevitable
failure demonstrates that the pupil flounders in a plethora of
masculinities in an agonised attempt to forge his own adolescent
identity.

For the rest of the poem, the narrator compounds this alienation from the male gang by initiating a creeping sense of his feminisation within working-class culture as a whole. The second stanza forms an elegiac and miniature *Bildungsroman* in verse, in which the boys successfully enter the world of girls whereas he is left to masturbate in his study. In the first line of the second stanza, the young boys play (laik), and eat fish and chips (p.116). By the second line, their activities have evolved into adolescent courting (*'tartin'*) on the back row of local cinemas, whereas the metrical breaks on the words 'on, on, on,' indicate the continuing isolation of the boy who is still, after all these years, reading about Labienus in Caesar's record of his campaigns in Gaul, *De Bello Gallico*.

His feminisation is complete when he unintentionally mimics Cicero by poking his head out of the skylight 'like patriarchal Cissy-bleeding-ro's'. As Carol Rutter writes in her notes to the poem in *Permanently Bard*, Marcus Tullus Cicero (106-43 BC) was an orator and lawyer killed, so legend has it, by sticking his head out of his carriage and asking Mark Antony's henchmen to do the business with their swords.[14] Also, it marks the pupil's femininity by his immersion in the 'feminine' world of learning and the Classics, since Cicero's rhetoric 'formed the core corriculum for the Elizabethan schoolboy and for generations of English schoolboys thereafter'.[15] Hence he, acting as Cicero, simultaneously becomes a 'Cissy' in his own eyes, and from the perspective of the working-class community he symbolically rejects (p.116). A masculine/feminine dialectic is momentarily formed by the insertion of 'bleeding' after 'Cissy', as the image of the orator's bloody head is superimposed with the more 'masculine' desire to swear. But this is then countered by the pun on the final syllable: the sound of '-ro's' evokes the word 'rose', a common poetic symbol for the feminine, epitomised by Robert Burns' famous line, 'O my Luve's like a red, red rose'.[16] And the pupil is also sissy in the sense of being a coward: by refusing to compromise the Classics, he thinks he has chosen a feminine fate, just as Cicero chose a death unbefitting an ancient male hero by opting for a castrating sword rather than the more noble demises on offer, such as armed combat.[17]

It could be argued that Harrison's feminisation of the process of learning adheres to a simplistically gendered binary between the masculine (activity/gangs) and feminine (passivity/academia). Moreover, this opposition might appear as a reductive fantasy when considered in the light of the fact that the number of grammar schools in which women were given an opportunity to learn the Classics is much smaller than their male equivalents. In this sense, Harrison might be seen as falsely feminising that which has been regarded as a male arena. However, such interpretations would ignore the clash of discourses which affect the scholarship boy when he operates in a space gendered by both the working-class community he is leaving, and the academic world he enters into. To the schoolteachers, he is the embodiment of their conception of working-class masculinity. For example, in 'Them & [uz]', he figures as a male barbarian who has infiltrated the more feminine and refined world of the grammar school. In contrast, in the 'School of Eloquence' sequence as a whole, the local Beeston community is suspicious of the pupil's passive study of culture after the gang has dispersed into male, working-class vocations.[18] Hence when Richard Hoggart argues in *The Uses of Literacy* that the scholarship boy is 'between two worlds' in the sense of class divisions, it is necessary to add that he also vacillates between two irreconcilable forms of gender politics.[19]

This vacillation continues in the later and long poem 'V'. Here, as in 'Me Tarzan', it goes beyond a simple masculine/feminine binary;

however, in 'V', 'popular' masculinity is figured by the prosopopoeiac character of the skinhead rather than the marginalised gang. Critics have often commented on the clash between the skinhead and the poet/narrator in 'V', but rarely have they done so in terms of its investigation of various modes of masculinity. For example, Terry Eagleton focuses on the opposition set up at the beginning of the dialogue between the yobbish skinhead and cultured poet, which Harrison then turns into dialectical interplay as the narrator begins to swear, and the youth 'comes up with the odd scriptural allusion which belongs to Harrison's culture, not his own'.[20] Such analysis is valid in itself, since 'V' does indeed dramatise Harrison's desire to forge a dialectic between his working-class upbringing, and the middle-class profession he has entered into. But it neglects the original clash between the 'masculine' skinhead and 'feminine' poet that Harrison then subverts throughout the dialogue.

Following the drama of 'Me Tarzan', 'V' immediately searches for role models of masculinity; however, in the latter poem, the textual figures of Geronimo, Caesar and so on are dropped in favour of the agonies of 'real' father/son relationships. Hence 'V' begins with an epigraph which consists of an extract from *The Sunday Times*:

> 'My father still reads the dictionary every day. He says your
> life depends on your power to master words.'
> > Arthur Scargill
> > *Sunday Times*, 10 January 1982[21]

Set in the midst of the Miners' Strike, the epigraph forms the first reference to the event in its framing of 'V' within the words of the then president of the mineworkers' union. Yet instead of then offering a leftist representation of the event, as Eagleton notes, 'The actual Miners' Strike impinges on *v*. hardly at all'.[22] This oblique reference to the miners actually frames the poem in terms of male genealogy. It originates from an interview with Scargill entitled 'Why "the king" spurns the commons', and constructs a father/son linearity in which his own eloquence benefits from the lexical and literary learnings of his predecessor:

> [My father] read about eight books a week. The home was full of books. Everything. The Bible, Shakespeare. My father still reads the dictionary every day. He says your life depends on your power to master words. I read Jack London and The Ragged Trousered Philanthropists. Those were the books that formed my political opinions.[23]

The word 'master', with its peculiarly gendered etymology, compounds this legacy of articulation in terms of working-class masculinity.[24] Indeed, the dictionary assumes a mythic status in working-class narratives about the struggle for eloquence, into which Harrison inserts his own text. For example, in Joseph Baron's *T'Yorksher Lingo: A Dickshonary ov Gooid Owd Tykes' Words*, the anonymous collector of dialect poetry recalls reading the dictionary in bed as a child, as his father requested, in order to 'better himself'.[25] Such patrilineal links, which exclude women and collude with male discursive practices (and therefore, institutions) then inform the first few stanzas of 'V'. Even though the poet asks the reader to look 'behind the *family* dead', we are then referred specifically to the male bread-winners, the 'butcher, publican, and baker, now me, bard/adding poetry to their beef, beer and bread' (p.7).[26] Linguistically, the poem also alludes to a 'masculine' aesthetic by employing 'masculine' rhyme (hard/bard; dead/bread) and monosyllabic words traditionally associated with men (beef/beer/bread).

If this chapter appears to be shifting towards a simplistic resistance to an exculpation of the male poet's silencing of matriarchy, then this is where the shifting ends. As in 'Me Tarzan', the poet's desire to identify with the father figure(s) entails a tender but fractured negotiation. He does not simply or immediately seat himself amongst the patriarchs, since he has to undergo a clash of gender politics similar to that in the 'School of Eloquence' poem. His own dislocation from his male forebears begins as soon as the third line: he is a 'bard' in the sense of being a modern skald, and also by being 'barred' from the family grave most obviously and bathetically because he is alive, and more symbolically because he has entered a middle-class profession considered to be feminine by his ancestry. This is where his identification with the skinhead character begins, who also senses a rupture with his forebears due to his loss of a perceived, stable identity within the *working* class. The unemployed skinhead's anger is directed not against the Tory government of the mid-1980s, but against the tendency of the dead to enjoy fixed, and advertised, vocations: '*Ah'll tell yer then what really riles a <u>bloke</u>./It's reading on their graves the jobs they did-*' (p.18).[27]

Both characters, for different reasons, feel emasculated by this dislocation from working-class history. In turn, this complicates the seemingly banal gender split between the 'masculine' skinhead and 'feminine' poet, since both are concerned with a threat to their conceptions of working-class masculinity. For example, the youth endorses phallocentricity by flourishing his phallic spray can (his 'tool') (p.10). However, the poet immediately undermines his own allusion to male anatomy by emasculating the skinhead: his 'V's daubed on gravestones' are also like the ticks 'they never marked his work much with at school'. It could be argued that his lack of achievement should be read in terms of male codes of adolescent masculinity, but the poet emphasises that from the viewpoint of the older narrator, his inability to get a job must be read back into his disastrous schoolwork in order to pinpoint the initiation of his future emasculation.

Such interplay between the cultural constructions of masculinity and femininity is epitomised in the following stanza:

> *So what's a* cri-de-coeur, *cunt? Can't you speak*
> *the language that yer mam spoke. Think of 'er!*
> *Can yer only get yer tongue round fucking Greek?*
> *Go and fuck yerself with* cri-de-coeur! (p.17)

On one level, the romance language familiar to the poet signifies his 'culturedness' and simultaneous effeminacy to the skinhead figure; hence the latter's contrasting articulation of 'masculine' monosyllables (the demotic stuff of male banter), and his likening of the poet to female genitalia. *Coeur* compounds the assumed femininity of French, since the heart has functioned as a sign for emotion in many western cultures. It has a particular resonance in the context of Harrison's *oeuvre*: in 'Cypress & Cedar', the poet argues that 'The head and the heart/are neither of them too much good apart'; in an interview with John Haffenden, he contends that his work enacts a fusion of the 'heart and the head', the sensual and the rational (p.233).[28] Hence the passage amalgamates the rational, pessimistic and subversive masculinity of the *Doppelgänger* skinhead with the femininity of aesthetic space.

On another level, this masculine/feminine dialectic might be regarded as problematic, since sex and gender identities are distinct in the sense that the 'feminine' heart is here the property of a male persona, but the passage still adheres to the patriarchal binaries Hélène Cixous outlines in 'Sorties'. 'Head/Heart' links with the other oppositions, such as 'Activity/Passivity' and 'Intelligible/sensitive', which western culture has opined for centuries as the defining aspects of male and female identities.[29] By associating the *coeur* with the feminine, Harrison, it could be argued, maintains a continuum between the (perhaps) distinct categories of sex and gender.[30] That is, unless Harrison's correlation between the aesthetic and effeminate highlights a cultural construction evident since Romanticism, in which poets in western societies are perceived as feminine, as opposed, for example, to the previously 'masculine perswasive force' of a Renaissance poet like John Donne.[31] The feminised figure of John Keats functions as a cultural icon with which contemporary male poets still have to negotiate in order to forge their own poetic identity, in a similar way to that in which modern homosexuals have had to deal with the legacy of Oscar Wilde's influence on the Victorian popular imagination.[32]

Moreover, the possible charge of simplistically conflating a sex/gender split is rendered even more dubious by Harrison's challenge to the gendered poles of his own head/heart dialectic. Even though the skinhead berates the middle-class poet as feminine due to his use of French in the first part of the passage, in the second line, the latter is attacked for being too masculine in the sense of attempting to forge, as in 'Me Tarzan', a genealogical link with the father. *'Can't you speak/the language that yer mam spoke'* refers both to his feminised 'culturedness', and to his rejection of the simple and refined aesthetics of his pre-nursery-school education (p.17). As I noted in relation to 'Me Tarzan', in another poem from the 'School of Eloquence' sequence, 'Blocks', Harrison commemorates the fact that his mother introduced him to poetry through nursery rhymes and, at a more basic level, by teaching him the alphabet (p.164). Paradoxically, then, the older writer's dialogic fusion of foreign cultures with Yorkshire dialect is read by the skinhead as enacting a gendered contradiction. He is 'feminine' when he speaks a romance language, but also 'masculine', since he simultaneously ignores the influence of his mother. And yet, if he sought a lost, pure source of 'feminine' aesthetics, the poet would thereby pander to the skinhead's dangerous, nationalistic and monologic attitude towards British culture by silencing the (equally feminised) alien 'other'.

By uncovering the indeterminate nature of the skinhead's confidently gendered assumptions about the role of the bourgeois poet, Harrison registers his inability to construct fixed gender identities in relation to class in 'V'. Hence he allegorically capitulates to a projected, self-referential fantasy of genderless identity in the last two lines of the passage. On the surface, '*Can yer only get yer tongue round fucking Greek?/Go and fuck yerself with* cri-de-coeur!' constructs the skinhead as the masculine ego of the poet's psyche, in which the demotic vies with the cultural 'other' (p.17). However, getting one's tongue around something recalls the pun on oral sex in Harrison's poem 'Following Pine', in which the narrator projects his sexual fantasies onto the 'tongue in groove' floorboards (p.228). Whether the object be a tongue or clitoris, the subtext of the third line suggests that the poet feminises himself - again, paradoxically - by spending his time writing poetry instead of engaging in sexual intercourse with females. This conviction is compounded by the fantastical resolution of the last line of the stanza, in which the narrator is condemned to a life of self-copulation ('*Go and fuck yerself...*') (p.17).

Such fantasies of genderless identity occur elsewhere in Harrison's poetry; for example, with the androgynous figure in 'Cypress & Cedar'. However, the poet rarely, in his work as a whole, displays a homoerotic undertone to his relationship with other men. Despite his interest in ancient Greek culture - in which homosexuality and patriarchy formed a fruitful (but not elided) relationship - Harrison appears to deliberately avoid confronting the gay or queer: for example, the play *The Common Chorus* engages with the plight of the Greenham women, but refuses to admit even the possibility of any lesbian or homoerotic relationship between women.[33] But in 'V', the poet enjoys a queer identification with (and exploitation of) the skinhead. During his altercation with the youth, the poet vituperates:

'the *autre* that *je est* is fucking you' (p. 19). Intertexuality refers the reader to Arthur Rimbaud's letter to Georges Izambard, which contains the famous claim: '*C'est faux de dire: Je pense. On devrait dire: On me pense [...] JE est un autre*'.[34] Endorsing Rimbaud's self-referential rewriting of Descartes, Harrison allows the 'abstract masculine epistemological subject' of 'man' (as opposed to Judith Butler's focus on 'woman') to fracture into two parallel, conceptual dialectics.[35] The 'masculine' (working-class) skinhead vies with the 'feminine' (middle-class) poet, a binary which synthesises, as I have demonstrated above, when the poet challenges the discursive assumptions of received gender roles. This initial dialectic incurs tropological 'fucking'. The narrator 'fucks' the youth both in the sense of exploiting his otherness in order to construct his identity as a poet, and in the sense of elicting an erotic bond in which - as condoned by Pausanias in Plato's *Symposium* - the elder statesman 'fucks' the younger pupil who requires his tutoring.[36] But there are actually two versions of fractured subjectivity in Harrison's appropriation of Rimbaud: the skinhead is also the poet at the same time as the poet is also the skinhead. Epistemological subjects here reach an absurd level of performativity in a literary enactment of the logical extreme of Butler's thesis in *Gender Trouble*: nobody is quite sure who is fucking whom. However, as this epiphany recedes, the narrator exposes it as a performative production of textual fantasy: at the end of the poem, the clash between the 'feminine' (middle-class) poet and 'masculine' (working-class) skinhead resumes when the narrator asserts his heterosexism by returning home to his 'woman', and the skinhead persists in his denunciation of him as a wanker (p.31).

'*Wanker!*' parallels masturbation and poetic self-referentiality. It derides the poet as feminine through his production of the masturbatory fantasy called 'V'. As Roger Horrocks argues persuasively in *Male Myths and Icons: Masculinity in Popular*

Culture, wankers are feminised by their intrinsic display of a lack of sexual fulfilment:

> men [...] buying porn [...] are 'caught in the act',
> not the act of oppressing women, but the act of
> admitting to their own needs, and their own lack of
> fulfilment. They are 'wankers'. That word is one
> of the great put-downs of men in our culture,
> hurled by car drivers at each other, and by
> politicians and academics at each other in private
> [...] porn is the literature of wanking [...][37]

In 'V', poetry is the literature of wanking. Shouting a word designed, between men, to give the maximum offence, the skinhead derides poems as symptoms of frustrated desire. By confessing this through his *Doppelgänger*, the poet violates the supposedly laminated consciousness of the 'perfect' male. Yet again, class and gender politics intersect in Harrison's poetry, since this incompleteness manifests itself, for the skinhead, in the simultaneously bourgeois fetish of literature. Such intersections contrast with the lacuna of class consciousness, as I stated at the beginning of this chapter, in much of the writing about masculinity. Another example, Robert Bly's *Iron John*, remains one of the most famous recent books on men, despite its insistence on the mythopoeic nature of masculinity. Historicity remains subordinate to the perennial in this study, to the extent that references to Vietnam, Nagasaki, drug barons, King Arthur and Medieval French knights clump together in the space of three pages.[38] Such a totalising framework can only conceive of the mythic man, not male bodies located in societies where class matters.

[1]Quoted in Lynne Segal, 'Look Back in Anger: Men in the Fifties', in *Male Order: Unwrapping Masculinity*, ed. by Rowena Chapman and Jonathan

Rutherford (London: Lawrence and Wishart, 1988), p.83. The comment was oral, so there is, in a sense, no 'original' textual source. Segal takes the quotation from Alan Sinfield, *Society and Literature 1945-1970* (London: Methuen, 1983), p.177. Sinfield does not give an accredited textual reference for Maugham's speech.

[2]Tony Harrison, *Selected Poems* (London: Penguin, 1987), p.122.

[3]See Ken Worpole, 'Scholarship Boy', in *Tony Harrison*, ed. by Neil Astley (Newcastle: Bloodaxe, 1991), pp.61-74. Worpole discusses the poetry in terms of the effects of the 1944 Education Act, which 'brought in the tri-partite system - grammar, technical and "modern"- ', and includes an anecdote about his own grammar-school experience, in which working-class pupils 'sat at a separate table [during school dinners] and afterwards cleared up the other boys' dirty plates' (p.64).

[4]Roger Horrocks, *Masculinity in Crisis* (London: Macmillan, 1994), p.1.

[5]Lynne Segal, *Slow Motion: Changing Masculinities, Changing Men* (London: Virago, 1990), p.68.

[6]Eve Kosofsky Sedgwick, *Between Men: English Literature and Male Homosocial Desire* (New York: Columbia University Press, 1985), p.24.

[7]See, for example, *Manliness and Morality: Middle-class Masculinity in Britain and America* (Manchester: Manchester University Press, 1987), and Norma Fuller's Ph.D. thesis 'The Cultural Constitution of Masculine Identity Among Peruvian Urban Middle-class Men' (University of Florida, 1996).

[8]Judith Butler, *Gender Trouble: Feminism and the Subversion of Identity* (London: Routledge, 1990), p.xi, 3. Butler's exposition of 'woman' as the 'abstracted masculine epistemological subject' can be equally applied to 'man', since they are the product of the same (and dialogic), phallogocentric discourses (p.11). An anti-foundationalist approach to 'man', instead of 'feminisms', would uncover a Foucauldian genealogy of the 'male', and 'masculinities' as fluid identities which cannot be unified into a pre-ordained, coalitional assemblage (p.15). Such discursive practices are beyond the theoretical limits of this chapter.

[9]Butler, p.3.

[10]*The Oxford English Dictionary*, 2nd edn.

[11]Richard Hoggart, *The Uses of Literacy* (Harmondsworth: Penguin, 1957), p.295.

[12]*The Oxford Classical Dictionary*, ed. by Simon Hornblower and Antony Spawforth (Oxford: Oxford University Press, 1996), p.809.

[13]Hoggart, p.295.

[14]Tony Harrison, *Permanently Bard*, ed. by Carol Rutter (Newcastle: Bloodaxe, 1995), p.127.

[15]Rutter, p.127.

[16]Robert Burns, *Poems* (Harmondsworth: Penguin, 1972), p.228.

[17]*The Oxford English Dictionary*, 2nd edn. Even though Cicero chooses a 'feminine' death, it is worth noting that he is still described as an archetypal male patriarch (p.116).

[18]In an Arena interview, Harrison argues that this feminisation of culture was a common response by his Beeston friends and family. Hoggart also remarks on the jealousy and distrust mixed with a grudging respect for education in Holbeck's working-class culture in *The Uses of Literacy* (p.85).

[19]Hoggart, p.301.

[20]Terry Eagleton, 'Antagonisms: Tony Harrison's *v.*', in Astley, p.349.

[21]Tony Harrison, *V* (Newcastle: Bloodaxe, 1991), p.7.

[22]Eagleton, p.350.

[23]John Mortimer, 'Why "the king" spurns the commons', *Sunday Times*, 10 January 1982, p.17.

[24]*The Oxford English Dictionary*, 2nd edn.

[25]Joseph Baron, *T'Yorksher Lingo: A Dickshonary ov Gooid Owd Tykes' Words* (London: Milner & Co., c.a. 1900), p.i.

[26]My italics.

[27]My italics. 'Bloke', as with many words in 'V', has a particularly gendered etymology.

[28]John Haffenden, 'Interview with Tony Harrison', in Astley, p.227.

[29] *The Hélène Cixous Reader*, ed. by Susan Sellers (London: Routledge, 1994), p.37.

[30]For a return of the biological in this perennial debate, see Matthew Pateman's discussion of the separate yet linked categories of sex and gender in his chapter in this book. Perhaps there is also a pun on *coeur*/cur in this passage. The specifically male, cowardly 'cur' would then support the skinhead's conception of the poet's femininity.

[31]John Donne, 'Elegie: On his Mistris', in *The Metaphysical Poets*, ed. by Helen Gardner (London: Penguin, 1972), p.52.

[32]Harrison's poetic debt to Keats is registered in the poem 'A Kumquat for John Keats'. For a discussion of Wilde's influence on the popular conception of the homosexual, see Ed Cohen, *Talk on the Wilde Side* (London: Routledge, 1993).

[33]See Sedgwick's discussion of homosexuality and ancient Greek culture in relation to K. J. Dover's study *Greek Homosexuality* in *Between Men* (pp.4-5). Exceptions to Harrison's avoidance of homosexuality include the poem 'The White Queen'.

[34]*Rimbaud*, ed. by Oliver Bernard (Harmondsworth: Penguin, 1962), p.6.

[35]Butler, p.11.

[36]See Sedgwick's discussion of the homoerotic continuum of same-sex relationships in relation to ancient Greek culture in *Between Men* (p.4).

[37]Roger Horrocks, *Male Myths and Icons: Masculinity in Popular Culture* (London: Macmillan, 1995), p.119.

[38]Robert Bly, *Iron John: a Book about Men* (Shaftesbury, Dorset: Element Books, 1991), pp.154-56.

9

MEN AGAINST MASCULINITY: THE FICTION OF
IAN McEWAN

> I am uncomfortable with the formulations that imply
> some utopic or normative masculinity outside crisis.
> In this respect, I would argue that masculinity,
> however defined, is, like capitalism, *always* in crisis.
> And the real question is how both manage to
> restructure, refurbish, and resurrect themselves for
> the next historical turn.[1]

Metaphysics, as Derrida would have it, predicates erasure.
Its fundamental concepts secure value at the expense of their
rhetoricity, which is worn away through their continual
circulation. To rent for a moment his own monetary figure
which captures this process, the soft metal of metaphor is
gradually forged into the metonymic certainty of reason. 'White
mythology - metaphysics has erased within itself the fabulous
scene that has produced it, the scene that nevertheless remains
active and stirring, inscribed in white ink, an invisible design
covered in the palimpsest'.[2] Nowhere are these erasures more
striking than in those concepts that, in Zygmunt Bauman's
phrase, are central to the 'legislative knowledge' which
characterises the hierarchies of Western modernity: concepts
such as Englishness, 'whiteness', and masculinity.[3] Subjecting
them to a critical gaze is like looking at an old coin whose face
has been eroded by years of fingering and exchange. All that
appears is a blank disc; the insignia and date of minting have
disappeared through use. Its surface reveals little about where
the coin came from, its conditions of possibility, but we know at
least that it is of value. Until recently, the cultural critic was
faced with a similar blankness when interrogating the
abstractions of masculinity, or Englishness, or 'whiteness': each

is tendered as lucrative cultural capital, each is its own palimpsest. Here are treasured concepts in the negotiation and circulation of power, but for too long they have been taken blankly at face-value. How do we account for their profit? Which 'invisible designs' first stamped them as priceless concepts? What rewards accrue to those who maintain their trade?

It has been inevitable, yet still suspiciously a long time coming, that postcolonial enquiries into 'race' have thrown 'whiteness' into crisis by inflecting it with the rhetorics of ethnicity, and the post-national diasporic writings of metropolitan migrants have disarticulated the tautology that connects 'race' to nation in the discourse of an authentic English national identity.[4] Similarly, developments in feminist and gay and lesbian theory have, through the critique of the social processes of gendering that define our 'proper' roles as men and women, triggered a rethinking of the origins and operations of masculinity as a social discourse. Until recently, 'masculinity has stayed pretty well concealed', writes Antony Easthope. '[It] tries to stay invisible by passing itself off as normal and universal'.[5] The blank palimpsest of masculinity as a concept has been peeled away in order to discover the rhetorics of power that remain active and stirring beneath its seemingly neutral surface. So today, as Abigail Solomon-Godeau puts it in the quotation that prefaces this essay, masculinity is in crisis. For some, its critique has robbed men of a normative role in contemporary society, to which they must be urgently reconnected. Others have made the liberating discovery that masculinity is not an inert fact of men's identity but a discourse of power that profits in valuable cultural capital, one that demands repeated public and private performances if its dividends are to be enjoyed. Yet Solomon-Godeau's sense of 'crisis' encapsulates more than these historical responses. In describing masculinity as *always* in crisis, she also points to its persistently volatile mechanics, the fact that its social articulation is not now nor never was a simple, uncontested operation. Masculinity, like capitalism, requires a means of production that must function to order. It is maintained by 'invisible designs' that stir actively below its blank palimpsest. Yet these designs are flawed.

I shall be examining some of the designs of masculinity in the work of the novelist and short story writer, Ian McEwan, with particular attention to how they inflect the language of his narrators. As a writer who has persistently explored the operations of masculinity from a variety of angles, and who has become increasingly sympathetic to the causes of the women's movement in recent years, his prose, I would suggest, is particularly interesting to examine in the context of masculinity. On the one hand, it attempts to bring masculinity to crisis by exposing and travestying the rhetorics that maintain its design - while, on the other, it articulates an indecisive response to the crisis of masculinity; one that, as Solomon-Godeau suggests, can result in the problematic recuperation of the ideologically suspect.

Ian McEwan's fiction to date consists of two short-story collections, *First Love, Last Rites* (1975) and *In Between the Sheets* (1978), and six novels, *The Cement Garden* (1978), *The Comfort of Strangers* (1981), *The Child in Time* (1987), *The Innocent* (1990), *Black Dogs* (1992) and *Enduring Love* (1997).[6] His work is remarkable both for his subject matter and his economical and compelling modes of narration. His material is often controversial - the burial in cement of a mother by her children, the murder and dismemberment of a human body, the traumatic loss of child in a busy supermarket - but McEwan rarely writes for gratuitous effect or for the cheap thrill of shock-value. As Clare Hanson has argued in her discussion of the short stories, McEwan's prose is predicated upon the tension 'engendered by the contrast between the subject matter and the modestly controlled narrative tone'.[7] Unsavoury incidents are usually described through narrative voices that, in their seeming blankness, their lack of overt moral outrage or compassion, demand precisely that the reader thinks about them in moral, if not political terms. His work frequently returns us to those shifting and disturbing borders that we are otherwise happy to forget or avoid - between life and death, childhood and adulthood, innocence and experience. Yet, these issues are not articulated as if remote from the agency of gender identities and relations. McEwan's work persistently examines the psychic and social articulations of masculinity as they interface with these liminal conditions. Masculinity impacts at a variety of levels, from the private realm of the nuclear family in *The Cement Garden* to the public sphere and the threat of nuclear war in *The Child in Time*. This is not to suggest that his understanding of masculinity is unitary. To borrow again Derrida's terminology, McEwan's work peels back the blank cover of the normatising palimpsest to reveal the 'fabulous scenes' of masculinity in production.

As R.W. Connell suggests, we should always talk about plural masculinities rather than a singular, uniform masculinity. Connell splits masculinity into four categories - hegemonic, subordinate, complicit, and marginalised masculinity - whilst also realising that 'to understand gender [...] we must constantly go beyond gender' and consider the relations between masculinity, 'race' and class.[8] His schematisation inevitably oversimplifies a more complex set of relations, but is nonetheless useful. Hegemonic masculinities function to legitimate the dominant social position of men and women's resultant subordination. Subordinate masculinities deal with the unequal relations between men of different gender identities, such as the material subordination of gay men in relation to heterosexual men.[9] Complicit masculinities are the possession of men who uphold the patriarchal status quo without seeming to embody the worst aspects of hegemonic masculinity. Marginalised masculinities are those which are demonised by the operations of social power (Connell gives the example of 'black' masculinities). The wide range and effects of the social relations of gender outlined by Connell go some way to uncovering the extensive influence of masculinity on both men and women. For my purposes, his schema provides a useful critical vocabulary with which we might approach the fiction of McEwan that I examine. Taking one story as an example, I shall argue that McEwan's earlier work tends to unveil the production of hegemonic masculinity, yet is at a loss to interrupt its successful functioning and bring it to crisis. His later writing contains moments where he endeavours to reconfigure gender relations with recourse to a Utopian social agenda; yet the result is in danger of becoming yet another complicit masculinity which (unwittingly perhaps) restructures and refurbishes certain elements of hegemonic masculinity while seeming to dissent from its claims.

'Homemade', the opening story in *First Love, Last Rites* is a veritable *Wunderkammer* of the social rhetorics of hegemonic masculinity.[10] In particular, it examines with much candour how hegemonic masculinity takes possession of male heterosexuality as an important part of its design. Its narrator is a fourteen-year-old boy who tells of his first experience of sexual intercourse with his younger pre-pubescent sister. As Abigail Solomon-Godeau argues, masculinity as a normative social role 'is something to be acquired, achieved, initiated into - a process often involving painful or even mutilating rituals'.[11] 'Homemade' can be read in these terms as a particularly grotesque travesty of a young boy's initiation into hegemonic masculinity through the required sexual congress of the acquiescent female. Yet, as the narrator admits, his is not just a story of 'virginity, coitus, incest and self-abuse' (p.9). Of equal import is his relationship with his older friend Raymond to which he draws our attention at the beginning of his narrative. Although incest is declared at the beginning of the story as the narrative's ultimate *end*, Raymond occupies 'the beginning and the middle' because it is Raymond who makes possible the siblings' repugnant coupling that rents their childish innocence (p.9). As the story unfolds, it becomes clear that Raymond is the narrator's interface with hegemonic masculinity; he is its principal representative from whom the narrator learns about gender roles and relations in a masculinist framework, and in whose company he accumulates expectations and experiences of a masculinist world. The story examines that interface in its exploration of how hegemonic masculinity interacts with male heterosexuality in order to highlight the pressure-point in its design. We first see Raymond on Finsbury Park bending and unbending his finger before our baffled narrator in a crude gesture of copulation. Raymond introduces him to cigarettes and alcohol, masturbation and soft drugs, theft and - in trying to bribe the famed Lulu Smith to indulge the boys' aroused sexual curiosity - prostitution. The boys are on the threshold of a

society where male fantasies of sexual congress have objectified
women into a series of abstracted bodily postures:

> Lulu! Her wobbling girth and laughing piggy's eyes,
> blooming thighs and dimpled finger joints, this
> heaving, steaming leg-load of schoolgirl flesh who
> had, so reputation insisted, had it with a giraffe, a
> humming-bird, a man with an iron lung (who had
> subsequently died), a yak, Cassius Clay, a marmoset,
> a Mars Bar and the gear stick of her grandfather's
> Morris Minor (and subsequently the traffic warden).
> (p.13)

Lulu is cast as the willing provider of sexual experience
required by the boys to enable their performance of hegemonic
masculinity. Yet, as a consequence of the role in which she is
cast by hegemonic masculinity, she *must* be contained. Her
ability to satisfy male heterosexual desire makes her attractive
but also dangerous, the focus for anxieties. As the fulcrum upon
which a domineering hegemonic masculinity must rest, her
performance is also a source of distress as she is granted a
perverse empowerment as a willing sexual subject. To
compensate for her agency, the narrator participates in a wider
realm of extravagant talk and bravado in order to enact through
narrative a necessary containment which converts the sexual
subject into an object of control. This is an impossible task, one
that breeds anxieties, yet one that the males are compelled to
pursue. The potency of the narrator's extravagant language
attempts to compensate for their sense of powerlessness. Lulu is
an object of both desire and derision. She is wanted for her
sexual potency and agency but is deemed disgusting for
precisely this same reason. Her sexual appetites are represented

as animalistic, as indicated not only by her alleged bestial partners but also her 'piggy's-eyes' and concomitant wobbling flesh. The list of indecent and improbable couplings strive to neutralise Lulu's sexual agency as a subject by disempowering her as an obscene object. But note how the narration is fundamentally agitated in its verbal profundity. The accumulation through breathless repetitions of her range of lewd partners registers the impossibility of her containment. The representation of Lulu demonstrates how, on the one hand, hegemonic masculinity makes heterosexual congress with women one of its important required rituals; yet, contrariwise, female sexuality returns to haunt the narrative voice which is disturbed as much by anxiety as ardour. Here, then, emerges the flaw in the 'invisible design' of hegemonic masculinity: the contradictory positioning of the sexual active female as both a subject with agency and the object of control. Her agency must be both acknowledged and disavowed.

McEwan exposes how hegemonic masculinity creates a heightened use of language that is both tantalised and traumatised by the sexually acquiescent female. One of the boys' favourite haunts is a cafe near Finsbury Park where the narrator is exposed to a whole rhetoric of hegemonic masculinity voiced by adult males, noteworthy not least for the histrionic mantras of heterosexual congress:

> we listened to who and how the dustman fucked, how the Co-op milkmen fitted it in, what the coalmen could hump, what the carpet-fitter could lay, what the builders could erect, what the meter man could inspect, what the bread man could deliver, the gas man sniff out, the plumber plumb, the electrician connect, the doctor inject, the lawyer solicit, the

> furniture man install - and so on, in an unreal
> complex of timeworn puns and innuendo, formulas,
> slogans, folklore and bravado. I listened without
> understanding,   remembering   and   filing   away
> anecdotes which I would one day use myself, putting
> by histories of perversions and sexual manners - in
> fact a whole sexual vocabulary [...] (p.14).

These grotesque, crudely punning stories reveal language as an important cog in the mechanics of hegemonic masculinity, and the extent to which it can become marbled with masculinist rhetoric. Language is inflected with the thought of sexual congress to such an extent that all the signifiers seem to slide to this ultimate signified, endowed through puns with a specific level of meaning. In this sexual vocabulary, each clause casts the male as the dynamic subject of an activity for which no female needs be specified, acknowledged only in her absence. This is the contradictory task of hegemonic masculinity - the 'editing out' of the woman as an agent in the proceedings. The length of the first sentence quoted above, its building to an impossible climax through the demented incantation of short subordinate clauses, demonstrates how language - like the boys - has been traumatised, over-excited, placed under a seemingly unbearable pressure.

In the 'fantastic scene' of the coupling between the narrator and his sister, ten-year-old Connie, the anxieties which the narrator's agitated style tries to bury come to the surface as the flaw in the design of hegemonic masculinity is uncovered. Its pressures have led the narrator to consider his sister as a possible acquiescent female with whom his initiation via coitus can be achieved. The scene is engineered by the narrator exploiting Connie's favourite game of 'Mummies and Daddies' in which she has frequently in the past implored her brother to participate, but to no avail. The game involves the performance of gendered familial roles. On hearing that they are at last to play her favourite game, Connie fetches her toys - 'prams, dolls, stoves, fridges, cots, tea-cups, a washing machine and a kennel' (p.20) - and arranges a typical British suburban family home in miniature. The narrator is then required to perform a series of 'masculine' roles as defined by the domestic arrangement which mimics the adult world:

> I was plunged into the microcosm of the dreary, everyday, ponderous banalities, the horrifying, niggling details of the life of our parents and their friends, the life that Connie so dearly wanted to ape. I went to work and came back, I went to the pubs and came back, I posted a letter and came back, I went to the shops and came back, I read a paper, I pinched the bakelite cheeks of my progeny, I read another paper, pinched some more cheeks, went to work and came back. And Connie? [...] She was the inter-galactic-earth-goddess-housewife, she owned and controlled all around her, she saw all, she knew all, she told me when to go out, when to come in, which room I was in, what to say, how and when to say it. (p.20)

The same agitated, repetitive mode of narration common to the previous passages about sexualised women reappears in the description of the imaginary home and underlines the seeming disempowerment acknowledged by the narrator before his all-knowing, all-seeing sister. Like the previous two passages, the narration in this passage emphasises the narrator's pressurised sense of embattlement and barely contained frustration that he seeks to diffuse through his use of repetitive, sardonic phrases. The promise of intercourse offers him an opportunity to wrest control of the situation back from his all-powerful sister through the performance of his required hegemonic masculine role that will convert her from the orchestrator of this fantastic scene to the sexualised object of his own design. Yet the narrator's initiation is a disaster. After coercing Connie into bed without her clothes, his attempts to penetrate her initially prove fruitless. His explanation of why mothers and fathers have sex is greeted with amusement and bafflement by Connie who fails to see what could be special about it. Further hilarity ensues when she spies his erection: ' "It looks so . . . it looks so . . ." [she] sank back into another fit, and then managed in one high squeal, *"So silly, it looks so silly,"* after which [she] collapsed back into a high-pitched, squeezed-out titter' (p.23). The ultimate sign of masculine sexual virility, the erect penis, becomes a figure of mockery, an absurdity on the narrator's body. Connie's actions here index why hegemonic masculinity struggles to represent women as contradictory objects of both desire and derision; they provide the means by which the boy is initiated into hegemonic masculinity, but can also confiscate those means and turn him into an absurd object of her mocking gaze. The scene reveals how, by making sexual congress so central to its performance, hegemonic masculinity is fractured from within by locating women as objects to be controlled but also subjects that threaten masculinist control. The narrator, like the language he uses, flounders desperately in trying to neutralise female agency in his quest for her containment. Yet the failure ever to do so successfully is suggested by the fact that it is Connie who eventually takes control of the situation and initiates her brother into hegemonic masculinity, simultaneously performing and surrendering her power: ' "I know where it goes," she said, and lay back on the bed, her legs wide apart, something it had not occurred to me to ask her to do. She settled herself amongst the pillows. "I know where the hole is" ' (p.23). Ultimately, she unwittingly facilitates the feelings of pride he admits to when eventually experiencing intercourse, 'lying in that manly position, proud in advance of being able to say "I have fucked", of belonging intimately and irrevocably to that superior half of humanity who had known coitus, and fertilised the world with it' (pp.23-24). Like the men in the cafe, the narrator looks forward to narrating his activity in a short clause with a subject, a predicate, but no object. The sexually acquiescent female who announces 'I know where the hole is' is edited out of the narrator's 'official' version which declares 'I have fucked'. That erasure of the woman-as-subject is part of the invisible design of hegemonic masculinity, the impossibility of which is responsible for its fatal flaw which is the focus of McEwan's story.[12]

In these terms, McEwan does much to subvert the designs of hegemonic masculinity by uncovering its destructive and grotesque consequences. His narrator is ultimately a pathetic creature, whose loss of virginity is a sordid, ugly affair rather than the victory he is anxious to declare. If Raymond plays the part of a masculine 'Mephistopheles', then the narrator is a modern-day Faustus who sacrifices his childish innocence for carnal knowledge, and perhaps is repentant as the story closes (p.12). Indeed, he begins the story washing after the incest he performs at the end, almost as if seeking absolution for what he has done. But the contrition this detail promises is never made available. McEwan's subversion is of limited impact; at another level there is little sense that hegemonic masculinity has been effectively challenged. It remains a carceral structure that entraps men within its suffocating, repressive confines - not dissimilar from the dreary miniature domestic scene which the narrator laments as utterly futile and banal (the narrator constantly refers to his feelings of futility throughout the story). According to Easthope, 'In so far as men live the dominant version of masculinity [...] they are themselves trapped in structures that fix and limit masculine identity. They do what they *have* to do'.[13] By beginning with its ending, 'Homemade' seems to seal the characters inside the agitated hegemonic rhetorics of masculinity it travesties. The narrator confesses that, after fucking his sister, he no longer wants to see naked girls for a while and wishes to cancel the appointment with Lulu. But Raymond 'would not want that at all', and the narrative ends with the impression that the narrator will have to disguise his disquieted, confused feelings behind the rhetoric of masculinity he has previously filed away, if his camaraderie with Raymond is to be maintained (p.24). Ironically, his first knowledge as an initiated male 'adult' is that it will not seem proper to pass up the opportunity to enter into sexual relations with an 'acquiescent' woman.

So, although McEwan can lampoon the languages of hegemonic masculinity and satirise the appropriation of heterosexual desire, its authority remains intact as its ability to reproduce itself is not threatened. There is the sense of frustration on the part of McEwan who, adjacent to his narrator, also finds himself locked inside the very languages he seeks to question. He can reveal the mechanics of hegemonic masculinity in unflattering terms, but at this stage of his career he is unable to offer any way of breaking out of the structure suggested by the self-repeating, if flawed, circuitry that connects the story's beginning to its end.

The opposition of hegemonic masculinities requires a new narrative; at least, that is the lesson of *The Child in Time*.[14] The novel calls for 'new times' where the social conditions are possible for new forms of relations between men and women that escape the roles made available to them in hegemonic masculinity. In addition, and keeping in mind the inflection of the narrator's language in 'Homemade', it also experiments with the relationship between narrative time and narrated time in an attempt to release language from the stranglehold of hegemonic masculinity. This also revolves around the symbolic importance of a 'fabulous scene'.

As McEwan would have it, linear time is masculine. In the Introduction to his oratorio 'or Shall We Die?', he attacks the ideas of Newtonian physics for their dependency on linear structure. 'We conceive of ourselves moving through time in an orderly, linear fashion in which cause invariably precedes effect. When it does not so, as in, say, a precognitive dream, we are quick to dismiss the experience, or ridicule as superstitious those who do not'.[15] These views enshrine 'patriarchal values' that are single-handedly blamed for having brought the world to the brink of nuclear destruction. Against this is set an alternative view represented by Einsteinian physics which conceives of the world as in 'constant flux' (pp.12, 15). This view is linked to a 'female principle' that is proffered as a way of avoiding the threat of nuclear annihilation (p.15). This choice for humanity is stark, according to the oft-quoted words of the oratorio: 'Shall there be womanly times, or shall we die?' (p.17). *The Child in Time* attempts to realise a narrative that engenders 'womanly times' by simultaneously constructing and subverting a linear,

regulated society where men will be rescued from the confines
of hegemonic masculinity. Yet in so doing, McEwan's attempt
to write the new 'womanly times' is in danger of refurbishing
masculinity in ways that work contrary to his intentions.

Stephen Lewis works on the Parmenter Committee, a sub-
division of the British Government's Official Commission on
Childcare. The Committee exists to regulate the raising of
children through an agreed set of standards. One of the extracts
from the Government's *Authorised Childcare Handbook*
cements the relationship between time, regulation and gender
roles: 'Make it clear to him that the clock cannot be argued
with and when it is time to leave for school, for Daddy to go to
work, for Mummy to attend her duties, then these changes are
as incontestable as the tides' (p.27). This is a world in miniature
barely different to that imagined by Connie in 'Homemade' as
she constructs her game of Mummies and Daddies. The
interesting extra detail is time - the clock cannot be argued with,
its order is incontestable. *The Child in Time* disobeys this
maxim by deliberately 'arguing with the clock' at several levels.
The incontestable, regulated world of much of the novel is
made intolerable by the disappearance of Kate, the daughter of
Stephen and his wife Julie. This takes place in a busy
supermarket, where Stephen attends to his 'mundane errands,
and all about him shapes without definition drifted and
dissolved, lost to categories' (p.16). The orderly world of the
supermarket seems particularly sinister when read in the context
of the narrator's repetitive lists favoured by the anxious narrator
of 'Homemade':

> The people who used the supermarket divided into
> two groups, as distinct as tribes or nations. The first
> lived locally in modernised Victorian terraced houses

which they owned. The second lived locally in tower
blocks and council estates. Those in the first group
tended to buy fresh fruit and vegetables, brown
bread, coffee beans, fresh fish from a special counter,
wine and spirits, while those in the second group
bought tinned or frozen vegetables, baked beans,
instant soup, white sugar, cupcakes, beer, spirits and
cigarettes. [...] What else did [Stephen] buy?
Toothpaste, tissues, washing-up liquid, and best
bacon, a leg of lamb, steak, green and red peppers,
radice, potatoes, tin foil, a litre of Scotch. And who
was there when he reached for these items? Someone
who followed him as he pushed Kate along the
stacked aisles [...]. (p.15)

In this description, the crudely-drawn, bifurcated world of
'Homemade' haunts the seemingly sophisticated depiction of
late-twentieth-century, post-Thatcherite Britain. Later in the
novel, Thelma Darke - Einsteinian physicist and friend of
Stephen - will scorn 'rational' science in similar terms as a
'whole supermarket of theories [...] One offering has the world
dividing every infinitesimal fraction of a second into an infinite
number of possible versions, constantly branching and
proliferating, with consciousness neatly picking its way through
to create the illusion of a stable reality' (p.117). Kate is the
victim of this orderly environment in a way that literalises the
loss of Connie's (and indeed the narrator's) innocence in
'Homemade'. But in *The Child in Time*, the absent female so
desperately required by the objectifying rhetoric of hegemonic
masculinity becomes a nightmare for 'new men' like Stephen,
out 'doing their bit' at the supermarket on a Saturday morning
(p.15).

Kate's disappearance is the measure of the cruel, masculine world of *The Child in Time*. Jack Slay is right to argue that the novel 'is more than Stephen's search for his lost daughter; it also presents the search for the lost child that exists within every adult', but he misses the gender politics of McEwan's purpose.[16] McEwan wants lost childhoods back again, as if their reclamation will instantly defeat hegemonic masculinity and the patriarchal society that it engenders, allowing men to join women in a new union of 'womanly times'. For the Government, childhood is 'a physically and mentally incapacitating condition, distorting emotions, perceptions and reason' (p.179). McEwan requires these distortions to break out of the male order he contests, and for this purpose the manipulation of narrative becomes paramount. According to the incontestable face of linear time, childhood is an historical stage. The anonymous characters we meet at the beginning of the novel are described as 'ex-children' (p.8). They have had their time. The sense of childhood loss is intensified by the fortunes of Stephen's student friends whose youthful aspirations have been ravaged by the torpor of adult life in an uncaring society:

> A couple of acquaintances, once truly free men, were resigned to teaching English to foreigners. Some were facing middle age exhaustedly teaching remedial English or 'lifeskills' to reluctant adolescents in far-flung secondary schools. These were the luckier ones who had found jobs. (p. 27)

The phrase 'truly free men' can never be completely neutral in McEwan's economic, and meticulously crafted, prose. The implication is that, for men, childhood may promise a freedom from the incarceration of regimented society within which they live. Stephen's friends' aspirations die with their youth, as indeed do Stephen's; his time in Africa as a young child is remembered as a 'five-year idyll' that ends with his attendance at boarding school which signified 'a period of his life, a time of unambiguous affinities, was over' (p.73, 74). A reconnection with childhood energies is attempted by forging a narrative structure that refuses to consign childhood to the past and makes it simultaneous with the lived presence of the adult.

This manifests itself severally. Although the novel has an anonymous third-person narrator, the point of view is in the main with Stephen, and it aligns itself quite closely with his memories and digressions. The novel's 'present' is never fully clear, only that it is set somewhere in the near future (as the novel was published in 1987, we assume this to be the mid-1990s or the early years of the next millennium).[17] Little information about dates is provided, and the time that elapses between episodes is rarely counted. In terms of narrative, McEwan creates a discordance between narrative time and clock time. As Gerard Genette points out in a discussion of Proust, this discordance can be achieved by variations in the 'acceleration, deceleration, stasis and ellipsis' of historical time by the narrator.[18] Two examples are worth contrasting in *The Child in Time*. Acceleration occurs in the synopsis of the Olympic crisis, in which an argument between a Russian and an American sprinter escalates almost into nuclear war in the short space of twelve hours (pp.34-35).[19] The impression of the speed with which the crisis arises is reflected in the sudden rapidity of the narrative that covers the incident in six paragraphs that span less than two pages. Yet, time is decelerated at the beginning of Chapter five when Stephen is involved in a car-crash with a lorry. In this scene the narrator notes how 'the rapidity of the event was accompanied by the slowing of time', as if Stephen experiences his collision in slow motion (p.93). Between the time of the lorry becoming out of control and the point where he brings his car to a halt, Stephen's mind flicks between concentrating on his driving and thinking of his family. Like the narrative of the Olympic crisis, the narration is concluded in approximately two pages, but here the events last roughly five seconds. Borrowing from McEwan's terminology, the narration of these incidents foregrounds Einsteinian 'womanly' time to support the words of Thelma Darke to Stephen:

> Time is variable. We know it from Einstein who is still our bedrock here. In relativity theory time is dependent on the speed of the observer. What are simultaneous events to one person can appear in sequence to another. There's no absolute, generally recognised "now" - but you know all this. (p.118)

The discrepancies between narrative time and historical time are part of the novel's wider narrative fabric that derives its pattern from Stephen's mystical experience at The Bell, which dovetails the distortions of time with the distortions of childhood. Wandering through the English countryside, Stephen comes across a pub where he has a peculiar, mystical experience. Looking through the window, he sees - improbably - his mother and father deep in conversation. As he learns later from his mother Claire, the fantastic scene he witnesses did indeed occur years before. It was the moment when Claire, pregnant with Stephen at the time, decided to keep her baby. Her decision was predicated on her seeing through the window the face of a child looking in. She was convinced she 'was looking at my own child' (p.175). The concept of linear time is refused at this point in the novel as it yokes together the adult and childish versions of Stephen. Indeed, Stephen is present in at least three forms here - as the child seen by Claire, as an adult looking in, and as an unborn embryo whose foetal motion suffuses the narrator's description of the experience:

> His eyes grew large and round and lidless with desperate, protesting innocence, his knees rose under him and touched his chin, his fingers were scaly flippers, gills beat time, urgent hopeless strokes through the salty ocean that engulfed the treetops and surged between their roots; and for all the crying, calling sounds he thought were his own, he formed a single thought; he had nowhere to go, no moment could embody him [...]. (p.60)

In these terms, the marking of a passage of linear time conjured by the symbolic associations of the pub's name - the 'bell' that rings on the hour - is superseded by the sense of the verb 'to bell'; that is, to swell when pregnant. The embryonic gills attempt to 'beat time', but their effort is urgent and hopeless because the logic of the 'moment' no longer applies. The fabulous scene has no absolute, generally recognised 'now'.

The simultaneous conjuring of the child and adult selves *within the male* is proffered as a means of impacting positively on social relations, of connecting again the severed line between 'public policy and intimate feeling' (p.9). Women, it seems, simply do not have this problem: Thelma Darke knows all about Einsteinian 'womanly times', while Julie already has faith in flux, 'in endless mutability, in re-making yourself as you came to understand more' (p.54). This is an aspect of 'her femininity', whereas men remain the sad creatures of linearity 'froze[n] into place' once they pass a certain age. Here is the 'womanly' version of selfhood men must aspire to, if there is to be any hope of social change (in so doing, McEwan seems uncharacteristically insensitive to the age-old patriarchal association between 'female irrationality' and children's irrationality that he is in danger of maintaining). Both Stephen and his friend, Charles Darke, attempt to bridge the gap between childish and adult selves, but with differing consequences. Stephen is surprised to learn that Charles spends some of his free time living secretly a childish life, dressing as a young boy, complete with toys and tree-house. But his attempts to make his childhood self simultaneous with his adult self flounder because his aping of childhood occurs within the conventional confines of a boyish masculinity.

On one occasion, Charles invites Stephen to his tree-house where he shows his collection of toys, including a compass, a fish-hook and two oval pebbles:

> Looking down at these items spread before him on the planks, uncertain what to say next, Stephen was impressed by what appeared to be very thorough research. It was as if his friend had combed libraries, diligently consulted the appropriate authorities to discover just what it was a certain kind of boy was likely to have in his pockets. It was too correct to be convincing, not quite sufficiently idiosyncratic, perhaps even fraudulent. (p.113)

As a child, Charles remains 'a certain kind of boy' whose invented childhood is an inventory of male-childish possessions, a world still lost to categories. McEwan uses Charles to point out how the connection with childhood he is advocating is not simply the stuff of masquerade, as childhood is just as gendered as adulthood. Charles' homemade tree-house is not very remote from Connie's domestic doll's house in the gendered stereotypes they both enshrine. Stephen fares better. He fuses his childish and adult selves by indulging in his idiosyncratic childish fantasies as an adult. When he thinks he sees Kate playing in a schoolyard, he follows 'her' into school and joins one of the classes (the teacher assumes he is taking part in a parental participation scheme). When Stephen leaves the class part-way through the lesson, he is performing a fantasy that has been his since childhood:

> These were moments of intense pleasure, the time it took Stephen to walk to the classroom door; to step out of the fantasy, to cease colluding in the teacher's authority, simply to turn his back and come away at his own pace, confident of immunity - this was his schoolboy daydream, nurtured through many dull hours, enacted at last, thirty years late. (p.146)

In triggering his 'schoolboy dream', the moment marks an end to his depression, despite the fact that the girl he followed was not Kate. He begins to write again. He refuses to have lunch with the Prime Minister due to his opposition to the Government's policies. Another reminder that his younger self is awakening is his decision to learn Arabic; his early ambitions as a writer were based upon an unwritten novel, *Hashish*, set in the Arab lands of Turkey and Afghanistan. Similarly, on learning that his wife Julie is pregnant again - as a result of their lovemaking significantly just after Stephen's experience at The

Bell - he travels to her country retreat by hitching a lift in the driver's compartment of a train, a 'boyhood dream' (p.212). He arrives a 'new' man, remade and remodelled with recourse to his childhood self, liberated and energised through his experiences which have delivered him into 'womanly times' by reconnecting the child with the adult. He becomes a child (just) in time.

Or so it seems. The final scene in chapter nine, when Julie gives birth, is one of the most symbolically rich yet problematical in the novel. Stephen arrives at Julie's country residence fresh from the news that she is about to have a second child. The couple speak emotionally about their lost daughter, then make love. Their coitus triggers Julie's contractions, and in a moving scene that is a testament to McEwan's brilliance as a writer, Stephen helps to deliver Julie's child. The novel closes with the three lying together looking through the bedroom window at the approaching dawn, and at the planet Mars, 'a reminder of a harsh world' (p.220). Significantly, the gender of the new child is not specified. The final paragraph ends just as this fact is about to come to light: ' "Well?" Julie said. "A girl or a boy?" And it was in acknowledgement of the world they were about to rejoin, and into which they hoped to take their love, that she reached down under the covers and felt' (p.220).

Compelling as these final moments undoubtedly are, their impact is altered by a tension between two different ways of reading them that bear witness to the collision between, on the one hand, McEwan's attempt to deliver up his 'new man' to 'womanly times', and on the other, the extent to which his aims can result in Connell's 'complicit masculinities'. To first take what I assume is McEwan's intended purpose, the union between Stephen and Julie and the birth of a new child represents the possibility of new relations between men and women. This is because the male has successfully experienced as first-hand the 'womanly' version of time in the novel as expounded by Thelma. In forging a simultaneity between his child and adult selves, Stephen has embraced the flux and continual re-invention of the self associated with Julie. Whereas during Kate's birth his attendance had 'been more symbolic' than urgent, in this second birth he is a practical and vital presence that helps to deliver the new child (p.216). He acknowledges 'the mother's absolute right to order her own domain', and - crucially - he is admitted as a vital part of this order. Indeed, the birth of the child could be read as a metaphor of Stephen's rebirth in 'womanly times', a process begun nine months earlier at The Bell when he appeared almost as a foetus. Stephen's new self, as McEwan would have it, is much closer to Julie's 'femininity', and their new union will be a resource with which to oppose the hard world order signified by Mars that watches over the novel's final moments. The Utopianism of the scene is held in check by the fact that the novel's ending is not an escape from the social problems it has indexed. The phrase 'the world they were about to rejoin' conjures two moods. The first is the sense of healing the world, 'rejoining' its bifurcated halves (the two 'nations' in the supermarket, the two genders) into a new, 'womanly' whole. But second is the acknowledgement that there remain problems to be solved; society is still bifurcated, and Stephen, Julie and their child must join in it again to fight for a better life, equipped with their new hopes. 'Womanly times' must struggle in the face of the harsh masculine world symbolically ruled by Mars. The narrator's refusal to name the gender of the child is an act of defiance with which to end the novel, one which points out how it is the current social order that bestows gender definitions. In the union made possible in 'womanly times' no such divisions need operate; men and women will not be subservient to the rationale of hegemonic masculinity.

But the terms within which McEwan's Utopian conclusion is voiced reveal a darker purpose. As Kiernan Ryan has pointed out, the novel's closing nativity can be read *not* as Stephen's attempt to be admitted to the domain of the mother, but as an effort to usurp the mother's 'absolute right' to order it, bringing it once again under male mastery:

> The long journey from ejaculation to parturition is telescoped into one short sequence which edits out the child's gestation within the mother. The scene arrogates control to the father, creating the illusion that the act of insemination instantly precipitates the birth. And because they are marooned in the country, the stage is set for Stephen to play the midwife and deliver his own child into the world.[20]

Stephen and Julie's homemade nativity, where they become once again Mummy and Daddy, is haunted by the spectre of the hegemonic masculinity so spectacularly on display in the short story we examined earlier. In this scene also, the female is in danger of being 'edited out' of the proceedings, allowing Stephen to father the new child in himself in a way perhaps not too remote from the older men in 'Homemade' who father the next generation of masculine males by passing on their rhetoric which seeks to elide the female in the masculine mantra 'I have fucked'. There is a difference, of course - Stephen would no doubt abhor the men in 'Homemade' - but the trace of the invisible design of hegemonic masculinity remains. For this reason, the conclusion to the novel is perhaps pulled towards the assertion of a complicit masculinity, one that draws the patriarchal dividend without seeming to declare its interest. This is not to condemn McEwan out of hand for his well-intentioned gender politics, as Adam Mars-Jones enjoys doing. For this sanctimonious critic, 'Ian McEwan may be one of the few literary examples of the New Man [...] but in his vision of the relationship between the sexes there is much that is atavistic, patriarchal, even parasitic'.[21] Kiernan Ryan's opinion is smarter when he asserts how *The Child in Time* demonstrates that 'the desire to transfigure masculinity cannot be disentangled from the deep-rooted feelings it seeks to abolish'.[22] Indeed, perhaps some of the value of this remarkable novel, in addition to its progressive gender politics, is its unwitting demonstration of how hegemonic masculinity - in Solomon-Godeau's words quoted at the beginning of the essay - can restructure, refurbish and resurrect itself for the next historical turn.

As the select examples taken from his fiction evidence, McEwan is a writer who seeks to unmask hegemonic masculinity. He uncovers its hidden designs and points out its flaws, taking a stern if fascinated view of its material effects in the lives of men and women, be they adult, child, or at that uncomfortable space somewhere in-between. Masculinity becomes the motor behind a wealth of social phenomena, from the ways in which heterosexuals have intercourse to the social organisations of capital and government, and the regulation of time. The cleavage between the rational, orderly stasis of men and fluid, 'womanly times' may on occasions be too crude and convenient for comfort, but as the conclusion to *The Child in Time* wants to assert, the aim of this is a 'rejoining' where bifurcation is a thing of the (linear) past. Yet, for all of this, hegemonic masculinity is never fully dislodged. As 'Homemade' indicates, it continues to function successfully, and no amount of irony and travesty can constitute a spanner in its works. The narrator has no position outside of it, and can only beat its incarcerating walls from within on those occasions when his enthusiasm for it lapses. *The Child in Time* seems more optimistic and determined to junk masculinity for once and for all, yet the means by which this is achieved allows for the formulation of a complicit masculinity which continues to threaten the female with elision. That McEwan is yet to think of a way out of this quandary is evidenced in *Black Dogs*, where once again 'womanly times' are posited as the salve to post-war Europe ravaged by Nazism and neo-fascism, yet here the assertion is less convincing, almost as if McEwan has lost some of his faith in his redemptive model of 'womanly times'. As his fiction ultimately demonstrates, masculinity may well be in crisis as the designs which stamp it with authority are revealed, yet - exasperatingly - its value as cultural capital still endures.

[1] Abigail Solomon-Godeau, 'Male Trouble', in *Constructing Masculinity*, ed. by Maurice Berger, Brian Wallis and Simon Watson (New York and London: Routledge, 1995), pp.69-76, (p.71). I am grateful to my colleague Stephen Gregg for his helpful comments on an early draft of this essay.
[2] Jacques Derrida, *Margins of Philosophy*, trans. Alan Bass (Brighton: Harvester, 1982), p.213.
[3] Zygmunt Bauman, *Intimations of Postmodernity* (London and New York: Routledge, 1992), p.11.
[4] For inquiries into 'whiteness' and ethnicity, see Vron Ware, *Beyond the Pale: White Women, Racism and History* (London and New York: Verso, 1992). For critiques of the relations between 'race' and nationhood in discourses of Englishness, see Paul Gilroy, *'There Ain't No Black in the Union Jack': The Cultural Politics of 'Race' and Nation* (London: Hutchinson, 1987) and Anna Marie Smith, *New Right Discourse on Race and Sexuality: Britain 1968-1990* (Cambridge: CUP, 1994).

[5]Antony Easthope, *What a Man's Gotta Do: The Masculine Myth in Popular Culture* (Boston: Unwin Hyman, 1986), p.1.

[6]For an excellent short summary of McEwan's career that is sensitive to the contradictions and continuities throughout his work, see Kiernan Ryan, *Ian McEwan* (Plymouth: Northcote House, 1994), pp.1-5.

[7]Clare Hanson, *Short Stories and Short Fictions, 1880-1980* (London: Macmillan, 1985), p.160.

[8]R. W. Connell, *Masculinities* (Oxford: Polity, 1995), pp.76-86, (p.76).

[9]On this point Connell is perhaps in danger of making a slippage between gender identity and sexuality.

[10]Ian McEwan, *First Love, Last Rites* (London: Picador, 1975).

[11]Solomon-Godeau, p.71.

[12]Several of McEwan's other stories also travesty this flawed design, such as 'Dead as They Come' in *In Between the Sheets*. The most chilling example is 'Solid Geometry', where the narrator sorts out his domestic difficulties with his wife by making her literally disappear.

[13]Easthope, p.7.

[14]Ian McEwan, *The Child in Time* (London: Picador, 1987).

[15]Ian McEwan, *A Move Abroad: 'or Shall We Die' and 'The Ploughman's Lunch'* (London: Picador, 1989), pp.11-12.

[16]Jack Slay, Jr., 'Vandalising Time: Ian McEwan's *The Child in Time*', *Critique*, XXXV (4), 1994, (pp.205-218) p.210.

[17]Adam Mars-Jones has proudly undertaken the rather pointless task of figuring out the novel's 'present' as 1996, although the proof he gives is circumstantial. See Adam Mars-Jones, *Venus Envy: On the Womb and the Bomb* (London: Chatto & Windus, 1990), pp.19-20.

[18]Gerard Genette, 'Time and Narrative in "A la recherché du temps perdu"', in *Aspects of Narrative*, ed. by J. Hillis Miller (New York and London: Columbia, 1971), pp.93-120, p.99.

[19]The image of two male sprinters competing to be the quickest at running in a straight line, and coming to violent blows is another example of McEwan's 'thick description' of the character and consequences of a masculinist society.

[20]Ryan, pp.52-53.

[21]Mars-Jones, p.32.

[22]Ryan, p.53.

10.

MAKING THE 'PUBLIC' MALE: PERFORMING MASCULINITIES, POWER AND TRADITION IN GRAHAM SWIFT'S *WATERLAND* AND PETER CAREY'S *THE TAX INSPECTOR*

Graham Swift's *Waterland* (1983) and Peter Carey's *The Tax Inspector* (1991) are both subtle investigations into cultural constructions of masculinity articulated by the structural effects of empire, citizenship and nationality. That this is not immediately apparent on an initial reading is testimony to the skill of both authors, who set out to show precisely how this history is the target of cultural forgetting, or is repositioned into alternative memories, and who show how this history constantly returns. Both novels use the history of a family or families to tell of wider histories, and have the theme of incest as a crucially symbolic yet displaced centre. Increasing and deepening crises in the construction of traditional models of masculinity are narrated, as these are threatened within the private areas of the home, and in the political arenas of citizenship, nationality, and, in Carey's novel, multiculturalism. In other words, as questions are raised about a variety of identities, the stability of masculine identities is challenged.

There is a marked tendency to see Swift's novel as enabling some kind of abstract game in which various historiographical methodologies are allowed to compete, with little at stake. John Schad, for example, views it as 'an allegorical exploration of postmodern theories of the end of history, treating those theories as the novel's intertexts, or subtexts'.[1] Similarly, George P. Landow suggests that '*Waterland* questions all narrative based on sequence, and in this it agrees with other novels of its decade'.[2] This is in many ways true, and the articles alluded to analyse these aspects very well, but they ignore the fact that the novel deals specifically with English history, particularly the history of empire building and its aftermath.

Waterland is read here as an interrogation of constructions of various masculinities, linked to ideas of citizenship, constituted over the course of 'the Long Century', which began with Britain at war with France, and ended with Britain anxiously eyeing its competitors and contemplating decline. Key aspects of nineteenth-century politics are signalled by the novel, and institutions flood into and back from personal and private lives, modified and adapted by them. One of the most significant moments in the construction of citizenship is found in the Reform Act of 1867, accounts of which tend to be read purely in terms of British internal politics, but, as Catherine Hall demonstrates in her analysis of the act, 'critical moments in the construction of the British nation cannot be made outside of the colonial context'; debates both in and outside the two houses of parliament focused equally on the colonies as much as on the rights or problems of constructing the working-class male as subject and citizen.[3] The fact that it is the male who is constructed as citizen, and therefore brought into a formal relationship with the state, is significant. It provides the possibility of articulating an intertextual dialogue with Carey's novel, in which the construction of masculine identity in a settler colony as both insider and outsider is a major concern, and is tied to debates on the multicultural state. The wider franchise in Australia worried members of both houses of the British parliament in the nineteenth century, who viewed its extension as ushering in anarchy.

The statement that *Waterland* is concerned with English history needs qualifying, because the novel is built around several events which shape this history from the outside.[4] These include the French Revolution, empire, and two world wars which did not take place on British soil (the Blitz notwithstanding), and, as these demonstrate both Britain's growth and decline, it is significant that Dick's dive from the dredger and subsequent disappearance, whilst not chronologically at the end of the events in the novel, is narrated at its end, and is witnessed by two American airmen. Within these displaced centres it is possible to read the cultural articulations of forms of British masculinity, both central and marginal. The novel proposes an engagement with public and private masculinity, its relationship to sexuality, its connection with various forms of history, and its class articulations.

The two main families are the Atkinsons and the Cricks. The Atkinson family is shown as making and shaping history, is symbolically linked to empire through its creation of a brewery empire and its expansionism, is far-sighted, and connected with rationality and planning. They are the embodiment of public and civic masculinity, and, in the course of its history, build two asylums, the last of which shelters the damaged male victims of the First World War, who are characterised by their forgetting. The Crick males are linked to nature, both land and water, and are characterised by story-telling and superstition, fatalism and passivity. They work for the Atkinson family in various capacities, and end with Tom who, after his future wife has an abortion, will not experience fatherhood, and, through his job as a history teacher, is characterised by remembering.

The decline of the Atkinsons is deliberately charted through a period of history which saw extensions in the franchise, and debates over citizenship, events which challenged a specific form of masculinity. Exemplary representatives of their class, they are public to the extent that they hold office, and campaign to be elected to parliament; events, celebrations and commemorations revolve around their presence. The end of the public life of the Atkinson males is made apparent in 1918, when there is no celebratory drink to mark the end of the war, as 'there was no brewery to make it [...] and a large part of the beer-drinking population was no more' (p.213).[5] Previously, the Atkinson males had been at the centre of town festivities, and the absence reveals the extent to which this type of masculinity was predicated on public display. This was a form of masculinity which has to be staged in order to endure. Before the war, Ernest, with his daughter Helen, had retreated to Kessling Hall, ostracised by the townspeople, who disliked his speaking 'out against empire-building and flag-waving' (p.215). Having rejected his tirades against a public, and national, form of history, the townspeople now turn to fairytale and myth in order to speculate about the beauty of the seldom-seen Helen: 'For young knights [...] need their damsels - especially the beleaguered, inaccessible ones in forbidden towers' (p.214). Another narrative involving the public display of masculinity is inscribed in these myths. Ernest invents and nurtures other myths concerning his daughter, but they are informed by incest, the 'private' which should not be made 'public'. Yet he believes that the inevitably male offspring will be 'the Saviour of the World', which necessarily involves a return to the public, and political, sphere. The child is the aptly named Dick, who is denied the tools of reading and writing, and only discovers his past through the intercession of his brother (the future history teacher) years later in the attic of a private family home. Dick is therefore the result of both a desire to withdraw from, and potentially to re-enter in some form, public masculinities. Nostalgia motivates this desire: history 'creates this insidious

longing to go backwards. It begets this bastard but pampered
child, Nostalgia' (p.136). This regression is also found in Tom's
remark on waiting for Mary's abortion, that they are 'waiting
for [...] nothing to happen. For something to unhappen'.
Nostalgia is a main plank for maintaining myths of masculinity
as the norm, and this will be examined more closely in the
discussion of *The Tax Inspector*, where it plays a larger part.
Suffice it to say here that it is a method of silencing counter-
histories and challenges to hegemony, and is also a form of
discourse that is employed by power interests that have nowhere
else to go. Therefore it is an inward and closed discourse, and is
linked in this way to the theme of incest in both novels.

The history of the Atkinsons, particularly leading to Ernest's
withdrawal from public life and into incest, has been a long time
playing itself out, for chinks in the armour of public masculinity
were felt by Thomas a century earlier:

> He is becoming a monument. Man of Enterprise. Man
> of Good Works, Man of Civic Honour [...] Thomas is
> becoming aloof. He can no longer stand by one of his
> new drains and clap the shoulder of the man who has
> helped dig it [...] He does not wish it - he cannot help
> it - but he feels himself measured up and fitted out for
> the stiff and cumbersome garments of legend. (p.75)

There are several examples of masculinity here, and there is a
tension revealed in the image of the men at work, for one man is
a citizen, whilst the other is a subject. The man who digs the
drains has few rights, and is excluded from citizenship, and
participation in democracy. His like could not, and would not
for a good while longer, exercise the right to vote and to make

demands; masculinity as a universal norm has excluded this man, and it is significant that this section dealing with Thomas' anxieties should include an image such as this. This is in 1819, when Thomas is recognising that he is growing old, and his withdrawal and sense of anxiety is linked to increasing jealousy of his much younger wife Sarah, and to the suspicion that she is seeing someone else. His perception of his wife displaces the performance of the male. She has

> a beauty which is apt to remind Mr Atkinson of the
> beauty of an actress - as if his wife occupies some
> strongly lit stage and he, for all his public eminence,
> watches from a lowly distance. (p.75)

One day, in 1820, in an incident 'for which no first-hand account exists yet which is indelibly recorded in innumerable versions in the annals of Gildsey', Thomas strikes Sarah who, after recovering consciousness, never utters another word and is said to have lost her wits (p.76). Myths start to accumulate around this mute, and henceforth seldom seen, woman, who is said to exert mystical and supernatural effects on future events. This happening, and its subsequent effects, bear some examination, particularly as it has become apparent that there is a pattern between Ernest and Thomas. Actions by a man (striking his wife, and withdrawing to Kessling Hall) who has traversed, even if in some unconscious way, some fault line in discourses and constructions of masculinity, lead to the withdrawal from the public sphere of a woman about whom various mythologies subsequently grow.[6] Thomas, manifested through the ways in which he views his wife, is in some way performing, and becoming aware of tensions between masculinity as something assumed to be natural, and as something to be maintained. As Patrick D. Hopkins puts it:

> Paradoxically, then, the 'naturalness' of being a man,
> of being masculine, is constantly guarding against the
> danger of losing itself. Unaware, the 'naturalness',
> the 'rightness', of masculinity exposes its own
> uncertainties in its incessant self-monitoring - a self-
> monitoring often accomplished by monitoring others.
> In fact, although the stable performance of
> masculinity is presented as an *outcome* of being a
> man, what arises [...] is that being a man, or
> continuing to be a man, is the *outcome* of performing
> masculinity.[7]

Masculinity as something engaged in control and fear of loss, self-monitoring, and denying the demands and rights of others, is a common thread in both novels. In *Waterland*, these aspects have been brought home to the Atkinsons because the years between 1820 and 1918 had seen the rise of the working class, extensions in the franchise (two Reform Acts and further legislation), the abolition of slavery, and debates about the rights to citizenship within the colonies. These events had challenged the 'natural' order, and also the 'rights' of particular males of a particular class, through the articulation of different voices. At the same time as the Atkinson males are characterised as public and civic embodiments of masculinity, they are narrated as distant fathers, who are uncomfortable (whenever they consider it) within the family environment. In fact, this withdrawal can be seen as an attempt to maintain masculinity in a pristine and uncontaminated form. As has been said of other forms of masculinity, for 'the husband to maintain his status and prestige in his social life with his peers, he must consciously distance himself from his wife, and be seen to do so'.[8] This is seriously damaging, and represents a closing off of something potentially valuable, and to which there can be no retreat, or to a distorted return to the family in the form of interest. When Thomas starts to feel threatened by the contradictory discourses of masculinity, he lashes out at his wife, and ends his family life; when Ernest feels similarly threatened, he withdraws from public life, and imprisons his daughter in an incestuous relationship.

Ultimately, as suggested, the withdrawal from public life, due to the experiencing of tensions within constructing and maintaining the idea of the male as the norm, culminates in the Atkinson name ending with Ernest and his daughter, who gives birth to Dick, both son and grandson of Ernest. The line continues biologically, but changes name, as Helen marries a Crick, Henry, the shell-shocked soldier whom she nurses back to health. The novel is ambiguous as to how much Henry knows, whether he does initially believe Dick is his own son, and when exactly he finds out about the truth.

Dick himself is a blocked personality. Renowned for having a huge penis, he is unable to respond to Mary's sexual education, itself prompted by a curiosity which disappears after she induces an abortion, because he 'won't fit'. Therefore paths through which he might take up traditional male roles in the future are blocked, and paths towards the discovery of the past are also closed off because, although he has been bequeathed a chest containing Atkinson ale and papers explaining the circumstances of his birth, these are rendered unavailable because of his inability to read. The supposed saviour of the world has nowhere to go, and no one to turn to, and spends long solitary hours by himself, and, it is said, too much time with his motorcycle, with which he is rumoured to be more intimate than is healthy. Images of him as Christ are also overdetermined by millennial fears. His isolated nature is confirmed during the game played by the young boys by the river, a swimming contest, the prize for which will be a glimpse of Mary's naked body. Dick, who has been on the periphery of the game, takes part to the others' surprise, and wins after diving in with an erection, which then subsides. Emerging from the water, Dick then refuses to claim his prize.

Concentrating on the history of a poor white family also coming to the end of the line, Carey's *The Tax Inspector* is an interrogation of the possibilities of renewing or reworking identities when older narratives lose their legitimacy. Identity is always somewhere else in the novel, and memory, tradition and communication are narrated by constant signals that language and silence are not always where they should be, and they are equally narrated through the encoding of claustrophobia, suffocation, and stagnation.

These are checked through constantly being mediated through larger narratives perceived to be wanting, or more pertinently, lacking, with the acknowledgement that there has been a conspiratorial silence in the invention of several traditions, and the acknowledgement that identities made up from the fracture of larger, previously 'secure' narratives, such as nationality and masculinity, are always somehow provisional. An Australian identity based on its history is impossible to sustain, as the pastoral idylls on which it was founded call for the silencing of the origins of White Australia: convict settlements and the slaughter of Aborigines. In one sense, this suggests that the original stories were 'wrong', or that there could have been alternatives, but this ignores the workings of ideology and hegemony, which give some discourses 'authority', and render some narratives appropriate, whilst silencing others.

Masculinity is implicated and bound up in these crises. If the white Australian in harmony with the land developed male-centred, 'natural' qualities of emotion and energy, and if Australian nationalism was constructed by its departure from English values and loyalties, then this has led to stereotypes. In turn, this suggests that whatever represents English culture as refined, intellectual and artificial, and Australians as robust, 'democratic' and authentic, is in crisis. The latter are defined predominantly around standard signs of masculinity departing from the English norm: they are wild, at ease and confident. This is complicated by the contradiction of an early, but weak, national feminism. In 1902, Australia became the second country to give the full federal franchise to women, yet 'early enfranchisement hardly left a vibrant feminist legacy in Australia, which remained a profoundly masculinist society'.[9] Some of the male characters in Carey's novel live out these fluid, and in some senses oppositional, identities, but do so in contradictory terms. They want to somehow stabilise them in terms of authority and tradition, linked by a form of nostalgia, and incestuous patterns which tragically construct stable ground. Pressure and unbearable contradictions emanate from the desire to chain, fix and give authority to these fluid and spontaneous signs of identity. This is the case for Benny, who, as the youngest Catchprice, is furthest away from the origins of grand narratives, living out their dead-ends; his attempts to articulate or generate identities are thwarted or interrupted. His visit to the Woolwash, motivated by instructions issued by his self-affirmation tapes, is interrupted by the arrival in a taxi of his gelignite carrying grandmother, symbolically said to be as old as the century (p.117).[10] Later, his attempt to re-invent himself as a successful salesman is disrupted, at the point of success, by Sarkis, a member of an immigrant Armenian culture, who defines himself according to race (p.175). Benny's attempts to resurrect himself as an angel are tragically overdetermined by power, sex, and incest, as well as confused, and he is unable to articulate or supply a coherent explanation about this when challenged (p.104).

The characters in the novel end up using languages which are not their own, signs which are imposed, stolen or borrowed. This echoes problematics in the rhetoric of men's groups trying to articulate a male identity, a process which involves using mythologies generated by women, African-Americans, Native Americans and other non-white or non-male Others. Fred Pfeil suggests that what these

> largely elided and unacknowledged appropriations from the wisdom traditions of the other tribes suggest is precisely the fundamental fear among those relatively upscale post-sixties boomers that white men as a whole are without traditions and bereft of wisdom.[11]

The Catchprices are far from being 'upscale', but the idea works here as well. Various centres of authority are tried on, and rejected. Benny, who for some of the time works in the Spare Parts section of the business, attempts a transformation which involves a physical escape, not from, but into, the heart of the family, the same business. Obsessionally driven to be recognised and affirmed through the uncritical recognition of others, for

Benny, his family and its business evolved over generations, and guarantee 'traditional' and 'legitimised' markers of identity, as does the pregnant, Greek-born Maria Takis, who fulfills Benny's vision of the eternal feminine.

At the same time, these traditional and authorised markers are suspect, leading to other experiments; he is superficially constructed through phrases he has picked up from his self-affirmation tapes, and through clothes; 'he undressed [...] and - zap - he lost it' (p.98). His identity needs to be confirmed through the recognition of others, but at the same time he seems scared that this interaction will somehow mould him; he is structured through fear. The abuse and rituals he goes through come from a strong need to exert control, hence often he is displayed negatively, through silence and unreachability. The first mention of him states that he 'worked with a Marlboro in his mouth [and] a Walkman on his head' (p.4). He cannot speak or hear, nor can he be heard; he cannot represent himself, nor can he be represented. This is linked to the impossibility of equal exchange exemplified by the Catchprice family, ranging from the very first line, which states that Cathy makes eggs for Benny in the morning, and sacks him in the afternoon, to the latter's attempts to form partnerships through coercion, and the statement that Jack is only attracted to women he would treat badly, or who would despise him (pp.3, 166). It is useful to think of the motif of silence in the novel, particularly in relation to Benny, the young, white male, in terms of Stuart Hall's statement that

> questions of identity are always questions of representation. They are always questions concerning the invention, not simply the discovery, of tradition.

> They are always exercises in selective memory and
> must always involve the silencing of something in
> order to allow something else to speak.[12]

The novel offers several examples, ranging from Benny's wearing of a Walkman to block other narratives, to Vish's 'silenced anger', and in Carey's deliberate, if ambiguous, breaking of the particular silences around the taboo of incest and child abuse (p.13). The absence of Sophie, Benny's mother, is significant, and this silence allows other family members to misrepresent the causes behind the incident when Benny, as a young boy, is shot inadvertently when she vents her anger on her husband, the abuser of their sons. There is a silencing of several constructions of identity in order that others can be developed, and silence does serve as a vehicle for denial, but there is the problem of how, and from which materials, these 'new' identities can be made. There is a desire for these identities to be self-generated, autonomous, and self-controlled, as evidenced by Benny's anger on discovering that Maria has been listening to the same self-affirmation tapes and uses the same language and vocabulary from them. Benny does not seem to realise that these tapes came from somewhere else, that they are themselves constructed as products to be consumed. Identity and money are never far apart in the novel. Benny's discovery of someone else using his language does not validate his identity, as it might, which suggests that any searched for is not communal. This is contradictory, as Benny also desires the traditional, communal identities, even if they are steeped in denial. The self-affirmation tapes are, however, Benny's attempts to remake a new identity after older ones become suspect.

Benny's very maleness, and that of others, is subject to a crisis, and needs to be looked at it in relation to the invention of Australian masculinity going back over a century, an example of which is Frank Fowler's description of the Australian boy as

> a slim, dark-eyed, olive-complexioned young rascal, fond of Cavendish, cricket, and chuckpenny, and systematically insolent to all servant girls, policemen, and new-chums. His hair is shiny with grease, as are the knees of his breeches and the elbows of his jacket. [...] Lazy as he is though, he is out in the world at ten years of age, earning good wages, and is a perfect little man, learned in the ways and by-ways of life at twelve or thirteen.[13]

A version of this ideal develops into another as the male grows older into a self-sufficient, centred family man, as suggested by Anthony Trollope in 1871-72:

> I must say of this colony [...] that it is Paradise for a working man compared with England. The working man can here always eat enough food, can always clothe and shelter himself, and can also educate his children. His diet will always comprise as much animal food as he can consume - and, if he be a sober, industrious man, he will never find himself long without work.[14]

The novel in many ways narrates a distortion of the masculine ideal, which is not discarded, and the constructions of various masculinities are lived out as marginal, as attempts are made to make a journey back to a more central and knowable masculinity. The two constructions of masculinity above, and departures from them, are highly significant in the novel, perhaps in particular the suggestiveness of the mention of 'Paradise' and the 'systematic' nature of these versions, especially as these lead to repeated, almost institutionalised, behavioural patterns. They feed into myths, and it should be recognised that the stereotype is a fixed representation circulated repeatedly to arrest the flow of a history deemed uninhabitable and dangerous. This is linked to the use of nostalgia. An ache for the past, and the frustration of trying to grasp the intangible and absent, are often evoked through images of a stereotypical style and feel. It needs to be asked why this should be so: a useful starting point is that both are historical. Nostalgia, as the attempt to capture a lost past, is linked to the stereotype, which is the present use and retention of previously constructed, fixed images. The stereotype involves the comforting fantasy projection onto a real, unwanted and uncomfortable historical process. Hence for racist and colonial discourse the stereotypical construction of black people as lazy, smiling and unhistorical people blurs and replaces the real history of blacks as colonised, and struggling against colonialism for autonomy and independence. The stereotype legitimises a version of history and displaces/replaces another. Once it is constructed it remains fixed, for if it changed it would no longer be a stereotype; this would be the implicit admission of the existence of historical change, and anti-hegemonic struggle. The stereotype is linked to nostalgia: it is a fixed discourse which remains unchanged over time, and could not function if it did change, and involves a fantasy projection which seeks to make absent a real history. In *The Tax Inspector*, nostalgia is linked to foundation myths of the pastoral and 'mateship'

This has a place in debates on multiculturalism, as a phenomenon, and as something to be legislated about in political arenas; in Australia, after the 'celebrations' of the bicentennial. The ruling Anglo-Celt ethnic group still 'man' the institutions organising and framing the debates, and are able to use multiculturalism to further their hegemony by using it to distance England, admittedly by displacement into more continental European ideas of cosmopolitanism, and by using it to blur or bypass Aboriginal land-claim issues.[15] In other words, the privileged narratives are still those foundation myths of 'mateship', and the pastoral, narratives which obviously exclude much more than they include, especially in contemporary Australia. Myths which privilege nostalgic tropes of white male identity are evoked in order to silence the competing voices of the unheard majority, women and immigrants. Monocultural myths which identify an identity which is at once national *and* male come under increasing pressure, and the tensions on which they were built start to make themselves felt. It is significant that Benny's negotiations with his masculinity, his aggressive and violent methods of gaining control and 'consent', should be directed at people from immigrant cultures.

The masculinity evoked in Trollope's statement seems to be a place longed for by Benny's father and abuser, Mort, abused by his father before him, who enters the tale tired and angry, imagining himself away, running a country garage where he could be

> the guy who drives the school bus, delivers the
> kerosene and fuel oil, cuts the rust spots out of the
> school teacher's old car, fixes the butcher's brakes
> with used parts, is handy with a lathe, is a good shot,

> a good bloke, a scout master, the coach of the football
> team, someone who, when looking for a screw or bolt,
> upturns a drum full of old saved screws and bolts on
> to the workshop floor and can find - there it is - a 3/8
> Whitworth thread with a Philips head. (p.43)

In many ways this is a qualified pastoral image, or at least some combination of the modern and the pastoral, whereby the harshness of modernity is absorbed into some workable, and knowable, tradition. Again this is the crux of the novel, the realisation that traditions have been invented, and the realisation that this revelation strips tradition of authority, and exiles those who were rooted and formed within it. The pastoral is a very complex and highly structured motif; it is not nature passively reflected, but a version of nature organised in very specific ways, which arises, and is reused, in times of crisis. Displayed and inverted, it is offered as a provisional nostalgia which inevitably slips into dystopia in *The Tax Inspector*.

A significant number of pastoral and dystopian motifs are gathered around Frieda Catchprice, who is bitter because she has smothered her own dreams of having a flower farm in order to show her husband how a motor business, 'with the smell of rubber radiator hoses, fan belts, oil [and] grease', could be run instead (p.60). A wilful blindness is also apparent in Frieda, as she is forced to answer accusations that she did nothing to prevent systematic incest and child abuse. Mort fills in details she probably already knows, telling her that her husband made her son dress as an angel and abused him. He asks 'what would that have done to you [...] what sort of person would you have become?' (p.247). Earlier, he has suggested to Maria that Benny would himself become an abuser of his children, and says 'it is common because it is natural. No, I am not saying it is natural, but if it is so common how come it is not natural ?' (p.158). There is a suggestion that the maintenance of masculinity can be caught in the image of abuse and incest, and that it is both a performance, and an attempt to 'act' out something which has to be presented as natural. The language here ties into authority, nature and hegemony, given that it is the role of ideology to construct made traditions and imposed authority as natural. Mort is no King Lear, to whom a disguised Gloucester can offer his services precisely because he displays, in his body and features, 'authority'; he is subject to manipulation by those he has abused, as evidenced by Benny's seduction and threats towards him. This raises the question of where male authority lies, in personal and 'natural' demonstrations, or in some structural form through which the characters are decentered. The pastoral visions played with by his father are not available to Benny, who is caught in spirals of shifting sites of identity and authority, which are either turned inwards, or exercised in external displays of control and abuse he himself does not fully understand. The ritualistic and institutionalised child abuse itself becomes a tradition, which is accepted because it is known and established. Horrifically, child abuse works in the same way, or as nostalgia and its attendant repetition of previously established fixed images, as the tradition and repetition provide stable centres of authority and identity.

Dominant fictions of sexual difference offer various phallic sounds and images within which the male subject can find himself. Kaja Silverman reminds us that male subjectivity rests not only upon a mis-recognition, but also on a failure to recognise, which takes two forms:

> The subject classically refuses to recognise an
> unwanted feature of the *self* by projecting it onto the
> other, i.e. by relocating it. He [...] refuses to recognise
> an unpleasurable or anxiety-inducing aspect of the
> *other* by disavowing it, a process which sometimes
> requires the support of a fetish.[16]

Benny's failure to recognise takes the shape of denial, and is
arranged through wilful imagination, and the fetish of the
customised surf board on which he terrorises the Armenian
Sarkis Alaverdian and the Greek Maria Takis, significantly both
from marginalised immigrant cultures.

The obsession Benny has for Maria is partly explained by the
fact that, as a visibly-pregnant woman Maria, bears the past
mark of the sexual act; her pregnancy also carries with it the
future life of the child. Perhaps too for Benny the unborn child
signifies some blank uncontaminated site on which an identity
can be inscribed in an unproblematic way. The impossibility of
this is symbolised during the novel's apocalyptic ending by
Benny holding Maria's baby, still attached to her by the
umbilical cord, to his face and naming it 'little Benny', as if to
imprint it (p.276). The context of abuse, and the repetition of
the name, suggests the continuation rather than disruption of
cycles. Benny's blindness is thrown into relief by the fact that
Jack is attracted to Maria precisely because she carries someone
else's child, '[s]he had arrived complete [...] with a child that
was not, in any way, a reproduction of himself' (p.213). If
Benny can gain Maria's consent and affirmation, Benny's
identity will be deeply rooted and legitimised, with hegemony
over past, present and future. His need for consent and
affirmation is expressed bizarrely by the suggestion that he will

make her make him have sex: '[h]e wanted her to stroke his
hair, maybe, kiss him on his eyes, that sort of thing. Not fuck,
not unless she made him' (p.260). At this point in the narrative,
he has kidnapped Maria and is holding her prisoner at gunpoint
in the bowels of the business, where the walls are covered in the
names of angels written by Benny, symbols of the history of
abuse. In this scene, central to the display of the contradictions
in maintaining masculinity as both performance and as natural
authority, consent, hegemony and submission are caught in
vicious contradictions.

What are at stake in the novel are identity, power and
hegemony, and these are motivated by the shifts and the
contradictions arising from the realisation that identities
legitimised by tradition and authority are threatened and deeply
suspect. Hegemony can only work through tacit or unconscious
consent, or by the attempt to negotiate new identities out of the
fracture of the old. The 'staging' of this process in the novel
goes beyond the argument that men in the late twentieth century
are having deep problems in adjusting to the demands made on
them both by various feminist movements, and by the erosion of
traditional roles, an argument in part summed up by the fact that

> [m]en have an interest in preserving the status quo,
> because - like women - they have constructed their
> personal identities, values and ideas of themselves in
> terms of the options socially available. For men to
> become supporters of women's liberation, or to
> become committed to stopping environmental
> degradation, means becoming aware of the scale of
> both sexism and gratuitous destruction - both of
> which can be painful.[17]

It was suggested earlier that Maria Takis offers Benny a site where he can re-establish a concrete identity within tradition and authority, partly through her symbolising the eternal feminine. This process needs some negotiation of the specific identities she herself performs. She holds some power as a tax inspector, which is modified by the fact that she is becoming marginalised through office politics; she is also a member of the tightly knit Greek diaspora, whose family 'bonds stretch across oceans as easily as across a village street'.[18] The figure of diaspora, of the margins, and of exile, is a strong element in Greek cultural memory, symbolised, as James Pettifer suggests, by Odysseus, the wily wanderer who manages to return home to rescue his wife from unwanted suitors, and by Alexander the Great, who conquered the known world from Macedonia, but did not return. Benny is, initially, perhaps always, unaware of the cultural overdeterminations that constitute Maria: for him, she is constructed through the male gaze as she walks across the carpark to begin her audit of the family business.

There is a wider structural concern in the novel aimed at some narration of the nation: the founding moments and the confidence in the various constructions of Australian identity have been misplaced or badly deployed (p.84). A final quotation on the Australian identity as masculinity can lead to some conclusions:

> In the bush the Common Man had at last decisively proved himself. His victory depended on the simple fact that in the frontiers of the New Countries the Common Man could beat the gentleman. He could stand firm on his own feet and cock snooks at the refined tenderfoot. He was no longer the underfed,

> pallid, uncertain product of the slums. Successful life
> in the bush depended on the individual's cunning of
> hand and stoutness of heart. Here at last he had
> proved himself a man - and he was pretty sure he had
> proved himself a better man.[19]

As stated earlier, the traditional markers of Australian identity coincide with core images central to the construction of a masculine identity, defined as oppositional to Englishness, but nonetheless still exclusive and hegemonic. The confident tone of these has evaporated, and if the characteristics of the 'gentleman' embody vested interests, then Carey's novel reveals those vested interests squarely in place. Characters in the novel do try to get by on 'individual's cunning', but it is not enough, and often involves trying to position fluid and potentially oppositional identities as hegemonic and authoritative; attempts to gain strength reveal vulnerability. There is no possibility of return, as identities have been revealed as inventions, and any attempt to return or reconstruct involves intolerable contradictions between power, authority and submission. These contradictions are thoroughly staged in the final, violent confrontation between Benny and Maria, who has 'no idea that he was as near as he had ever been to love. She saw only some pretty, blonde-haired, Aussie surfer boy' (p.278). Benny's attempts to find some coherent and stable identity, ranging from trying to maintain the traditions of the family and the business, to stepping outside them, have utterly failed.

Stitching the two novels together, it is revealed that the contradictions inherent in public and civic nineteenth-century English forms of masculinity are taking a long time to play themselves out. Yet they are constantly challenged and slipping,

under both external and internal pressure, into incest, their final
exhaustion, and destruction in a devastated garage in Australia,
a settler colony struggling over various narratives of the state.
Both novels display and narrate tensions within codes of
masculinity when these are confronted by challenges from
groups who are excluded from definitions of the masculine as
norm. Perhaps not everyone would feel it appropriate to talk of
a crisis or crises within cultural constructions of masculinity,
given the time scale of two centuries, and the fact that males
have controlled legitimising discourses which define the norm
and exclude others. However, a case can be made for
considering masculinity as labouring under a permanent crisis,
and both novels in question do reveal dominant codes of
masculinity as being erected on fundamentally contradictory
discourses. Together they chart two male lines within families,
from the executive class in nineteenth-century Britain, to a
'white trash' family in twentieth-century Australia, which
disappear as they labour under the circumstances of maintaining
constructions of masculinity which must be maintained and
performed, 'produced' as being 'natural', and which are
ultimately attacked by other cultural constructions and identities
which they exclude.

[1] John Schad, 'The End of the End of History: Graham Swift's *Waterland*',
Modern Fiction Studies, 38:4 (Winter, 1992), 911-925 (p.911).
[2] George P. Landow, 'History, His Story, and Stories in Graham Swift's
Waterland', *Studies in the Literary Imagination* (1990), pp.197-211
(p.203).
[3] Catherine Hall, 'Rethinking Imperial Histories: The Reform Act of 1867',
New Left Review, 208 (November/December 1994), 3-29 (p.29).
[4] At times this is pointed towards by following the narration of private
family moments acted out in the isolated fens with a list of what has been
happening in the arenas of world politics.

[5]Graham Swift, *Waterland* (London: Picador, 1984 [1983]).

[6]Obviously this has helped lead to the arguments that Swift is primarily engaged in letting various types of discourse compete: here public history, civic duty, masculinity, myth and superstition.

[7]Patrick D. Hopkins, 'Gender Treachery: Homophobia, Masculinity, and threatened Identities', in *Rethinking Masculinity*, ed. by L. May, R. Strikwerda, P. D. Hopkins (Lanham and Boulder: Rowman and Littlefield Publishers, 1996), pp.107-8.

[8]Lynne Segal, 'Look Back in Anger: Men in the 50s', in *Unwrapping Masculinity*, ed. by R. Chapman and J. Rutherford (London: Lawrence and Wishart, 1988), p.75.

[9]Ellen Dubois, 'Antipodean Feminism', *New Left Review*, 206 (July/August, 1994), 127-32 (p.127).

[10]Peter Carey, *The Tax Inspector* (London and Boston: Faber, 1991). Many thanks to students at the University of Leeds and Université de Liège, and to Andrew Norris and Marc Delrez, for discussing the novel with me.

[11]Fred Pfeil, 'Sympathy for the Devils: Notes on Some White Guys in the Ridiculous Class War', *New Left Review*, 213 (September/October 1995), 115-24 (p.117).

[12]Stuart Hall, 'Caribbean Identities', *New Left Review*, 209 (January/February 1995), 3-14 (p.5).

[13]Frank Fowler, quoted in G. A. Wilkes, *The Stockyard and the Croquet Lawn* (London: Edward Arnold, 1981), pp.87-88.

[14]Anthony Trollope, quoted in Wilkes, p.24.

[15]For a debate on this subject, see Sneja Gunew, 'Denaturalising cultural nationalisms: multicultural readings of 'Australia'', in *Nation and Narration*, ed. by Homi Bhabha (London: Routledge, 1990), pp.99-120.

[16]Kaja Silverman, *Male Subjectivity at the Margins* (New York and London: Routledge, 1992), p.45.

[17]Caroline New, 'Man Bad, Woman Good? Essentialisms and Ecofeminisms', *New Left Review*, 216 (March/April 1996), 79-94 (p.92). The issue of the destruction of nature and the ecosystem would be highly relevant to an analysis of this novel, which deals with the pastoral becoming a dystopia.

[18]James Pettifer, *The Greeks* (London: Penguin, 1993), p.219.

[19]A. A. Phillips, quoted in Wilkes, p. 35.

NOTES ON CONTRIBUTORS

DANIEL DUFFY teaches at the University of Leeds; his main research area is Victorian theatre.

STEPHEN GREGG teaches at the University of Leeds. He is currently researching the work of Daniel Defoe, and issues of nationhood; a chapter of his will appear in *Images of Manhood in Early Modern Literature*.

LIZ HEDGECOCK researches narrative mastery and sexual selection in the male-authored Victorian novel at the University of Salford. Other interests include the process of adaptation, and genre fiction. She has a chapter appearing in *New Larkins for Old* (Macmillan), and is editing an anthology of Victorian dramatizations of Victorian novels.

EMMA LIGGINS lectures at Edge Hill University College. She has published on Sensation fiction in the *Journal of Victorian Culture*. Her main research areas are in Victorian popular fiction, fictional representations of death and murder, and marriage plots in nineteenth-century novels.

SCOTT McCRACKEN is a Senior Lecturer at the University of Salford. His key publications are *Cultural Politics at the Fin de Siècle* (CUP, 1995, with Sally Ledger), and *Pulp: Reading Popular Fiction* (MUP, 1998). He is currently working on a book about masculinity and modernist prose.

JOHN McLEOD lectures on Commonwealth and Postcolonial literatures at the University of Leeds. His published work includes articles on J. G. Farrell, Timothy Mo and Kazuo Ishiguro, and he is writing a book for Manchester University Press entitled *Beginning Postcolonialism*.

MATTHEW PATEMAN lectures at University College Scarborough. He has published work in these areas: pornography, masculinity and Julian Barnes.

ANTONY ROWLAND lectures at the University of Salford. His main research areas are contemporary poetry, Holocaust Studies, and masculinity. He is currently writing a book for Liverpool University Press on the poetry of Tony Harrison, and editing a collection of essays on the Frankfurt School.

WILLIAM STEPHENSON teaches at the University of Central Lancashire. He is editing a book with Bruce Woodcock on Queer Theory.

ERIKS USKALIS lectures at the University of Liège. He is interested in African literature and Marxist theories of the post colonial, and has published on Ngugi in *Critical Survey*.

INDEX

JEANNE D'ARC
ENTRE LES NATIONS

Etudes reunies par Ton Hoenselaars et Jelle Koopmans

Amsterdam/Atlanta, GA 1998. 146 pp.
(CRIN 33)
ISBN: 90-420-0338-3   Hfl. 45,-/US-$ 23.50

Editions Rodopi B.V.

USA/Canada: 2015 South Park Place, Atlanta, GA 30339, Tel. (770) 933-0027, *Call toll-free* (U.S.only) 1-800-225-3998, Fax (770) 933-9644

All Other Countries: Tijnmuiden 7, 1046 AK Amsterdam, The Netherlands. Tel. + + 31 (0)20 6114821, Fax + + 31 (0)20 4472979 *E-mail:* orders-queries@rodopi.nl — http://www.rodopi.nl

POSTMODERNISM AND THE HOLOCAUST

Ed. by Alan Milchman and Alan Rosenberg

Amsterdam/Atlanta, GA 1998. VII,325 pp.
(Value Inquiry Book Series 72)
ISBN: 90-420-0591-2   Bound Hfl. 160,-/US-$ 84.-
ISBN: 90-420-0581-5   Paper Hfl. 45,-/US-$ 23.50

This book is the first sustained inquiry into the ways in which postmodern thinkers have grappled with the historical bases, implications, and methodological problems of the Holocaust. The book examines the thinking of Arendt, Levinas, Foucault, Lyotard, and Derrida, all of whom have recognized the centrality of the Nazi genocice to the epoch in which we live. The essays written for this volume constitute a wide-ranging study of the efforts of postmodernism to articulate the Holocaust.

Editions Rodopi B.V.

USA/Canada: 2015 South Park Place, Atlanta, GA 30339, Tel. (770) 933-0027, *Call toll-free* (U.S.only) 1-800-225-3998, Fax (770) 933-9644

All Other Countries: Tijnmuiden 7, 1046 AK Amsterdam, The Netherlands. Tel. ++ 31 (0)20 6114821, Fax ++ 31 (0)20 4472979 *E-mail:* orders-queries@rodopi.nl —— http://www.rodopi.nl

LE SIÈCLE DE GEORGE SAND

Textes réunis par David A. Powell
avec l'assistance de Shira Malkin

Amsterdam/Atlanta, GA 1998. XII,373 pp.
(Faux Titre 153)
ISBN: 90-420-0473-8   Hfl. 120,-/US-$ 63.-

Sont réunis dans ce volume trente-sept essais traitant de la place occupée par George Sand dans la société de son temps, tant sur la plan politique, historique et social que littéraire. Ce recueil, édité par David A. Powell, chercheur en littérature française du XIXe siècle et spécialiste de George Sand, présente pour la première fois un ensemble de textes qui attestent le rôle fondamental joué par l'auteur berrichon à son époque, mais aussi après sa mort. L'envergure de son influence ne saurait se restreindre au domaine de la littérature comme en témoigna le Colloque International sur George Sand organisé par Hofstra University dans l'état de New York en 1996. Les textes publiés ici furent d'abord présentés sous forme de communications lors de ce colloque. Le chercheur, qu'il s'intéresse à l'histoire culturelle, sociale, politique, littéraire ou à d'autres domaines, trouvera dans la richesse de cette collection d'essais la preuve que l'œuvre de George Sand constitue véritablement une source intarissable de réflexion.

Editions Rodopi B.V.

USA/Canada: 2015 South Park Place, Atlanta, GA 30339, Tel. (770) 933-0027, *Call toll-free* (U.S.only) 1-800-225-3998, Fax (770) 933-9644

All Other Countries: Tijnmuiden 7, 1046 AK Amsterdam, The Netherlands. Tel. + + 31 (0)20 6114821, Fax + + 31 (0)20 4472979
E-mail: orders-queries@rodopi.nl —— http://www.rodopi.nl

THE ARCHIVE OF DEVELOPMENT

Ed. by Annette W. Balkema and Henk Slager

Amsterdam/Atlanta, GA 1998. 187 pp.
(Lier en Boog. Series of Philosophy of Art and Art Theory 13)
ISBN: 90-420-0441-X   Bound Hfl. 100,-/US-$ 52.50
ISBN: 90-420-0431-2   Paper Hfl. 35,-/US-$ 18.-

In the current debate on art, thought on time has commanded a prominent position. Do we live in a posthistorical time? Has objective art historical time and belief in a continual progress shifted to a more subjective experience of the ephemeral? Has (art) history fallen away and, if so, what does this mean for the future of art? How does a visual archive relate to artistic memory?
This volume investigates positions, arguments and comments regarding the stated theme. Philosophers and theorists explore the subject matter theoretically. Curators articulate the practice of art. The participants are: Hans Belting, Jan Bor, Peter Bürger, Bart Cassiman, Leontine Coelewij, Hubert Damisch, Arthur C. Danto, Bart De Baere, Okwui Enwezor, Kasper König, Sven Lütticken, Manifesta (Barbara VanderLinden), Hans Ulrich Obrist, Donald Preziosi, Survival of the Past Project (Herman Parret, Lex Ter Braak, Camiel Van Winkel), Ernst Van Alphen, Kirk Varnedoe, Gianni Vattimo, and Kees Vuyk.

Editions Rodopi B.V.

USA/Canada: 2015 South Park Place, Atlanta, GA 30339, Tel. (770) 933-0027, *Call toll-free* (U.S.only) 1-800-225-3998, Fax (770) 933-9644

All Other Countries: Tijnmuiden 7, 1046 AK Amsterdam, The Netherlands. Tel. ++ 31 (0)20 6114821, Fax ++ 31 (0)20 4472979
E-mail: orders-queries@rodopi.nl —— http://www.rodopi.nl

Friendship
A special issue of SAQ
Peter Murphy, special issue editor

On Friendship in Aristotle
Pierre Aubenque

Ancient Friends, Modern Enemies
Dwight David Allman

Friendship in a Local Vein: Montaigne's Servitude to La Boëtie
Tom Conley

Spectral *Philia* and the Imaginary Institution of Needs
Marios Constantinou

Intellectual Friendship and the Elective Affinities of Critical Theory
John Ely

The Beauty of Friendship
Agnes Heller

Friendship's Eu-topia
Peter Murphy

On Friends and Enemies
Louis A. Ruprecht, Jr.

Monarchs, Minions, and "Soveraigne" Friendship
Laurie J. Shannon

Please send ___ copies of *Friendship* (*SAQ* Volume 97, Number 1; Winter 1998) at $12 each.
In the U.S. please add $3 for the first copy and $1 for each additional copy to cover postage and handling.
Outside the U.S. please add $3 for each copy to cover postage and handling.

☐ I enclose my check, payable to Duke University Press.
☐ Please bill me. (No issues can be sent until payment is received.)
Please charge my   ☐ MasterCard   ☐ Visa   ☐ American Express

---
Account Number   Expiration Date

Signature   Daytime Phone

Name

Address

City/State/Zip   SQ8E0

Send orders to Duke University Press, Journals Fulfillment, Box 90660, Durham, NC 27708-0660.
To place your journal order using a credit card, call toll free 1.888.DUP.JRNL (1.888.387.5765).
Fax: 919.688.3524, http://www.duke.edu/web/dupress/

THE FANTASTIC OTHER

An Interface of Perspectives

Ed. by Brett Cooke, George E. Slusser and
Jaume Marti-Olivella

Amsterdam/Atlanta, GA 1998. VII,276 pp.
(Critical Studies 11)
ISBN: 90-420-0401-0   Bound Hfl. 150,-/US-$ 78.50
ISBN: 90-420-0400-2   Paper Hfl. 45,-/US-$ 23.50

The Fantastic Other is a carefully assembled collection of
essays on the increasingly significant question of alterity in
modern fantasy, the ways in which the understanding and
construction of the Other shapes both our art and our
imagination. The collection takes a unique perspective, seeing
alterity not merely as a social issue but as a biological one.
Our fifteen essays cover the problems posed by the Other,
which, after all, go well beyond the bounds of any single
critical perspective. With this in mind, we have selected studies
to show how insights from deconstruction, Marxism, feminism,
and Freudian, Jungian and evolutionary psychology help us
understand an issue so central to the act of reading.

Editions Rodopi B.V.

USA/Canada: 2015 South Park Place, Atlanta, GA 30339, Tel. (770)
933-0027, *Call toll-free* (U.S.only) 1-800-225-3998, Fax (770) 933-9644

All Other Countries: Tijnmuiden 7, 1046 AK Amsterdam, The
Netherlands. Tel. ++ 31 (0)20 6114821, Fax ++ 31 (0)20 4472979
E-mail: orders-queries@rodopi.nl —— http://www.rodopi.nl

ISABELLE DE CHARRIÈRE
SAINTE ANNE

Edition établie, présentée et annotée par Yvette Went-Daoust

Amsterdam/Atlanta, GA 1998. 123 pp.
(Faux Titre 148)
ISBN: 90-420-0451-7   Hfl. 40,-/US-$ 21.-

Isabelle de Charrière publie *Sainte Anne* et 1799, sous le pseudonyme de l'Abbé de la Tour. Les cinq romans qui composent ce cycle expriment avec une franche liberté les idées que la romancière a développées au cours des aléas de sa vie personnelle et de l'histoire. Le trait qui distingue cette idéologie est l'anticonformisme. *Sainte Anne* donne à lire une réflexion sur le bien-fondé de la lecture et de l'instruction en général. Les discussions s'engagent entre les personnages, les idées se heurtent sur fond d'intrigues amoureuses, de prérogatives de classe ou de sexe. Le ton de la conversation, tantôt raisonneuse, tantôt désinvolte, gouverne le discours romanesque.

Editions Rodopi B.V.

USA/Canada: 2015 South Park Place, Atlanta, GA 30339, Tel. (770) 933-0027, *Call toll-free* (U.S.only) 1-800-225-3998, Fax (770) 933-9644

All Other Countries: Tijnmuiden 7, 1046 AK Amsterdam, The Netherlands. Tel. ++ 31 (0)20 6114821, Fax ++ 31 (0)20 4472979
E-mail: orders-queries@rodopi.nl —— http://www.rodopi.nl

THE SOCIETY TALE
IN RUSSIAN LITERATURE
From Odoevskii to Tolstoi

Ed. by Neil Cornwell

Amsterdam/Atlanta, GA 1998. 197 pp.
(Studies in Slavic Literature and Poetics 31)
ISBN: 90-420-0329-4   Hfl. 65,-/US-$ 34.-

This collection of essays is the first book to appear on the society tale in nineteenth-century Russian fiction. Written by a team of British and American scholars, the volume is based on a symposium on the society tale held at the University of Bristol in 1996. The essays examine the development of the society tale in Russian fiction, from its beginnings in the 1820s until its subsumption into the realist novel, later in the century. The contributions presented vary in approach from the text or author based study to the generic or the sociological. Power, gender and discourse theory all feature strongly and the volume should be of considerable interest to students and scholars of nineteenth-century Russian literature. There are essays covering Pushkin, Lermontov, Odoevsky and Tolstoi, as well as more minor writers, and more general and theoretical approaches.

Editions Rodopi B.V.
USA/Canada: 2015 South Park Place, Atlanta, GA 30339, Tel. (770) 933-0027, *Call toll-free* (U.S.only) 1-800-225-3998, Fax (770) 933-9644

All Other Countries: Tijnmuiden 7, 1046 AK Amsterdam, The Netherlands. Tel. ++ 31 (0)20 6114821, Fax ++ 31 (0)20 4472979
E-mail: orders-queries@rodopi.nl —— http://www.rodopi.nl

GERLINDE RÖDER-BOLTON

George Eliot and Goethe:
An Elective Affinity

Amsterdam/Atlanta, GA 1998. 290 pp.
(Textxet 13)
ISBN: 90-420-0359-6   Hfl. 90,-/US-$ 47.-

In the first half of the nineteenth century in England there was a strong
interest in German literature and German scholarship. George Eliot studied
German and German literature from the age of twenty. Her first
publication, in 1846, was a translation of Friedrich Strauss's *Das Leben
Jesu*; followed, in 1854, by the translation of Ludwig Feuerbach's *Das
Wesen des Christentums*. That same year George Eliot left England with
George Henry Lewes on her first visit to Germany. During the next three
months they visited Frankfurt, Weimar and Berlin to collect material for
Lewes's biography of Goethe. In this study, Gerlinde Röder-Bolton explores
the impact of Goethe on George Eliot, whose "elective affinity" with
Goethe was both ethical and artistic, and analyses George Eliot's
responsiveness to Goethe's moral vision and the literary uses she makes of
her familiarity with Goethe's work. *George Eliot and Goethe: An Elective
Affinity* concentrates on *The Mill on the Floss* and *Daniel Deronda*,
showing how the intertextual relationship with *Die Wahlverwandtschaften*
holds the key to an understanding of the latter part of *The Mill on the
Floss*, while the first part of *Faust* and *Wilhelm Meisters Lehrjahre* throw
new light on *Daniel Deronda*. This study, with its close analysis of a range
of works by George Eliot and Goethe, is essential reading for anyone
interested in both or either of these authors or in Anglo-German literary
relations.

Editions Rodopi B.V.

USA/Canada: 2015 South Park Place, Atlanta, GA 30339, Tel. (770)
933-0027, *Call toll-free* (U.S.only) 1-800-225-3998, Fax (770) 933-9644

All Other Countries: Tijnmuiden 7, 1046 AK Amsterdam, The
Netherlands. Tel. ++ 31 (0)20 6114821, Fax ++ 31 (0)20 4472979
E-mail: orders-queries@rodopi.nl — http://www.rodopi.nl

JOYCE: FEMINISM / POST / COLONIALISM

Ed. by Ellen Carol Jones

Amsterdam/Atlanta, GA 1998. 290 pp. + 6 ill.
(European Joyce Studies 8)
ISBN: 90-420-0771-0   Bound Hfl. 150,-/US-$ 78.50
ISBN: 90-420-0761-3   Paper Hfl. 45,-/US-$ 23.50

James Joyce is located between, and constructed within, two worlds: the national and international, the political and cultural systems of colonialism and postcolonialism. Joyce's political project is to construct a postcolonial contra-modernity: to write the incommensurable differences of colonial, postcolonial, and gendered subjectivities, and, in doing so, to reorient the axis of power and knowledge. What Joyce dramatizes in his hybrid writing is the political and cultural remainder of imperial history or patriarchal canons: a remainder that resists assimilation into the totalizing narratives of modernity. Through this remainder - of both politics and the psyche - Joyce reveals how a minority culture can construct political and personal agency. *Joyce: Feminism / Post / Colonialism*, edited by Ellen Carol Jones, bears witness to the construction of that agency, tracing the inscription of the racial and sexual other in colonial, nationalist, and postnational representations, deciphering the history of the possible. Contributors are Gregory Castle, Gerald Doherty, Enda Duffy, James Fairhall, Peter Hitchcock, Ellen Carol Jones, Ranjana Khanna, Patrick McGee, Marilyn Reizbaum, Susan de Sola Rodstein, Carol Shloss, and David Spurr.

Editions Rodopi B.V.

USA/Canada: 2015 South Park Place, Atlanta, GA 30339, Tel. (770) 933-0027, *Call toll-free* (U.S.only) 1-800-225-3998, Fax (770) 933-9644

All Other Countries: Tijnmuiden 7, 1046 AK Amsterdam, The Netherlands. Tel. + + 31 (0)20 6114821, Fax + + 31 (0)20 4472979 *E-mail:* orders-queries@rodopi.nl —— http://www.rodopi.nl

Masculinity is becoming an increasingly popular area of study in areas as diverse as sociology, politics and cultural studies, yet significant research is lacking into connections between masculinity and literature. *Signs of Masculinity* aims at beginning to fill the gap. Starting with an introduction to, and intervention within, numerous debates concerning the cultural construction of various masculinities, the volume then continues with an investigation of representations of masculinity in literature from 1700 to the present. Close readings of texts are intended to demonstrate that masculinity is not a theoretical abstract, but a definitive textual and cultural phenomenon that needs to be recognised in the study of literature. It is hoped that the wide-ranging essays, which raise numerous issues, and are written from a variety of methodological approaches, will appeal to undergraduate, postgraduates and lecturers interest in the crucial but under-researched area of masculinity.

ISBN 90-420-0603-X

9 789042 006034